Womb with a Window

Ethical Reflections on the
Personhood of the Unborn
Through Scripture and Science

Printed in 2019 by Shanway Press, 15 Crumlin Road, Belfast BT14 6AA

Cover design: DavidLee Badger

ISBN: 978-1-910044-21-6

Prayer for the Child in the Womb

Lord Jesus, you are the source and lover of life. Reawaken in us respect for every human life. Help us to see in each child the marvellous work of our Creator. Open our hearts to welcome every child as a unique and wonderful gift. Guide the work of doctors, nurses and midwives. May the life of a mother and her baby in the womb be equally cherished and respected. Help those who make our laws to uphold the uniqueness and sacredness of every human life, from the first moment of conception to natural death. Give us wisdom and generosity to build a society that cares for all. Together with Mary, your Mother, in whose womb you took on our human nature, help us to choose life in every decision we take. We ask this in the joyful hope of eternal life with you, and in the communion of the Blessed Trinity. Amen.

ACKNOWLEDGEMENTS

I wish to place on record the services of many people who magnanimously helped make this venture a reality. I am deeply indebted to His Beatitude Major Archbishop Mar George Cardinal Alencherry, His Grace Eamon Martin, Archbishop of Armagh, His Excellency Noel Treanor, Bishop of Down and Connor for diligently going through the text and writing insightful messages and Foreword, in spite of their heavy schedule.

I am grateful to several other people who have provided valuable assistance in helping me, the staff of St. Paul's parish. In particular, I would like to single out Very Rev Father Tony Devlin who has always been an inspiration. My deepest gratitude to all my brother priests of St Paul's Presbytery: Fathers Paul Morely, Andrew Black, Aloysius Lumala for whom I have no words to express.

I express my thanks to Roisin Lynch for giving her insightful comments and perspicacious suggestions. I also thank Shanway Press for its careful supervision of this work.

Finally, I thank everyone who contributed in one way or another to the completion of this work and pray that the book proves useful to everyone who reads it. I hope, however, that what I say can stimulate somebody to reimage his/her understanding of the value of human life from its origin to its natural end and I dedicate this book to the cherished memory of my beloved parents, George and Annam Perumayan, for receiving me as a valued gift from God's hands.

Message from George Cardinal Alencherry

The quality of human life and its sanctity are topics of intense discussion among some philosophers and moral theologians of our times. When many question the relevance of human life which is not marked with quality, others strongly stand for the God-gifted nature of human life and for its sanctity. Some argue that human life which is totally vegetative is not beneficial to anyone. They further argue that such lives can be eliminated without any prick of conscience. To them human lives are insignificant so long as they are medically unfit to live or in a comatose state. However, lots of miraculous recoveries have happened in such cases which are beyond human imagination and logic. We have to bear in mind that the quality of human life is not under our control. Human life is a gift of God and is sacred.

Man, even though he thinks that he is the crown of the creation, has to acknowledge his limitations. First of these limitations is the fact he cannot create life. Procreation is neither a creation nor a production but a process that is synchronised with nature. His second limitation is that he cannot prevent or overcome death. The life expectancy and the quality of life are not human achievements. Nor can one control death. This reveals the truth, 'Life is a precious gift of God'. This revelation has scientific and biblical evidences. Aruna Ramchandra Shanbaug, an Indian nurse, who was at the centre of attention in a court case on euthanasia spent 42 years in a vegetative state as a result of sexual assault. Even though she was bed ridden for 42 years nobody wanted to put an end to her life. Besides, everybody tried to preserve her life in the expectation of the possibility of her recovery. This possibility is beyond human capacities and in the hands of God. Here, arises the moral conflict. The same society that respected the sanctity of life in the case of Aruna Ramchandra Shanbaug engages in legalising abortion.

May this book by Monsignor Antony Perumayan help people to open their eyes to the helplessness of the unborn, to respect human life and to accept the sanctity of life. Hearty congratulations to Msgr. Antony Perumayan!

+ *GrAlencherry*

George Cardinal Alencherry
Major Archbishop of the Syro-Malabar Church

5

Message from Archbishop Eamon Martin

The human person created 'in the image and likeness of God' (cf. Gen 1: 26-27) is endowed with a precious and inalienable dignity. This dignity is not dependent on anything or anyone, because the Creator has conferred it in such a way that others are called to recognise and acknowledge that dignity as opposed to granting it.

Monsignor Perumayan's extensive study applies the teaching and wisdom regarding the dignity of the human person to the question of the personhood of the unborn. This is a timely consideration since in a so-called 'throwaway culture' one could easily forget to recognise and acknowledge the personhood of the unborn baby. Instead, some are inclined to argue that, this is something that might or might not be conferred on the foetus. The teaching of the Catholic Church on the sanctity of unborn life is, ultimately, rooted in the dignity of the personhood of the unborn person. Pope Francis states unequivocally that the Church's insistence on this teaching rests on, 'the conviction that a human being is always sacred and inviolable, in any situation and at every stage of development' (Evangelii Gaudium 213).

I commend the ongoing study of the important topic of the personhood of the unborn and the consequent obligation on us all, individually and collectively, to cherish that dignity and to foster it when it is undervalued. As Pope Benedict observed, 'If personal and social sensitivity towards the acceptance of the new life is lost, then other forms of acceptance that are valuable for society also wither away' (Caritas in Veritate 28). This gentle and clear protecting of the life of the unborn will lead to building a society which cares for the weak, the poor, and so many others who can be easily forgotten. The witness of all believers and indeed of all men and women of goodwill on this issue will be essential to 'building a civilisation of love'.

+ Eamon Martin

Eamon Martin, Archbishop of Armagh

Foreword

This book is a courageous and remarkable undertaking by its author, Monsignor Anthony Perumayan. It is courageous in that it seeks to explore and elucidate the mystery of human life from its inception at a juncture in human history when many grey and undeclared forces seek surreptitiously to blunt human sensibility to the mystery of human life, to its transcendental quality and to its sacred nature.

Through the prisms of the three thematic sections of the book, anchored respectively in explorations of the status of the unborn in Scripture, Science and Ethical theory, the author takes the reader to the threshold of the intelligibility of the origins and status of human life. The subject of the book is indeed a liminal subject and its consideration requires an epistemological approach that is open minded, investigative of all epistemological vehicles of meaning and is therefore both inter-disciplinary and intra-disciplinary in its methodology.

Each of the three thematic sections deserves close reading. In each the author expounds his insights with clarity and skill. Of particular interest for the reader is the manner in which the book highlights how contemporary scientific and medical insights clarify and legitimise anthropological, ethical and moral questions regarding the personhood of the unborn. With the advance of science and with the ever growing potential of science and technology, the amplitude, pertinence and ultimate significance of the inescapable moral dimension of human consciousness and action acquires ever greater importance for civilisation, society and indeed for human history. Therein also lies the timeliness of this publication.

Abortion is the subject of debate in several countries. Whether in Korea, the UK, or in the Republic of Ireland, citizens of our global society, awash with forces manipulative of ethical and moral sensibility, need the synthesis of wisdom, science, ethical theory and insight offered by this book.

Monsignor Perumayan's work will enable readers to realise ever more clearly that abortion is one of the greatest derelictions of human rights of all time and a further tragic societal instance of humanity's ultimate failure of itself.

+ Noël Treanor

Noel Treanor, Bishop of Down and Connor

CONTENTS

Human life, grounded in its divine origin and in the image of God, is the basis of all human rights and the foundation of civilised society. A society itself is to be judged by its protection of and the solicitude it shows for the weakest of its members. In the first part we try, with the help of Scripture, to establish the personhood of the unborn and the moral worth of the human person. For this we will have recourse to the Biblical doctrine of man – being created in the image and likeness of God; standing in relation to God as their personal Creator and the life affirming ethos seen in the Scripture etc. – to understand the sanctity and dignity and thus the moral worth of human person.

The Biblical teaching on personhood will lead us to the specificity of a human being as fashioned by God in His image and likeness which will help us conclude that the foetus is a human being and that human being is a human person. The relationship with God makes a human being's value and worth constant: whether strong or weak, conscious or unconscious, healthy or unhealthy, socially useful or useless, wanted or unwanted, born or unborn. Since human life begins at fertilisation, the full moral worth afforded to every human being is equally afforded from fertilisation onward, throughout the development. After that, we will address and respond to the various objections usually raised against the personhood of the unborn. Therefore, vague notions of personhood or social utility have no place in decisions regarding the worth, dignity, or rights of any human being, born/unborn. Thus we will arrive at the conclusion that human being's life may not be sacrificed for the economic or political welfare or convenience of other individuals or society.

*"One who is a fan of science will also be
a fan of human life – at all of its stages."*
In the second part we will show that an embryo is a complete human – an individual, unique, self-directing organism. All it needs is food and suitable shelter and it will grow into an adult human being. Unfortunately approximately 3,500 persons lose their lives every day at the hands of trained killers. Many of the questions that arise from the abortion controversy are directly related to the scientific knowledge regarding the beginning of human life. Hence, it is primarily a scientific and medical issue. So we need to have recourse to scientific and medical facts. The moral and legal status of the unborn depends on a careful examination of the process of prenatal

development. Now the science of foetology is able to prove, that a living, fully human, and unique individual exists at the moment of fertilisation and continues to grow through various stages of development in a *continuum* until death.

Hence one of the great powers of science is that it is able to help clarify moral issues like personhood of the unborn. Science is clear on this point. It is most unfortunate that scientific facts known for decades or longer have been quietly ignored by many proponents of abortion. Our aim here is to show that the positions like unborn child is simply "part of the woman's body," or that human life does not begin at conception, do not accord with the well established scientific facts. Experts in this field and even those personally sympathetic to abortion, also acknowledge that.

Part Three: Ethical Reflections on the Personhood of the Unborn
Page 127
The onslaughts of postmodernism and pluralism have caused many ordinary people to doubt their shared traditions and deep-seated moralities. Here we seek to find a common basis on which moral acquaintances may build a view of personhood. Such an approach, we hope, will confer a dignity upon human beings that all parties inwardly know they possess. We will examine the insights from a number of writers to demonstrate a commonly-held understanding of human value. This moral sense is limited by our own ability to understand the *telos* built into the universe.

We try to defend the personhood of the unborn with the 'endowment account of personhood'. Defining person as a member of a kind of being that is rational and free, we will establish that humans are rational and a member of a species *Homo Sapiens*. This will help us to arrive at the conclusion that human beings begin to exist at conception and every zygote is a human person. We will seek the support of the 'constitutive property' argument. In the final analysis, the problem we face is not a lack of knowledge; rather it is a moral unwillingness to act on it: Most modern ethical thinking assumes that we don't know what's right and wrong and are trying to find out. But natural law theory assumes that the problem is mainly volitional – that it has to do with the state of our will. It holds that by and large we know what's right and wrong but wish we did not, and that we try to keep ourselves in ignorance so that we can do as we please.

Introduction

Attempts to render an entire group of human beings as "non-persons" based upon arbitrary qualities – such as IQ, age, place of residence, etc. – in order to discriminate against that group is immoral and unjust. History is full of infamous examples of governments legalising the discrimination of an entire group of human beings by rendering them "non-persons." Jews were rendered "sub-humans" in Germany in the 1940s and colonial slave owners bought and sold Africans as "property." As a matter of fact, in 1857 the Supreme Court of a country ruled that Dred Scott, a black slave, was not a "person" with rights, but the "property" of his master. Was the Court wrong then? Of course it was! Throughout history, certain groups have felt the brunt of a system which denied their humanity, stripped their personhood, and subjected them to horrors beyond measure.

While the legal framework that made such horrors possible has now been removed, it remains firmly in place for the babies still in the womb. In some countries today, there is only one group of human beings – the "unwanted," unborn children – for which being human is not enough. There, the pre-born have no protection under the law and are being killed *'en masse'* every day. It is truly astounding, but not wholly unprecedented. The inconvenience of their existence has resulted in a legal loophole of shameful proportions. The (US) Supreme Court of 1973 legalised abortion nationwide with its *Roe vs. Wade* decision. It was just as immoral and unjust where they dehumanised an entire class of human beings in order to legitimise wholesale discrimination against them. Abortion may go down in history as the greatest human rights abuse of all time.

As some countries' founding documents make clear, the right to life is God-given and inalienable. "Is it ever legitimate to categorise specific members of the human community as "non-persons"? If it's morally reprehensible to kill a developing human being after birth, why is it morally permissible to kill a developing human being before birth? The right to live cannot be legitimately usurped. No government or individual has the right to deprive one of life or liberty without a trial by jury, regardless of skin colour, age, stage of development, level of dependence upon others for survival, or place of residence.

If the courts were to consider 'the humanity' of the pre-born child, it could end this age-based discrimination and restore the legal protections of personhood to the pre-born. Governor Mike Rounds I of South Dakota signed bill HB1215 into law on 6th March 2006. Effective from 1st July 2006, nearly all abortions in South Dakota will be criminal acts. Any doctor performing any abortion at any time between conception and childbirth runs the risk of a heavy fine and lengthy jail sentence, unless she/he can prove that the procedure was necessary to save the life of the woman. That is, the guarantee of due process of law under the Constitution of South Dakota applies equally to born and unborn human beings, and that under the Constitution of South Dakota, a pregnant mother and her unborn child, each possesses a natural and inalienable right to life. When signing the bill, Rounds implied his belief that human personhood starts at conception. Rounds said: "In the history of the world, the true test of a civilisation is how well people treat the most vulnerable and most helpless in their society. The sponsors and supporters of this bill believe that abortion is wrong because unborn children are the most vulnerable and most helpless persons in our society. I agree with them."[1]

But, "the fact is, too many people are afraid to stand up for the most vulnerable and most helpless members of our society or even acknowledge their existence. However, South Dakota defined the foetus as a member of our species. It legislatively made the unborn a person, making abortion akin to murder. At least South Dakota had everyone's best interests in mind. If you do too, go out and get educated on the horrors going on behind closed doors. You may be surprised."[2]

As we know, for Catholics and pro-lifers human life is a sacred continuous "process" from conception, through pregnancy, birth, growth to adulthood and on to natural (or accidental) death. To deliberately destroy an innocent human being at any point after conception is, in God's eyes, wrongful killing. Therefore, discarding spare embryos, terminating a pregnancy, starving the differently–abled child to death (or giving a lethal dose of a powerful drug to end the earthly life of an elderly or incurably diseased person) are all prohibited by the teaching of the Bible. They are all acts which intentionally destroy innocent human life, and such acts are forbidden by the commandment: 'Thou shalt not kill'. Hence Catholics and the pro-lifers oppose abortion, embryo disposal, infanticide and euthanasia.

The real question today is not when human life begins, but what the value of human life is. "The abortionist who reassembles the arms and legs of a tiny baby to make sure all its parts have been torn from its mother's body can hardly doubt whether it is a human being."[3] The legality of abortion entirely centres on the question as to whether and at what point, [an embryo or] a foetus is a person. For Paul Campos, professor of law at the University of Colorado, this is a question that cannot be answered logically or empirically. The concept of personhood, according to him,[4] "is essentially a religious or quasi-religious idea, based on one's fundamental (and therefore unverifiable) assumptions about the nature of the world."[5] "In a world where man must learn more and more to recognise and to respect his brother, the [Catholic] Church wishes to make her own contribution to the service of the human community, while pointing out... the relationship that binds each person to the Creator of all life and the source of the inalienable dignity of each person, from conception to life's natural end."[6]

This book will give scientific, ethical and scriptural support to what South Dakota has attempted. It is a treatment of the subject of human life from its initial stage to birth thus establishing the sacredness of human life especially at its nascent stage. It is expected that it will drive home the eternal truth of the sacredness and dignity of human life at all stages from the time of conception to its (natural/accidental) end.

---

1 John-Henry Westen, "Abortion Ban Signed into Law by South Dakota Governor," 2006-MAR-06, LifeSiteNews.com. See also, Chet Brokaw, "S.D. Governor Signs Abortion Ban Into Law," Associated Press, 2006-MAR-06, at:http://my.earthlink.net/

2 Eric Versluys, "South Dakota law is clear," The Rocky Mountain Collegina, 2006-MAR-09, at:http://www.collegian.com/

3 President Ronald Reagan, "Abortion and the Conscience of the Nation," The Human Life Review, 1983-Spring, Online at: http://www.nationalreview.com/

4 The explanation of 'personhood' will be given later.

5 Paul Campos, "Opinions: PAUL CAMPOS: Abortion and the rule of law," Scripps Howard News Service, 2002-JAN, at: http://www.nandotimes.com

6 "Dignity of man, from conception until natural death, is primary, says Pope Benedict XVI," Catholic News Agency, 2005-JUN-01, at: http://www.catholicnewsagency.com.

PART ONE
The Personhood of the Unborn: Scripture

'Man then is not man because of what he does or what he accomplishes.
He is man because God made him'. 'Cogito(r) ergo sum'
We are "fearfully and wonderfully made." (Psalmist) 139

Introduction: Personhood Starts at Conception

The issue of personhood informs opinion on abortion issues. We must therefore, reflect on these questions: when does a life which deserves moral and legal protection as a human being really begin, and at what point do we attribute moral status to a human being? A strong pro-life stance believes that human personhood begins at conception. That is, a newly formed zygote – a 'just-fertilised ovum'– is a full human being and must be protected as such that it has rights including the right to not be deprived of its own life.

Some pro-lifers are reluctant to define the advent of personhood at a point later than conception, because this might lead to a "slippery slope" situation: the public might reach a consensus that abortions should be legal and freely available at progressively later times in gestation.

The Moral Worth of Human Life

The question "why is life good?" is found everywhere in the Bible and from the very first pages it receives a powerful and amazing answer. The life which God gives (wo)man is quite different from the life of all other living creatures. (Wo)man, although formed from the dust of the earth (cf. Gen 2:7, 3:19; Job 34:15; Ps 103:14; 104:29), is a manifestation of God in the world, a sign of his presence, and a trace of his glory (cf. Gen 1:26-27; Ps 8:6). This is what Saint Irenaeus of Lyons wanted to emphasise in his celebrated definition: man fully alive, is the glory of God.

Man has been given a sublime dignity, based on the intimate bond which unites him to his Creator: in man there shines forth a reflection of God himself. Humans, reflecting this divine image, possess certain qualities which set us apart from other things created by God, qualities such as "rationality, creativity and spirituality, for instance."[7] This fact affirms the Christian view of the essential dignity of human life.

A recurrent theme in the Bible is that it is good to be alive. Human beings are accorded the greatest dignity: they are said to be the pinnacle of creation (Gen. Chs 1&2, Zech. 12:1); made in God's image and likeness (Gen. 1:26-31, 5:1,

9:6, Wis. 2:23, 1Cor. 11:7, Jas. 3:9); with his spirit or breath (Gen. 2:7, Is. 42:5, 57:16, Job 27:3, 32:8, 33:4, 34:13-14, Acts 17:25) and so, are little less than gods themselves (Ps.8). The rest of creation is ordered to their good and only they are given dominion over it (Gen. 1:28-31, 9:1-7); they, in turn, are oriented to God, who alone is Lord of life (Hos. Ch.2, 2Mac.14:46).

The incarnation further dignifies human beings: The Son of God himself became human and died to redeem all people, to make them children of God and heirs of his kingdom and to renew them in his likeness (Jn. 1:14, 1Cor. 15:49, 2 Cor. 3. 17-18; Rom. 8.29; Col. 3.10; Phil. 2. 5-11; Eph. 4.22-24; Ch. 5). Because of this high estimation human being must be reverenced for what they are in themselves and never reduced to mere instruments for the advantage of others.

The title 'Womb with a Window' is a kind of thought experiment. If wombs had windows it would be more difficult to refuse to acknowledge the personhood of the unborn and to continue to rationalise the right to kill such a person. In our thought experiment we consider a womb with a window having two panes: one Scripture and the other science. If we look through a window we can see what is inside the room. Similarly, a sincere look through the panes of Scripture and science will enable one to be convinced that what is in the womb is a human person. Thus, the charade of whether there is "personhood" would more quickly cease. F. La Gard Smith rightly recollects: "For years, like millions of other Americans I had only the vague notion of what actually took place in an abortion. I assumed that the procedure to "terminate a pregnancy" was simply the removal of a blob of cells having no similarity whatever to a human being. But most of us would be shocked to see how highly developed the typical aborted foetus really is, even at very early stages."[8]

Pro-choice is nothing less than blind choice that slams the windows shut. Those who argue against abortion believe that if wombs had windows, the abortion debate would be over, once and for all. Here is an attempt to look through the panes of Scripture and Science that make up the window of the womb. This will help us to arrive at the conclusion that what is conceived in the womb is a human person.

Questions about the nature and value of life especially prenatal life in God's sight cannot be answered without an understanding of the Biblical doctrine of man. Hence we must begin by explaining the Biblical doctrine of man.

The Biblical Doctrine of Man

The Biblical doctrine of man can be summarised as follows: Being created by God, in His own image and likeness, human life is sacred and so it has dignity and the ensuing right to be respected and protected. An understanding of the concepts, 'sanctity' and the 'image of God' will help us to appreciate the moral worth of human life.

Sanctity and Dignity

"Once the principle of the sanctity of life is abandoned, there can be no criterion of the right to life, except that of personal taste."[9]

The word sanctity refers to something that is sacred or holy. People like Gerhard von Rad, Anthony Fisher, Huesman J., and J Wyatt believe that human life is sacred. They maintain that human life has value in itself, because it has been created by God and because of this, humans have responsibility to respect and protect all human life at all times. Others like Peter Singer, Ronald Dworkin, Vardy P, Grosch P and James Watson argue that the 'quality of life' concept is more important than the 'sanctity of life' principle. This approach asserts that humans are autonomous beings and have the ability to choose between life and death in certain circumstances. Peter Singer comments that if "the choice was between the sanctity of life ethic and the quality of life ethic, the decision has been unequivocally in favour of the latter."[10]

Sanctity of Human Life: Some Secular Views

Some secular philosophers do not accept that human life is sacrosanct. They opine that if a person's quality of life is so poor that they feel their life is no longer worth living, they should have the autonomy to decide to end their own life. Or in the case of an embryo, parents should be able to abort to prevent the unnecessary suffering of a child who may be born with severe disabilities. Ronald Dworkin in his book *"Life's Dominion"* outlines his belief that all people should have the right to decide for themselves whether they live or die. He explains the importance of personal autonomy in the following quote: "Freedom is the cardinal, absolute requirement of self-respect: no one treats life as having any intrinsic objective importance unless he insists on leading that life himself, not being ushered along it by others."[11] Peter Singer in his book *'Rethinking Life and Death'* argues: "The traditional religious view that all human life is sacrosanct is simply not able to cope with the array of modern medical dilemmas."[12] Singer believes that the "worth of human life varies" that we should "respect a person's desire to live or die" and "bring children into the world only if they are wanted."[13]

If these secular views are accepted, abortion and euthanasia will become morally acceptable, because these views do not believe in the sanctity of life.

Sanctity of Human Life: Christian View
The Biblical view on the sanctity of life (which we will see shortly) is shared by many of the Christian denominations. At the 1998 Lambeth Conference, the Anglican Communion declared: "life is God – given and has intrinsic sanctity, significance and worth."[14] In a booklet produced by the Board of Social Witness of the Presbyterian Church in Ireland, we read like this: "God is creator of life and He is sovereign. We are made in God's image and are unique. All human beings, regardless of age or disability, have infinite worth in His sight because they are made in His image. Being human requires us to be in relationship with other people who are necessarily different from ourselves."[15]

The Catholic Church promotes the sanctity of life. She embraces a "consistent ethic of life." This does not mean that all life issues have equal urgency. It does mean that all life issues are linked. Simply to list the "life issues" is a challenging task, because everything which impacts the dignity of the human person can be considered a "life issue." At times, however, we need to step back and examine the common thread that connects the "life issues." What is the foundation? What is the answer to the fundamental question, "Why should human life be defended in the first place?" The encyclical *Evangelium Vitae* states that human life is "the 'place' where God manifests himself, where we meet him and enter into communion with him".[16] This statement provides a starting point for profound meditation on the reason why life is sacred. When we think biblically about God "manifesting" Himself, we think of creation, of mighty deeds, and of the death and Resurrection of Christ. Deeper reflections on creation and on the cross help us see in what sense human life becomes a meeting place with God. The *Catechism of the Catholic Church* states: "Human life is sacred because from its beginning it involves the creative action of God and it remains forever in a special relationship with the Creator, who is its sole end."[17]

These considerations give the basis for the principle of dignity of human life. This principle supplies "what is noticeably lacking in secular discussions: a genuinely transcendent basis for recognising the dignity and value of human life".[18] Now we will begin with an examination of the biblical outlook on the value and dignity of human life, and then consider the texts that relate specifically to prenatal human life, concluding with the personhood of the unborn.

Sanctity of Human Life: Biblical View

The Bible includes a number of references which imply that human life is sacred. "Since the creation of the world, invisible realities, God's eternal power and divinity have become visible, recognised through the things he has made" (Rom. 1:20). At the height of creation, God manifested His "image" in the creation of man and woman. "God created man in his image; in the divine image he created him; male and female he created them" (Gen. 1:27).

In Genesis 1:26, God distinguished humans from the rest of the animal creation. Only of man did God say, "Let us make man in our image, according to our likeness." He appointed man then to rule over the other creatures on earth. In his address to the Consistory of Cardinals (April 1991) which dealt with the sanctity of life, Pope Benedict XVI, the then Cardinal Joseph Ratzinger, noted, "Man is created in the image and likeness of God" (Gn 1:26).

In the two accounts of creation recorded in Genesis 1 and 2, we are informed that human life is the high point of God's creation. In the first creation account we are told that God said: Let us make man in our image, in our likeness, and let them rule.... (Gen1:26). The implication of this is that human life is sacred. This reference implies that "human beings are unique in all the vast array of creation because they alone of all the creatures are made in God's image."[19]

The creation of human life has, essentially and from the beginning, a communitarian dimension. Much has been written about what the "image of God" means, which we shall see later. It is far more than simply the fact that human beings can think or that we have a spiritual soul. The "image of God" in the creation of human life includes our whole being, spiritual and physical, and the fact that we find ourselves by a gift of ourselves. "Male and female he created them." This is the "divine image" because within God, there is a giving, a pouring out of self from one person to another. That is reflected in the union of marriage, and in the many other manifestations of human love. The truth here is so obvious that it is easy to miss. We have the capacity to give ourselves freely to each other and to God. This makes us unique in creation. As said above, this makes us a manifestation of God, who is love, and who gives Himself freely to His creation.

The second account of creation expresses the same idea, saying that man, taken from the dust of the earth, carries in himself the divine breath of life. This creation account develops the profound and sacred character describing how God blew into man's nostrils the divine breath of life: "the Lord God formed the man from the dust in the ground and breathed into his nostrils the breath of life, and the man became a living being" (Gen 2:7). This account of creation informs us that God is responsible for the creation of human life: It is by this divine life force that an essential feature of man's being is his immediacy with God. Man is characterised by immediacy with God that is proper to his being; man is *capax Dei* and because he lives under the personal protection of God he is 'sacred'…" *Evangelium Vitae* develops this theme further in the following passage: "Life is always a good. This is an instinctive perception and a fact of experience, and man is called to grasp the profound reason why this is so". From these two accounts we can deduce the sanctity and dignity of human life from the very beginning of the Old Testament.

The concept of sanctity of life can be seen developed also in Job 10:8-12. It highlights that God is the author of life and therefore life is scared. "Your hands shaped me and made me .....You moulded me like clay.... You gave me life and showed me kindness." Then the prophet Jeremiah develops the idea that life is sacrosanct because it is created by God. Jeremiah 10:23 implies that because God alone gives life, he is the only one who can take it: "A man's life is not his own; it is not for man to direct his steps."

The New Testament also refers to the sanctity of life. It is clearly expressed by Paul in I Cor. 6:19: "Do you not know that your body is a temple of the Holy Spirit?" In Mathew's gospel, Jesus is recorded as having said that we should not worry about food or clothes because God will provide for our needs, just as he provides for the birds. Jesus then adds: "Are you not much more valuable than they?" (Mat. 6:26). It is implied that we humans have a unique relationship with God and this is the basis for the sacredness of our life.[20]

The Biblical view on the sanctity of life can be further developed when we consider the commandment 'not to take life' is consistent (with the exception of war and capital punishment, which were much part of the culture at that time) throughout both the Old and New Testaments. The commandment from Ex 20:13 "you shall not murder" is developed by God's words in Gen 9:6: "whoever sheds the blood of man, by man shall his blood be shed; for in the image of God has God made him." According to Heusman, the commandment not to kill was intended to "protect the very sacredness of human life by forbidding murder."[21]

That is, according to this scriptural view, human dignity is based not on social acceptance, intellectual capacity, maturity, independence or wantedness but on membership of the human race, that one 'family' with whom God has this special relationship.[22] Man being created in the image and likeness of God is the ground for this special relationship. This special relationship with the Creator is the source of man's inalienable dignity and his sanctity. This dignity is the basis for man's rights especially the right not to be killed. Now we shall turn to 'image of God', the ground for our special relationship with God, which is the source of human dignity, which is the basis for man's rights.

Image of God
From what has been said so far, it is clear that human beings are created in God's image and therefore have inherent value independent of their utility or function. The primary source and documentation for this concept of the essential nature of human beings is found first in Genesis 1:26, 27, and it appears in two other places also (Gen.5:1-3, 9:6).

The Image of God (Hebrew: צֶלֶםאֱלֹהִים; tselem elohim, lit. 'image of God', often appearing in Latin as *Imago Dei*) is a concept and theological doctrine within all Abrahamic religions. It asserts that before creating man God said: "Let us make a human in our image/*b'tsalmeinu*, as our likeness/*kid'muteinu*. And they will have dominion over [the animals] … And God created the human in His image /*b'tsalmo*, in God's image/*tselem* He created him, male and female He created them. And God blessed them and God said to them: Bear fruit and multiply and fill the land and occupy her, and have dominion over the sea's fish and the sky's birds and every animal crawling over the land". (Gen 1:27–28). The other two are the following: "On the day God created Adam, in His likeness/ *d'mut* God created him; male and female He created them, and He blessed them, and called their name Adam in the day of their being created. And Adam lived 130 years and bore in his likeness/ *bid'muto* like his image/ *k'tsalmo* and called his name Seth". (Gen 5:1–3). "One who spills the blood of the human, through/by the human, his blood will be spilled, for in God's image/ tselem He made the human." (Gen 9:6) There have been many interpretations of this concept from ancient times until today.

Image of God: Biblical Interpretation

Biblical scholars still have no consensus about the meaning of the term Image of God. To assert that humans are created in the image of God may mean to recognise some special qualities of human nature which allow God to be made manifest in humans. For humans to have a conscious recognition of having been made in the image of God may mean that they are aware of being that part of creation through whom God's plans and purposes can best be expressed and actualised; humans, in this way, can interact creatively with the rest of creation. The moral implications of the doctrine of *Imago Dei* are apparent in the fact that, if humans are to love God, then humans must love other humans whom God has created (cf. John 13:35), as each is an expression of God.

The human likeness to God can also be understood by contrasting it with that which does not image God, i.e., beings who, as far as we know, are without this spiritual self-awareness and the capacity for spiritual / moral reflection and growth. We may say that humans differ from all other creatures because of the self-reflective, rational nature of their thought processes – their capacity for abstract, symbolic as well as concrete deliberation and decision-making. This capacity gives the human a centredness and completeness which allows the possibility for self-actualisation and participation in a sacred reality (cf. Acts 17:28).[23]

Image and Likeness

Theologians have been examining the difference between the concepts of the "image of God" and the "likeness of God" in human nature for more than 2000 years. Origen viewed the image of God as something given at creation, while the likeness of God as something bestowed upon a person at a later time. The theologian Irenaeus made a distinction between God's image and his likeness by pointing to Adam's supernatural endowment bestowed upon him by the Spirit.[24] The image was the human's natural resemblance to God, the power of reason and will. The likeness was a *donum superadditum* – a divine gift added to the basic human nature. This likeness consisted of the moral qualities of God, whereas the image involved the natural attributes of God. When Adam fell, he lost the likeness, but the image remained fully intact. Humanity as humanity was still complete, but the good and holy being was spoiled.[25] That is, the image referred to a natural, innate resemblance to God and the likeness referred to the moral attributes (God's attributes) that were lost in the fall.[26] The same image and likeness thus become the basis for the sanctity and sacredness of the person at any stage of development.

This Biblical account tells us that human life is a trust given into our stewardship by God, that we are called to choose life and the ways of life; not death and ways of death; that any killing demands justification and the taking of innocent human life is contrary to God's will, and that no one should usurp the role of God, who alone is the Lord of life and death.

Life Affirming Ethos

Accordingly, we can identify the following life affirming ethos in the Bible: a) Sanctity based on image of God, and b) Sanctity based on the prohibition of murder.

Sanctity Based on *Imago Dei*

The centuries have produced a wide range of interpretations of the image *(tselem)* and the likeness *(demuth)* of God in (wo)man.[27] "These interpretations have generally focused on features of man's consciousness as the seat of the *imago Dei*: man's intellectual, moral, and spiritual capacities. As we shall see later, such a view is one-sided in the light of the Biblical data and reflects the influence of a Greek understanding of human nature".[28] Generally, there are three ways of understanding the manner in which humans exist in *Imago Dei* – Substantive, Functional and Relational.

Substantive: The substantive view holds to the idea that there is some substantial characteristic of the human race that is like God. Some may argue that we are a mirror image of God's essential nature. Other substantive views suggest a spiritual commonality with God, God being a spirit and not having a physical body. Throughout the ages there have been different interpretations of substantive likeness to God.

Functional: The 'functional' view differs from the substantive and relational views in that it argues that the image of God imprinted on us resides in function rather than in form or relationship, this function being primarily our task of ruling over earth. Genesis 1:26 speaks of humankind being made in the image of God and given the function of naming and ruling over the fish of the sea and the animals on land, reflecting God's rule over all the universe, ourselves included. Here the point to be stressed is that the Biblical doctrine of the *imago* is primarily a relational one.[29]

Relational: The relational view argues that one must be in a relationship with God in order to possess the 'image' of God. In all his relations and acts, he is never man-in-himself, but always man in relation, in relation to this history of God's deeds in creation, to this origin of an inalienable relation to his Creator. If we seek to define man merely in terms of various qualities and abilities, we are not giving a biblical picture of man. This means, man, as *imago Dei*, possessing inalienable dignity and worth, is to be understood not primarily in terms of innate capacities or faculties – whether intellectual, moral, or spiritual – but in terms of his unique relationship to his transcendent Creator and covenant Lord. However, those who hold to the relational image agree that humankind possess the ability to reason as a substantive trait.

Theologians like Karl Barth and Emil Brunner argue that it is our ability to establish and maintain complex and intricate relationships that make us like God. Since other creatures do not form such explicitly referential spiritual relationships, these theologians see this ability as uniquely representing the *imago Dei* in humans. We repeat once again that it is not intrinsic powers of speech, imagination, and rational thought that lend transcendent worth to human nature, but man's unique calling to live in loving fellowship with the Triune God for all eternity.

Sanctity Based on Prohibition of Murder
The imposition of capital punishment for murder, in Gen. 9:6, presupposes the inviolability of man's life in the sight of the Creator, precisely because man bears the divine image: "Whoever sheds the blood of man, by man shall his blood be shed; for God made man in his own image. Shedding man's blood is a heinous offence for the very reason that an attack on the bodily integrity of man is an assault on the dignity and honour of the One who created him."[30]

The prohibition of murder forbids the outward act of violence, along with the hateful and malicious intentions of the heart that give rise to the act.[31] The N.T also attests to the fact that the sacredness of human life as the divine image precludes not only violent actions against others, but also harmful verbal expressions.[32] "Christ makes explicit the profound ethical implications of the Decalogue in his Sermon on the Mount (Matt. 5:28); the commandment prohibits not only the outward destruction of a neighbour's life, but even the attitude of contempt, which demeans his personal worth (Matt. 5:21,22)".[33] Referring to Genesis 1:26, James writes that cursing another human violates God's will, as man is made in the image of God. . . (James 3:8-10).

Gospels also make it clear that God's law represents more than negative prohibitions. It entails positive obligation to love God with all the resources of one's personality and one's neighbour as oneself (Matt.22:37-40; Mark

12:30,31; Luke 10:27,28). By ruling out thoughts and attitudes that demean and endanger our neighbour's life, it in fact implies a positive obligation to affirm and protect our neighbour, as circumstances and our abilities permit. According to Q.99 of the Westminster Larger Catechism: ". . .where a duty is commanded, the contrary sin is forbidden; and where a sin is forbidden, the contrary duty is commanded." Accordingly we can say, "abortion on demand, the deliberate killing of innocent prenatal human life, is clearly incompatible with that life-affirming ethos found in the Scripture".[34]

For a better understanding and appreciation of the 'personhood of the unborn', it is good to know how God deals with children and the least privileged. This can be better understood in the light of the paradigm shift, seen in the scripture. God uses a different measure in judging personhood. As humans, who are supposed to be the manifestation of God the Creator, we are also expected to understand this measure and use the same for assessing the personhood of the unborn.

A Paradigm Shift: Divine Standard vs Human Standard
Israel's God was concerned about those whom culture was prone to neglect as having little value. The frequent Biblical injunctions to show compassion toward the fatherless, the widow, and the sojourner (Deut. 10:18; 14:29; Ps. 10:14; Is. 1:17; Jer. 49:11) seem to question our current attitudes toward unwanted unborn children. Austen Ivereigh, author of a biography, *"The Great Reformer: Francis and the Making of a Radical Pope"* and founder of the *Catholic Voices* website, refers to Pope Francis' visits to impoverished and geopolitically insignificant countries and gives the following comment: "The point he wants to make ... is his conviction that often those on the margins are the most receptive to the Church, and he wants to give voice to those on the margins."[35]

God's concern for the fatherless challenges both the *'de facto'* abandonment of paternal responsibility by many fathers, and by implication the widespread abandonment of maternal responsibility toward the unborn. Abortion may well be the ultimate rejection of parental responsibility and compassion for one's own offspring. It is likewise an ultimate denial of the transcendent value of an unborn human being. But God's values are not society's values. Society may neglect the fatherless, but He does not and will not. "There could hardly be a more fitting paradigm of the electing love of God than today's unwanted unborn child, rejected by culture, but valued in the sight of God."[36]

God's standards are a striking contrast to the contemporary criterion of "viability" as a measure of the worth of the unborn child. Contrary to the view that an "unviable" infant is less valuable than a "viable" one, the Bible depicts human weakness, dependency, and helplessness as what most fully manifest the love of God for the most vulnerable of the earth. The Son of God came to minister to the weak and heal the sick. While some propose that severely handicapped infants be left to die from neglect,[37] God's Messiah would not break a bruised reed or quench a smouldering wick (Isa.42:3; Matt. 12:20).[38]

"In God's sight no human being is completely "viable" in the sense of having mastery over his own life or the independent capacity to overcome the dominion and guilt of sin; and yet it is in human weakness that the power of God is made perfect (2 Cor. 12:9). The God of Israel does not judge human worth on the basis of age, size, physical appearance, or "viability" (cf. 1 Sam. 16:7). By his sovereign grace, God can demonstrate his glory even in unwanted infants with birth defects such as blindness and deafness (Exod. 4:11; John 9:3)".[39]

Christ's words and actions pose a sharp challenge to conventional ways of assessing human worth. "Christ's attitude toward children cuts at the very root of the contemporary abortion ethos. While his disciples felt that the young children brought to him (Matt. 19:13-15; Mark 10:13-16; Luke 18:15-17) were not important enough to demand his time and attention, Jesus' actions proved otherwise. The disciples apparently did not regard the young children as persons 'in the whole sense.' But Jesus did".[40] For example, Jesus presented a child as the very paradigm of a citizen of the kingdom of heaven (Matt. 18:1-4; Mark 9:33-37; Luke 9:46-48).

According to the parable of the Good Samaritan (Luke 10:25-37), "love is to be understood in an inclusive sense, extending beyond the bounds of one's normal associations and natural sympathies".[41] "Patterned on the universal benevolence of the heavenly Father, a disciple's love is to far transcend the conventional perception of one's 'neighbour,' even to include the enemy who persecutes (Matt.5:43-48)".[42] In the modern world the unborn child, like the man in the parable, all too often falls prey to unexpected assaults on his life. Our Lord's teachings challenge us to ask whether neighbour-love ought to extend even to the unborn children of the world. St. Paul made this point very clear to the Corinthian Church (1Cor. 1:26-29). He said to them: "Consider your call, brethren; not many of you were wise according to worldly standards, not many were powerful, not many were of noble birth; but God chose what is weak in the world to shame the strong. God chose what is low and despised in the world, even things that are not, to bring to nothing things that are, so that no human being might boast in the presence of God".[43]

God's ways are not our ways, and his perceptions of personhood are different from ours. It is precisely in God's choice of what the world often sees as the "foolish" and the "weak," the "low and despised," and even "things that are not" *(ta me onta)* that his mercy and grace are thrown into sharpest relief.

Having seen the life affirming ethos and paradigm shift, now we shall turn our attention to the concept of personhood. As our topic of study is 'personhood of the unborn', an understanding of this concept will be helpful.

Humanness and Personhood: Scripture
There are essentially two issues which must be resolved concerning unborn embryos and foetuses. The first is, "Are they human beings?" The second is, "Should they be recognised as persons?" There is no debate on the first question. It is a matter of plain, objective science. Embryos and foetuses are fully and individually human from fertilisation on.[44] If this were not true, if unborn children were not genetically distinct human beings, there would be no need to even talk about rights of personhood; "Removing a foetus" would be the moral equivalent of pulling out a tooth. This, however, is not the case. In many controversial bioethical debates, the key point is whether or not a subject can be considered a person. This is a philosophical (including religious philosophy) and legal consideration. Science and medicine can't give the definition, but given a definition it may be possible (depending on the definition) to determine who and what is a person. How do you define what a person is? When does someone become a person? At what point do they stop being a person? Are there different stages/levels of personhood? Can a non-human be a person? Can you have a human that isn't a person? Could a non-biological entity ever be a person? Could a non-living entity be a person?

How do you decide the answers to these questions? Is it because of your religion? If so, what is your religion? Where in your religion do you get the answers from? Is it written in a sacred text or teachings?

In our attempt to define personhood, as Christians we have recourse to our sacred Scripture. Before going directly into what Scripture says about 'person', let us learn what the term means in common parlance.

'Person' in Common Parlance

If you look up the word "person" in your average dictionary (for example, Webster's), you'll find something like this: "Person (n), a human being." A person, simply put, is a human being. This fact should be enough. The intrinsic humanity of unborn children, by definition, makes them persons, and should, therefore, guarantee their protection under the law. Hence, an understanding of 'what it means to be human?' will be timely. The focus of our study is on the 'Scriptural and scientific support for the personhood of the unborn'. So, we will first look into Scripture and then will try to get the support of science to see how they qualify humanness and personhood. Then we will examine whether foetus qualifies itself to be called 'human' and thereby be a 'person'.

We all know and understand what it means to be human. Yet, when it comes to defining what being human means in the world of bioethics, the question does not quickly yield a simple answer. Our answer will shape our view on many important issues: scientific research on embryos, reproductive technologies, abortion, end-of-life decisions, care of patients with brain damage, and policies on animal rights, genetic engineering, and artificial intelligence. What does it mean to be human is at once a biological, theological, and ethical question?

The question, 'what does it mean to be human?' is more than a matter of academic interest. The question is relevant to everyday ministry situations pastors face. In hospital visitation, pastors encounter family members of patients struggling with decisions for care of preterm infants, car accident victims with brain damage, and the terminally ill. In the counselling office, pastors answer questions from couples about choice of birth control methods and reproductive technologies. In the pulpit, pastors address the difficult moral issues facing our society, such as how to protect the young, the disabled, and the elderly. To define what it means to be human as it relates to bioethical decisions, let us examine the Biblical answers to this question first.

Humanness: Biblical Basis

The Bible affirms that God is the Lord and giver of all life.[45] Human beings are uniquely made in God's image,[46] and each individual human being is infinitely precious to God and made for an eternal destiny.[47] The Christian attitude toward human life is thus one of reverence[48] from the moment of fertilisation to death. We can present the Biblical basis for the humanness of the unborn, in the following manner.

1. Procreation is acknowledged in the Bible to be the gift of God.[49]

2. The mandate for human procreation in Genesis 1:27-28 and 9:1,7 implies that the God-ordained means of filling the earth with human beings made in His image is the proper reproductive expression of human sexuality in marriage. Human beings do not merely reproduce "after their kind"; they beget or procreate beings that, like themselves, are in the image of God (see CMDA Statement on Reproductive Technology).

3. Human beings are created as ensouled bodies or embodied souls.[50] (Genesis 2:7). Together the physical and spiritual aspects of human beings bear the single image of God and constitute the single essential nature of human life.[51] A biological view of human life beginning at fertilisation is therefore consistent with the Biblical view of human life.

4. From fertilisation on, God relates to the unborn in a personal manner.[52] Fertilisation and birth are regularly linked in Biblical language.[53] God continues His activity in the unfolding and continuous development of the foetus.

5. The Bible assumes a personal and moral continuity through fertilisation, birth, and maturation.[54]

6. The Bible, the Church in all its formative Creeds[55] and Ecumenical Councils,[56] and the witness of the Holy Spirit attest to the beginning of the incarnation, wherein the second person of the Trinity took upon himself human nature, being conceived ("conceived" is to be understood as "fertilisation;)"[57] by the power of the Holy Spirit in the womb of the Virgin Mary.[58] The uniqueness of the event and its mode does not affect its relevance to the question of the beginning of human life. From conception the Son of God is incarnate, his human nature made like us in every way.[59] It follows that authentic human existence begins at conception or fertilisation.

Definition of Human Being

There is an acute need of defining humanness when discussing the subject of abortion. The following statement shows its urgency: "People who worry about the moral danger of abortion do so because they think of the foetus as a human being and hence equate foeticide with murder. Whether the foetus is or is not a human being is a matter of definition, not fact, and we can define any way we wish."[60] This statement is reprehensible. If we can define 'humanness' any way we wish, then no life is safe.

We are with no philosophical basis for protecting any life. D. Callahan observes: "A power group society could by use of this principle (of defining humanness any way we wish) define the chronically sick, the senile, the elderly as non-human, and thus justify the taking of their lives on grounds of the social good to be obtained."[61] The cogency of Callahan's rebuttal will be apparent to all who remember the German experience under Hitler, who defining the Jew as less than human justified their elimination.[62]

The Bible contains information that defines what it means to be a human being. Being created in His own image, God gave man special status and dominion over all other animals (Genesis 1:26-27). The Bible gives the reason for the moral seriousness of murder in the fact God made man in His image (Genesis 9:6). Being made in the image of God connotes that human beings have intrinsic moral value based on whom we are instead of extrinsic moral value based on certain functions and capabilities we possess.

The Bible also teaches that human beings have a spirit as well as a body. James states that the body apart from the spirit is dead (James 2:26). When Paul teaches about the resurrection, he distinguishes between the spirit and the body (1 Corinthians 15:44). If human beings have a spirit as well as a body, then a human being has value beyond the condition and developmental stage of his body. The identity of a human being involves more than just the state of the physical body or the measure of mental capacity.

Psalm 139:13–16 shows that God knows us even at the earliest stages of embryological development, before our organs have formed and our cells have differentiated. The Bible demonstrates that God cares for all human life, regardless of capacities. In demonstrating His providential care for the developing child within his mother's womb, God affirms the dignity of human life before birth. In addition, this passage supports the concept of human beings having intrinsic value bestowed on them by their Creator that is not contingent on attaining a certain developmental stage or acquiring certain functional abilities.

God's call on the lives of the prophet Isaiah (Isaiah 49:1) and the prophet Jeremiah (Jeremiah 1:5), as well as the apostle Paul (Galatians 1:15), originated before birth while they were still in the womb. In Luke 1:39–44, the Bible tells of John the Baptist at six months' gestation in his mother Elizabeth's womb leaping for joy as Mary, carrying the developing Messiah within her womb, came to visit. These Scriptures support the concept of an individual having personal and moral continuity from the beginning stages of human life within the womb to adulthood.

We shall start with an exegetical approach to the humanness of the foetus. This will help us to understand the specificity of being human. Then we will apply this specificity to the foetus to see whether the foetus can be considered human. If it satisfies we can conclude that the foetus is human and hence a person.

Humanness of the Foetus: An Exegetical Approach
We have two methods for proceeding to arrive at a Biblical definition of human: 1) we could exegete the two basic texts disclosing the origin and nature of man recorded in the first two chapters of Genesis and 2) we could study the crucial theological terms informing a Biblical anthropology about man's essential being, such as *basar* and *soma*, body,[63] *nephesh* and *psyche*, soul, *leb* and *kardia*, 'heart', and so forth.

We shall combine these two methods by considering the crucial theological words in connection with an exegesis of the two fundamental texts presenting the origin and nature of man. We shall take the familiar verse Gen.2:7 as the first text. "Then the Lord God formed man of dust from the ground, and breathed into his nostrils the breath of life; and man became a living soul." Here we can identify three clauses and we shall see them in turn. From the first clause, "the Lord God formed man of dust from the ground" it is clear that man is in part "dust", personally fashioned by God. We can easily deduce that man originated from the earth both by the fact that he must continually ingest the minerals of the earth through its produce in order to maintain its existence and by the fact that upon death man's body once again becomes part of the earth. The pertinent anthropological terms here are primarily *basar* (Hebrew) and *soma* (Greek), "body".
The second clause, "and breathed into his nostrils the breath of life", reveals that man's origin is not only from the earth but also from heaven. His life manifested by his breathing, derives from the eternally living God (Dt.32:39-41). The phrase "of life" (subjective genitive) denotes that man's breath is a manifestation of life. According to Hans Walter Wolff, "for Old Testament man, life is essentially manifested in the breath."[64] Here the key theological terms are *neshama*, breath and *ruah* and *pneuma*, 'wind'.

There are other texts also that teach that man's life, manifested by his breathing, comes from the spirit of God. Job, for example whose words the

Lord approved (Job 42:7), said: "For as long as breath is in me, and the wind from God is in my nostrils" (27:3). Likewise, Elihu said: "If he should determine to do so, if he should gather to himself his wind and his breath, all flesh would perish together and man would return to dust" (34:14f). Isaiah referred to God as the One "...... who gives breath to the people on it and wind to those who walk in it" (42:5). The Preacher, whose words are judged to be true (Eccl. 12:10), said: "Then the dust will return to the earth as it was, and the wind will return to God who gave it" (12:7).

The third clause, "and man became a living soul" shows that the result of this union of the clay with the breath of life is called *nephesh* (LXX *psyche*), "soul". *Nephesh* in its most synthetic sense denotes animated substance. Since soul is the *tertium*, the resulting state, it can be said that man does not have soul but that man is soul. It is clear in this basic text soul is not a distinct aspect of man's being but denotes his body animated by the life of God.

Specificity of Being Human

However, all that has been said thus far about man, the Bible also says about animals. They too derive their bodies from the earth. "Let the earth bring forth living creatures after their kind" (Gen. 1:24). They also derive their life from the spirit of God. "Thou dost send forth thy spirit (wind), they (animals) are created; and thou dost renew the face of the ground" (Ps.104:30). Many other texts affirm that animals owe their life to the wind or spirit of God (Gen. 6:17, 7:15, 22; Ez1:12,20, 10:17; Eccl. 3:19,21; Is.31:3). And so, these animated beings are also called "living souls" in scripture. For example, in Genesis 1:24 we read with reference to animals: "Let the earth bring forth living creatures". This traditional rendering, "living creatures", is for the same Hebrew expression, *nephesh hayya*, translated "living souls" with reference to man in Genesis 2:7. That is, animals are also called "living souls".

Then what is that which distinguishes man from the animals? For an answer to this question we have to go beyond Genesis 2:7 and turn to Genesis 1:26-28, the second basic text presenting the origin and nature of man. "Then God said, 'let us make man in our image, according to our likeness'...... So God created man in his own image, in the image of God he created him." That which distinguishes man from animals is that man, in contrast to animals, is created in the image of God, and not after their kind.

We cannot interpret the crucial phrase "image of God", literally. Because in the first place, we are told that God is a spirit (Jn. 4:24; Is. 31:3), and that he is ubiquitous (IKg. 8:27). In the second place a literal interpretation would leave us with all sorts of bizarre questions.[65] Thirdly, it seems unlikely that man's dignity above the rest of the animals (Gen. 9:5; Jas. 3:7-9) is due to his slight physiological differences from them. Finally, a literal interpretation seems not only contradictory to the rest of scripture, and unlikely, but also inappropriate. Gardener aptly observed: "But our anatomy and physiology is demanded by our terrestrial habitat, and quite inappropriate to the one who inhabits eternity."[66] Hence, we have to admit that the statement in Genesis 1:26-28 must be metaphorical of man's spiritual being.

Francis Schaeffer considers that this phrase 'image' refers to our personality: "Within the Trinity, before the creation of anything, there was real love and real communication......This God who is personal created man in his own image.... He is the image of this kind of God and so personality is intrinsic to his make-up. God is personal, and man also is personal."[67] However, this does not completely distinguish man from animals. They also possess intellect, sensibility and will, a normative definition of personality. We need to have more narrow definitions of the term. Kierkegaard states: "Essentially it is the God-relationship that makes a man a man."[68] Emil Brunner concluded that "the image of God is fundamentally relational." G.C. Berkouwer wrote: "The characteristic of the Biblical view lies precisely in this, that man appears as related to God in all his creaturely relationships."[69] This interpretation comes closer to a proper understanding of the metaphor as we have already seen.

We have to be still more precise. The term denotes man as a spiritual, rational and moral being and thus as related to God. Moses pointedly recalled that the Lord revealed himself on the Mount Horeb not as a corporeal but as a transcendent, spiritual, moral being. He describes: ".... Then the Lord spoke to you from the midst of the fire; you heard the sound of words, but you saw no form – only a voice...." (Dt. 4:11-13). God communicated his transcendence through the phenomena accompanying his revelation, and he revealed himself as a spiritual, moral being by appearing only as a voice – just the ten commandments. It is in the image of this spiritual, moral being that man is created; animals are created "after their kind", that is, who behave instinctively. But man is created as a moral being concerned about distinguishing between right and wrong. That is, man is concerned with values, meanings and morals.

Here the crucial words pertaining to man's nature are, *leb* and *kardia*, "heart", which denote man as a spiritual, rational, moral being. Bible frequently uses "heart", an anthropomorphism, with reference to God. In I Samuel 2:35, God resolved: "I will raise up for myself a faithful priest, who shall do according to what is in my heart and in my mind." The statements about the 'heart' of God are worth thinking about because they always concern God's relationship to man. The heart of God is most often mentioned as the organ of God's distinct will, against which man is judged.[70] Hence we say, man is clay personally fashioned by God, animated by breath manifesting the life of God, and in God's image as a spiritual, rational, moral being.[71]

Foetus is Human

Having seen what, it means to be human we turn once again to the Biblical statements regarding the foetus to determine whether the Biblical authors regarded it as a human being. That is, whether the qualifications – fashioned by God and image of God can be meaningfully be applied to 'foetus'.

Foetus is Fashioned by God

The Biblical authors believed that God personally fashions each individual in the womb. For example, Job uses the following metaphors:[72] "Thy hands fashioned and made me altogether, and wouldst thou destroy me? Remember now that thou hast made me as clay; and wouldst thou turn me into dust again? Didst thou not pour me out like milk, and curdle me like cheese, clothe me with skin and flesh, and knit me together with bones and sinews? Thou hast granted me life and loving kindness, and thy care has preserved my spirit" (Job 10:8-12).

Similarly, David sang: "For thou didst form my inward parts; thou didst weave me in my mother's womb. I will give thanks to thee, for I am fearfully and wonderfully made; and my soul knows it very well. My frame was not hidden from thee, when I was made in secret, and skilfully wrought in the depths of the earth. Thine eyes have seen my unformed substance; and in thy book they were all written, the days that were ordained for me, when as yet there was not one of them" (Ps.139:13-16). When Moses complained that he was slow of speech and slow of tongue, the Lord asked him, "Who has made man's mouth? Or who makes him dumb or deaf, or seeing or blind"? (Ex. 4:11).

Advanced knowledge about the DNA molecule and the genetic code fits comfortably into the Biblical revelation, which has much to say about man's sexuality.[73] The inspired writers do not contest the fact that there is a causal connection between intercourse and conception. They consider sexual intercourse as merely the means whereby God, the first cause of all things, gives his blessing. This Biblical view is well expressed by Claudius Matthias when he said: "It went through our hands, but comes from God."[74] So we can say that the foetus, like Adam, is in part clay personally fashioned by God.

However, the Biblical writers are of opinion that the life of the foetus does not come immediately from God but mediately from its parents, which can be inferred from Genesis 2:2, 'God ceased from his creative work'. If each life is an immediate act of creation from God rather than a mediate one through the seminal process, then this statement loses meaning. Paul said to the Athenians: "God has made from one all nations of men to dwell on the face of the whole earth" (Acts 17:26), thus he pointed to the unity of the human race. If each life is a separate creation not passed on mediately from Adam, this unity is called into question. Thus, solely on the doctrine of the unity of the human race we can conclude, that the original life breathed into Adam is passed on seminally and is present at the time of conception.

Then breath which is associated with life in the Bible, is only a later manifestation of life. In the case of foetus other symptoms, such as growth, indicate the presence of this life. An analogy will illustrate our point. A tree manifests its life by the presence of green leaves on it during the spring and summer seasons. During its dormant season we will have to look beneath its bark to determine whether or not it is alive. The absence of leaves on a tree during its dormant days will not indicate that during this period of its life cycle it was only a potential tree or less than a tree. Similarly, absence of breath in the foetus does not indicate that during that period of gestation the man is only potentially a man or less than a human being. Hence we can say that foetus consists both of clay fashioned by God and of biological life mediately derived from the creator, for these aspects of man are passed on seminally and are already present at the time of conception. Now, we shall see how the foetus qualifies itself to be the image of God.

Foetus is the Image of God
We can have three reasons supporting the statement that foetus is the image of God.

1) Scripture asserts that man's sinful nature, which seems to be related to his spiritual, moral nature, is passed on seminally. There are passages that suggest that the sinful spiritual state of man is passed on mediately from generation to generation. For example, passages like Ps. 58:3; Job 14:4; 15:14 suggest that the sinful spiritual state of man is passed on mediately from generation

to generation. And so, one can presume that they implicitly teach that the foetus is a spiritual, moral being.

On the basis of inherited sin also, we can see that man's spiritual element is passed on mediately from Adam and not as the immediate creation of God. In Romans 7:23, Paul speaks of a law that is universal for all men: "But I see another law in my members warring against the law of my mind and bringing men into captivity to the law of sin which is in my members." The psychical-spiritual unity of the human race is just as real as its biological unity.

2) Moses taught his people that God created Adam 'in his own image'. Later, he said that this image was passed on seminally: 'Adam fathered (*yolid* = 'father a child')[75] a son in his own image' (Gen.5:3). Hence we can conclude that the essential feature of humanness, that which relates man to God and separates him from the rest of nature, is handed down through sexual intercourse –seminally.

3) Reading Psalm 51:5ff, one is prone to think that at the time of conception man is in a state of sin and that man's spiritual, moral faculty is already present in the foetus. It reads thus: "Behold, I was brought forth in iniquity, and in sin did my mother conceive me." According to E.R. Dalglish, the psalmist is relating his sinfulness to the very inception of life; he traces his development beyond his birth, to the genesis of his being in his mother's womb, even to the very hour of conception.[76]

In the next verse David notes that already in his foetal state the moral law of God was present in him. According to the King James Version the text reads: "Behold, thou desirest truth in the inward parts: and in the hidden part thou shalt make to know wisdom." The words 'inward parts' and 'hidden part' modify David's mother's womb, which can be inferred both from the close connection of verse 6 with verse 5 and from the words used, which literally mean 'the covered-over parts' and the 'bottled-up place', words that more aptly describe his mother's womb than his own body. Hence Dalglish concluded: "In the depths of the womb the psalmist was wrought in the context of sin; but there is another factor: the psalmist knows the divine desire for truth to be a moral imperative even in the formulative stages of his being within his mother's womb and is conscious that even there wisdom was taught him, i.e., in his embryological state in the closed up chamber of the womb, the moral law was inscribed within his being."[77]

Hence one can conclude that the image of God is already present in the foetus. Nobody will deny that a baby is a human being and that it is made in the image of God, it has the capacity for spiritual, rational and moral response. The scripture says that the foetus has that capacity and that capacity was already present at the time of conception. Having established that foetus is human, our next attempt is to examine whether foetus can be considered person.[78] The question – whether God considers the unborn child a person? – takes precedence over essentially pragmatic considerations such as socioeconomic distress, mental anguish, and illegitimacy.

Foetus is Person

Quite recently only has the concept of "personhood" surfaced. There are some in our society who want to find a developmental stage where they can justify that the foetus is only a collection of organs, not really a person. Carl Sagan put that foetal stage at perhaps six months, when the cerebral cortex is in place. Only then, he feels, should we confer "personhood" on a foetus.[79]

Such ideas are clearly subjective. It would seem that these discussions of personhood only arose from a need to justify the act of abortion. Certainly, they are not expressed in the Bible. Quite to the contrary, the Bible story shows that "personhood", or reaching one's full potential, comes from knowing God. A person develops and is preserved through his communion with a personal God who reveals Himself to us in love. The Bible consistently links our "personhood" to the time we are formed (conception), or even before in God's "mind".

Biblical Teaching on Personhood: A *Continuum* from Conception to Birth

As seen before, Bible teaches that each and every human being is created in the image of God and therefore has intrinsic value. Biblical teaching also implies that an unborn child in the womb is a person in the eyes of God. Because of this many Christians feel that a human being must be treated with respect from the moment of conception. Wyatt comments: "The Biblical narrative insists that God's creative activity does not commence at the moment of birth. Instead, God is intimately involved in the hidden and mysterious process of foetal development within the womb."[80] This is illustrated by Ps. 139: 13-14.[81]

Other Old Testament texts (though discussed earlier are worth repeating) which imply that life is sacred from the moment of conception include: Job 31: 15 – "Did not He who made me in the womb make them?" Is. 49:5 – "And now the Lord says: he who formed me in the womb to be his servant .... for I am honoured in the eyes of the Lord." Jer. 1: 5 – "Before I formed you in the womb I knew you, before you were born I set you apart."

Luke's account of visitation, when Mary visits Elizabeth, also supports the claim that life in the womb has intrinsic value. Luke writes: "when Elizabeth heard Mary's greeting, the baby leaped in her womb and Elizabeth was filled with the Holy Spirit. In a loud voice she exclaimed. As soon as the sound of your greeting reached my ears, the baby in my womb leaped for joy" (Lk. 1:41-44). For Luke the unborn child is as important as a child that has been born because in the context of the visitation, Luke uses the Greek word *brephos* to describe the unborn child. He uses the same word to describe a newborn baby (2:12 and 16) and the children who are blessed by Jesus in 18:15.[82]

Therefore, the Biblical material implies that human life is sacred even in the womb. Wyatt argues: "The consistent witness of the Biblical material is that the foetus is the part of the human drama, a hidden actor on the human stage; one whom God is creating in secret, calling into existence and into relationship with himself."[83] The Bible always recognises the prenatal phase of life as that of a child and not as a meaningless product of conception.

Bible and the Unborn
Throughout the Bible children are presented as a great blessing and parenthood is highly esteemed: Truly children are a gift from the Lord, a blessing, the fruit of the womb (Ps. 127:3, Gen.4:1, 17:15-16, 18:11-14, 21:1-2, 28:3, 29:31-35, 30:22-23, 33:5, 49:25, 1Sam. Chs.2,9,10, Ps.103:13, 113, 127:3-5, 128, Jer.31:15, Is.29:22-23, 40:11, Mal 4:6).

"Jesus took a little child; set him in front of them, put his arms round him, and said to them: 'Anyone who welcomes one of these little children in my name, welcomes me .... for it is to such as these that the kingdom of God belongs." (Mk 9:33-37, 10:13-16, Mt.18:10, 19:13-15).

Some may ask, whether the Scriptural reverence for children and for all innocent human life extends to life before birth? In the Old Testament the existence of human being before birth is clearly recognised. (Gen.25:22, Ps.51:5, Eccles.11:5, Is.49:15). Unborn children are already known and loved by God. Samson: Judg.13:5-7, David: Ps.22:9-10; Solomon: Wis.7:1-6; Job: Job ch.10, Isaiah: Is.49:1,5,15; Jeremiah: Jer.1:4-5; Sir 49:7; all the people of Israel: Is 44:1, 24, 46:3, Ps. 71:6 and 139, all these characters trace their personal identity from adult life back to the time of their conception or life in the womb. For example, Jer.1:4-5 notes: "Before I formed thee in the belly I knew thee; and before thou camest forth out of the womb I sanctified thee, and I ordained thee a prophet unto the nations." Ps.139:1, 13-16 O Lord, you examine me and know me, you know when I sit and when I rise .... See also, Job 10:8-12.

On the cusp between the OT and NT John the Baptist heralds (as we have seen already) the embryonic Jesus while both are still in the womb: filled with the Holy Spirit the foetal John leapt for Joy (Lk. 1:13-15, 41-44). Christ Himself was an embryo, foetus, infant, child, adolescent, adult. Paul too, tells how he was chosen while he was still in his mother's womb (Gal.1:15). All these passages suggest that personal identity for Jews and Christians is continuous from when God gives life at conception through maturity until death and consequently that the moral claims of the 'neighbour' upon us are present in our fellow human beings even from their conception.

A *Continuum*: From Conception to Birth

The remaining part of the book will consider five kinds of Biblical texts which will enable us to arrive at the personhood of the unborn by showing that there is a *continuum* from conception to birth. They are: (1) those texts where personal pronouns and proper names are used to refer to the unborn (pre-natal personalisation); (2) those texts speaking of a personal relationship between God and the unborn; (3) provisions in the Mosaic law relating to the unborn, particularly Exodus 21:22-25; (4) texts reflecting the psycho-physical unity of man created in the *imago Dei*; and (5) those texts dealing with the incarnation of Christ.[84] After that we will examine a number of objections to the personhood of the unborn. Then we will try to give our answers to them.

1. Pre-Natal "Personalisation"

'In a number of texts, the Biblical writers freely apply personal language to the unborn. Genesis 4:1 says that "Adam knew Eve his wife, and she conceived and bore Cain." The writer's interest in Cain extends back beyond his birth, to his conception. That is when his personal history begins. The individual conceived and the individual born are one and the same, namely Cain. His conception, birth, and postnatal life form a natural *continuum*, with the God of covenant involved at every stage.[85] Genesis 5:3 states that "......... Adam begat a son in his own likeness, after his image; and called his name

Seth" (KJV). From this it seems clear that human reproduction was the means by which the image and likeness of Adam were transmitted to Seth..... A personal continuity between father and son is here linked to bodily existence, sexuality, and prenatal life.[86] When Rebekah was pregnant with Jacob and Essau, Scripture says, "The babies jostled each other within her" (Gen. 25:22). The unborn are regarded as "babies" in the full sense of the term. Jacob's personal involvement in covenant history thus begins before birth.

In the third chapter of Job we find Job cursing the day of his birth: "Let the day perish wherein I was born, and the night which said, 'A man-child *(geber)* is conceived'"(Job 3:3). Here we see a basic continuity between the individual born and the individual conceived. Job traces his personal history back beyond his birth to the night of his conception. The process of conception is described by the Biblical writer in personal terms. There is no abstract language of the "products of conception," but the concrete language of humanity. The Hebrew word *geber*, generally used in a postnatal context and has the meanings as "man," "male," or "husband" (e.g., Ps. 52:9; 94:12; Prov. 6:34). Here that word is freely applied from the moment of conception.[87]

Psalm 51 (psalm of penitence), is an especially important text for our discussion, particularly verse 5: Behold, I was brought forth in iniquity, and in sin did my mother conceive me.[88] By saying 'Surely I was sinful at birth', David goes back even further, back before birth to the actual beginning of his life. What he means to say, is this: 'he was sinful from the time his mother conceived him. Who but an actual person can have a sinful nature? Rocks and trees and animals and human organs do not have moral natures, good or bad. Morality can be ascribed only to a person. That there is a sinful nature at the point of conception demonstrates that there is a person present who is capable of having such a nature. "This application of moral and spiritual categories to David as a conceptus suggests a relationship to God and the moral law even in his embryonic state."[89]

"The repentant David realises his sin is not a superficial problem, limited to his outward act of adultery, but pervades the core of his being. The pervasive depravity of human nature, elsewhere spoken of in a postnatal context (e.g., Rom. 7:7ff; Eph. 2:3), is here traced back to David's prenatal state."[90] "David never excludes his prenatal life from his complicity in sin."[91] "David goes on to confess that already in his mother's womb the moral law of God was present with him."[92] The text of Psalm 51:6 reads, "Behold, thou desirest truth in the inward parts: and in the hidden part thou shalt make me know wisdom." Waltke, following the suggestion of Dalglish, argues that the Hebrew words rendered "inward parts" *(tehoth)* and "hidden part" *(satem)* properly refer not to David's body, but rather to his mother's womb.[93]

"This interpretation is supported by the close connection of Ps.51 verse 6 with verse 5, which clearly refers to conception and birth, and by a comparison of verse 6 with Psalm 139:15. Both Dalglish and Waltke understand Psalm 51:6 to say that even in his prenatal state David was being taught the moral law of God."[94] Dalglish translates the verse as follows: "Behold, truth thou desirest in the inward (being); and in the secret (part) wisdom thou teachest me."[95] He summarises: ". . . (T)he psalmist knows fully well the divine desire for truth to be a moral imperative even in the formative stages of his being within his mother's womb . . . and is conscious that even there wisdom was taught him, i.e., in his embryological state . . . the moral law was inscribed within his being."[96] These verses strongly imply that personal identity is a *continuum*, beginning in the womb and extending naturally into postnatal life.[97]

"The notion of estrangement from God at the very earliest stages of life is not unique to Psalm 51:5. The following texts illustrate the point: The wicked go astray from the womb, they err from their birth, speaking lies (Psalm 58:3). Who can bring a clean thing out of an unclean? There is not one (Job 14:4). What is man, that he can be clean? or he that is born of woman, that he can be righteous? (Job 15:4). How then can man be righteous before God? How can he who is born of woman be clean? (Job 25:4)."[98] In Biblical thought sin pervades every aspect of man's fallen being and is present prior to his conscious sinful acts.

Two objections may be raised against this prenatal "personalisation". The first is that David's language is merely poetic and therefore precludes strict conclusions concerning the personhood of the unborn. The second objection is that verses 13-16 (Ps.139) deal solely with divine foreknowledge and have nothing to say on the personal character of prenatal life.[99] These objections are not without weight. So we must be cautious in drawing inferences from such personal pronouns alone.

However, in the New Testament, "Luke in particular is sensitive to the development of the unborn. In chapter 1, Elizabeth greets her visiting cousin Mary with these words: "Behold, when the voice of your greeting came to my ears, the babe in my womb leaped for joy" (Luke 1:44). Two elements are noteworthy here. First, John the Baptist in his mother's womb leaped for joy in response to Mary's greeting. Human emotion is explicitly attributed to the unborn John. His mother Elizabeth was probably still in her sixth month, since it seems likely that Mary's visit followed closely upon the announcement by the angel Gabriel (cf. Luke 1:36,39). Elizabeth's statement should not be dismissed as poetic hyperbole, since Luke specifies that Elizabeth was speaking under the inspiration of the Holy Spirit (Luke 1:41)".[100] Furthermore, it is now well known that an unborn child can respond to touch at eight weeks and at 25 weeks can respond to human voices and feel pain and discomfort.[101] There is no scientific basis for precluding human emotion in John the Baptist at that stage of his prenatal life.[102]

Another point worthy of note is the use of the term *brephos* to describe John in the womb. As we said earlier, elsewhere in the New Testament the same term is used freely of infants and the newly born (Luke 18:15; 1 Pet. 2:2; Acts 7:19). Here again we have language indicating an implicit continuity between prenatal and postnatal existence. Such expressions combine with other lines of Biblical evidence to form a total outlook pointing to the personhood of the unborn from conception.[103]

2. God's Relationship to the Unborn
The second category of Biblical texts give evidence to personal relationships between God and the unborn. Capacity for this sort of relationships with God is precisely the foundational element of personhood. "If such relationships exist between God and the unborn, that would strongly imply their personhood."[104]

God's Involvement in Creation and His Providence
God knows how each day of our lives on earth will unfold. His love, concern and care go with us throughout life. The omniscient God who knows what happens to persons after their birth also knows what happens to these persons before birth. In the Scriptural view, as Delitzsch observes, "A creative act similar to the creation of Adam is repeated at the origin of each individual; and the continuation of development according to natural laws is not less the working of God than the creative planting of the very beginning."[105]

In the natural sphere God's creative and providential work in the womb is the precondition for life itself. Personhood, whether "natural" or redeemed, is not a possibility intrinsic to man, but comes from God's sovereign initiative. "In him we live and move and have our being" (Acts 17:28); both at prenatal and postnatal state. It seems reasonable to say that we are persons because God first related to us in a personal way.

The Bible repeatedly affirms that God's providence governs everything from the weather (Ps. 148:8; Job 37:6-13), to animals' food and behaviour (Ps. 104:27-29; Job 38:39-41; Jonah 1:17; 2:10), to seemingly random events, such as the rolling of dice (Prov. 16:33). Surely if God governs these relatively minor things, then He also governs the formation of people in the womb. As quoted earlier, The Lord tells Moses, "Who has made man's mouth? Or who makes him mute or deaf, or seeing or blind? Is it not I, the Lord?" (Exod. 4:11).

Concerning Leah, the wife of Jacob, Scripture indicates, "When the Lord saw that Leah was unloved, He opened her womb. . . So Leah conceived and bore a son" (Gen. 29:31, 32). When Job compared himself to his servants, he asked: "did not He who made me in the womb make them? Did not the same One fashion us in the womb?" (Job 31:15). In pointing out God's impartiality Job said: "Yet He is not partial to princes, nor does He regard the rich more than the poor, for they are all the work of His hands" (Job 34:19). Isaiah speaking for God wrote: "Thus says the Lord who made you and formed you from the womb, who will help you; 'Fear not, O Jacob, My servant'" (Is. 44:2). And again: "Thus says the Lord, your Redeemer, and He who formed you from the womb" (v.24). In Jeremiah we read as follows: 'Before I formed you in the womb I knew you, and before you were born I consecrated you' (1:5). Luke 1:15 says of John the Baptist: "For he will be great in the sight of the Lord; and he will drink no wine or liquor, and he will be filled with the Holy Spirit while yet in his mother's womb".

David summed it up well when he wrote Ps.139: 13-16. 'For You formed my inward parts; You wove me in my mother's womb. I will give thanks to You, for I am fearfully and wonderfully made; wonderful are Your works, and my soul knows it very well. My frame was not hidden from You, when I was made in secret, and skilfully wrought in the depths of the earth; Your eyes have seen my unformed substance; and in Your book were all written the days that were ordained for me, when as yet there was not one of them'. Commenting on this Psalm, Donald Shoemaker wrote: "This passage can only evoke holy caution and respect for unborn life. God is at work, and as we observe we must worship, for the place where we stand is holy ground. Such respect for the divine origin of life is not to be found among the pro-abortionists. Theirs is an unholy intrusion into the divine laboratory to interrupt and to destroy the handwork of the blessed Creator! God loves the unborn. This Psalm will never let us forget it".[106]

Now we come back to the same texts, the book of Job and Psalms to learn God's involvement in creation and providence. In Job 10:8-12, Job described the way God created him before he was born. The person in the womb was not something that might become Job, but someone who was Job, just a younger version. In verse Job 10:9 there is an allusion to Genesis 2:7 and the formation of clay into a vessel by the potter's hand. "The figure is that of a potter who has lavished infinite care upon his vessel, and now reduces his work of elaborate skill and exquisite ornament into dust again."[107]

"Job feels that his present distress is inconsistent with God's previous care for him from the very beginnings of life. The figure of the potter and the clay, elsewhere used in a postnatal context (as in Jer. 18:5, 6 and Rom. 9:20ff.), is here applied to Job's prenatal existence".[108] Job's language of personal identity reaches back into his mother's womb. In verses 10 and 11 Job likens his formation to the curdling of cheese and the process of weaving or plaiting. "Semen, poured like milk into the mother's womb, is wrapped in flesh and woven together by God into a human embryo."[109] The "steadfast love" (Job 10:12; *hesed*) that Job has known throughout his life began with God's special providential care in the womb. *Hesed*, a key word in Old Testament theology, and applied here to the unborn Job, speaks particularly of Yahweh's covenantal relationship.[110] "Even in his mother's womb Job is shown the same *hesed* extended by God in covenantal relationships to Abraham (Gen. 24:27), Jacob (Gen. 32:10), David, and Israel (cf. Ps.98:3)."[111]

To Isaiah, God says, This is what the Lord says – he who made you, who formed you in the womb (Is. 44:2). What each person is, not merely what he might become, was present in his mother's womb. As in Psalm 139:13-16, the development of prenatal human life is understood as the result of God's creative and sustaining effort. "In both Psalm 139:13-16 and Job 10:8-12 God's personal involvement in creation and providence personalises the unborn."[112] That is, human personhood is rooted in the creative and providential care of God, which begins in the womb. As he is creatively active in the birth process, to terminate a pregnancy is to destroy the work of God. In this context abortion becomes evil defiance of the Almighty. It is an indication of the depths to which a consenting society has fallen.

Unborn: The Subject of Divine Election and Call
The Bible recognises God has plans for the unborn child. Only He knows the potential of life in the womb. "A number of Biblical texts indicate that the unborn can be the subjects of God's election and the recipient of God's calling."[113]

When God called Jeremiah to his prophetic ministry He indicated that the ordination was prenatal. Jeremiah acknowledged that God formed him in the womb and knew him by name. "Before I formed you in the womb I knew you; before you were born I sanctified you; and I ordained you a prophet to the nations" (Jer. 1:5). When Jeremiah protested that he was only a youth (Jer.1:6), God's reply to the protesting Jeremiah indicates that age and experience, credentials, normally necessary for tasks of great responsibility, are transcended by God's sovereign purpose to equip Jeremiah for his task (Jer.1:8). God was actively preparing Jeremiah for that task even before birth, having foreknown the course of his life even prior to Jeremia's conception.

Jeremiah is not an isolated example. In Judges 13:2-7 we read that Samson was consecrated to be a Nazirite to God prior to his birth. Both his conception and consecration are described as acts not of parental will, but of the Lord's sovereign determination. In Isaiah 49:1,5 the servant of the Lord declares, "The Lord called me from the womb, from the body of my mother he named my name." "While Jacob and Esau were still in the womb of their mother Rebekah, the Lord declared to her, concerning their future. Two nations are in your womb and two peoples, born of you, shall be divided; the one shall be stronger than the other, the elder shall serve the younger. By God's sovereign choice, Jacob, while still in the womb, is given pre-eminence over his brother Esau and made the bearer of God's special covenant promises."[114] "The struggling of the children within Rebekah's womb (Gen. 25:22) anticipates the postnatal conflict between Jacob and Esau, and the later strife between Israel and Edom as nations."[115] As it is written, "Jacob I loved, but Esau I hated." (Romans 9:10-13). This text makes it clear that Jacob is elected for covenant blessings prior to birth. "Thus both as prenatal antagonists and as subjects of divine decree of election, Jacob and Esau before birth are recognised as actors in the drama of redemption."[116]

John the Baptist, prior to his birth, was given a name. He was set apart to be the prophet who prepares the way for the Messiah (Luke 1:13-17). When Zachariah the priest was ministering at the altar of incense, an angel announced that his wife Elizabeth would give birth to a son who should be called John. Thus, it was revealed that God had definite plans for this child even when he was in his mother's womb. He was to be a forerunner of Jesus (Lk. 1:11-17). Isaiah 49:1, 5 affirms the same thing about Messiah. The angel of the Lord, appearing in a dream to Joseph, while the child was still in Mary's womb, announced that his name was to be Jesus (Matt. 1:18-25). And the apostle Paul declares that he too, had been set apart for God's service before he was born (Gal.1:15). All these texts indicate that God's special dealings with human beings can long precede their awareness of a personal relationship with God.

"In electing some to special covenant privileges, he does not employ the usual human standards."[117] "What distinguishes the elect from non elect, according to Paul, is not mere physical descent from Abraham, but the sovereign purpose of God expressed in the promise:"[118] Both the postnatal application of divine election in 1 Corinthians 1:26-29 and the prenatal reference in Genesis 25:23 upset the usual human expectations as to who qualifies for a privileged relationship with God. "The normal ways in which human beings qualify themselves for privileges of various sorts – through personal initiative, planning, foresight, organisational ability, etc. – are here clearly excluded. The usual marks of "personhood" are here absent: physical development, speech, social relationships, ability to work, relative independence".[119] God chooses to establish the most crucial of all personal relationships – the one between a man and his Creator – as we have seen above, in the case of Jacob, prior to his birth. This displays God's sovereign initiative in election.

"God's election of the weak and the dependent challenges us to re-evaluate our culturally determined views of the unborn in the light of divine revelation. Even the unwanted child can be the object of an everlasting covenant love. God's electing love, not the shifting sands of cultural convention, should constitute the basis for defining human personhood."[120] Thus, it is clear that with divine election and calling and consecration to service, God's actions present a striking contrast to current notions of personhood.

From what we have seen above, it becomes clear that categories normally applied to postnatal man are applied also to the unborn from the moment of conception. While some allowance must be made for the possibly metaphorical nature of such Biblical statements, it is hard to resist the impression that God takes a deep interest in the unborn child. These texts do challenge traditional views of personhood and they seem to suggest that the unborn are persons from the moment of conception. Therefore, to destroy the life of an unborn child is flagrantly to disregard the plans God has for that life. It robs the unborn person of the privilege of choosing to be an instrument of God's design.

3. Linguistic Evidences (Exodus 21:22-25)

The most significant thing about abortion legislation in Biblical law is that there is none. It was so unthinkable that an Israelite woman should desire an abortion that there was no need to mention this offence in the criminal code.[121] The prohibition was completely covered in 'thou shall not murder'. Israelites well understood this to mean killing by sword, by strangulation, by poison, by abortion, and by all other means. Later, as the Church began to spread to the gentile cultures that did not share the Israelite traditions, specific prohibitions were written. Church leaders and others consistently forbade the practice of abortion based upon their understanding of the Bible.

Nevertheless, there is a passage in Old Testament law (Exodus 21:22-25) that sheds light on the status of the unborn child. "This text, has been the subject of a number of competing interpretations. Assuming a 'miscarriage' the translators of the Revised Standard Version (RSV) translate the passage as follows:"[122] 22) "When men strive together, and hurt a woman with child, so that there is a miscarriage, and yet no harm follows, the one who hurt her shall be fined, according as the woman's husband shall lay upon him; and he shall pay as the judges determine. 23) If any harm follows, then you shall give life for life, 24) eye for eye, tooth for tooth, hand for hand, foot for foot, 25) burn for burn, wound for wound, stripe for stripe."

The King James Version sees the possibility of a premature live birth instead of miscarriage: 22) "If men strive, and hurt a woman with child, so that her fruit depart from her, and yet no mischief follows, he shall surely be punished, according as the woman's husband will lay upon him; and he shall pay as the judges determine. 23) And if any mischief follows, then thou shalt give life for life." "The phrase 'so that her fruit depart' of the KJV is a more literal rendering of the Hebrew than the RSV's 'so that there is a miscarriage'. The New International Version also takes the passage to refer to a premature live birth."[123]

We have the two most common lines of interpretations. We designate them simply as "Position I" and "Position II." The circumstances described in verse 22 will be designated as "Case A", and the circumstances of verses 23-25 designated as "Case B".

Those who adopt Position I take Case A to mean that if a pregnant woman suffers a non-fatal injury in the strife, and as a result suffers a miscarriage, then monetary compensation is to be rendered for the loss of the child and for the woman's injury. Case B is taken to mean that if, in addition to the miscarriage, the woman is fatally injured, then the provisions of the *lex talionis* apply, and capital punishment may be in view.[124] "On this view, the lack of a capital penalty for causing the death of the unborn child by miscarriage would suggest that Old Testament law placed a higher value on the life of the mother than on the life of the unborn child. If so, it is argued, then difficult circumstances might justify taking the life of the child through deliberate abortion as the lesser of two evils."[125]

Those who adopt Position II argue that the "miscarriage" translation is inaccurate.[126] They believe that Case A refers not to a miscarriage but to a premature live birth. In Case A, the child is born alive, and the woman sustains a nonfatal injury. Monetary compensation is rendered for the trauma of premature birth and for any harm suffered by the woman. In Case B, the "harm" *(ason)* is taken to refer to either mother or child. The death of either mother or child comes under the rule of the *lex talionis*, and the assailant is subject to the capital penalty. Accordingly, the Mosaic law makes no distinction between the value of the life of the mother and that of the unborn child. The loss of either life comes within the purview of the *lex talionis*. Old Testament scholars Keil and Delitzch forcefully argue that the word "fruit" in Hebrew clearly means "child".[127] Position II, then, sees Exodus 21:22-25 as teaching the full legal status of the unborn child as a human life (v.23b) from the time of its origin.[128] That would make Exodus 21:22-25 in fact a very strong anti-abortion passage.[129]

Interpreters who hold Position II point out a number of exegetical difficulties involved in Position I. The verb translated "depart" or "come out" *(yatsa)* usually refers in the Old Testament to live birth.[130] The usual Hebrew verb for miscarriage *(shakol)*, found in Exodus 23:26 and Hosea 9:14, is not used here. Furthermore, the term *yeled* in verse 22, "child" or "fruit," is not the usual Old Testament designation for the product of a miscarriage. O.T uses *yeled* to refer to the unborn (Ex 21:22-25). It is a word that "generally indicates young children, but may refer to teens or even young adult.[131] Old Testament people did not have or need a separate word for unborn children. They are just like other children, only younger. In the Bible there is no such a thing as potential, incipient or 'almost' child. There is a third position which is more or less akin to the second.[132]

Thus the linguistic evidence favours the view that verse 22 indicates not an accidental miscarriage, but rather a premature live birth. One scholar states:

"Looking at Old Testament law from a proper cultural and historical context, it is evident that the life of the unborn is put on the same par as the person outside the womb."[133] Far from justifying permissive abortion, Ex 21: 22-25, in fact grant the unborn child a status in the eyes of the law equal to that of the mother. The passage is thus consistent with the high regard for prenatal life manifested elsewhere in Scripture.[134]

4. Man: A Psycho-Somatic Unity

The Scriptures teach the psychosomatic unity of the whole person, body, soul and spirit (I Thes. 5:23). "The relation of the physical and spiritual aspects of man's nature is relevant to the status of the unborn before God."[135] "The older questions concerning the time of ensoulment and whether the child receives his soul from his parents (traducianism) or by the immediate creative activity of God (creationism) have their secular counterparts in the contemporary abortion debate. They now reappear as questions about the time at which the unborn child becomes a "person," whether at conception, implantation, formation of the cerebral cortex, "quickening," viability, or birth."[136]

"All but the first of these suggestions – conception – separate to some degree personhood from biologically human existence. They suggest a dualistic understanding of man that has more kinship with Greek and certain modern European philosophies than with the Biblical outlook."[137] The Greek tendency to disassociate the body from man's personality conflicts with Biblical thought. Man's flesh *(basar)* and his soul *(nephesh)*, as we have seen, are not dichotomised entities, but are complementary aspects of a unified psychosomatic being.

All such dualisms are fundamentally foreign to the Biblical outlook. John A.T. Robinson observes: "Man does not have a body, he is a body. He is flesh-animated, soul, the whole conceived as a psycho-physical unity."[138] Similarly, Edmond Jacob states that "the unity of human nature is not expressed by the antithetical concepts of body and soul but by the complementary and inseparable concepts of body and life."[139] "The essence of human personality is not man's spiritual or intellectual capacities in distinction from his "lower" physical nature".[140] "The Old Testament's unitary conception of man is also a key to understanding man as the *imago Dei*. As Gerhard von Rad comments, the image *(tselem)* and likeness *(demuth)* "refer to the whole man and do not relate solely to his spiritual and intellectual being."[141] "Though man's intellectual, moral, and spiritual capacities are of course crucial, the image of God extends beyond them, to his total existence as a psycho-physical unity."[142]

Thus man is to be valued not merely as a "thinking substance," but as the bearer of the transcendent image of God – an image that includes the bodily aspects of life too. In Biblical thought, man's "personal" life is not separated from his bodily life. As already said, "he is animated flesh, and where there is animated human flesh, there man is. Consequently, "this consideration of the Biblical understanding of man as a psycho-physical unity, again leads us to question approaches that define personhood in purely mental or psychological terms."[143] This more holistic understanding of man found in the Bible points to the transcendent value and dignity conferred on man from the very first moments of his bodily existence.

"The New Testament anthropology presupposes and builds on the Old Testament view of man as a psychosomatic unity. There is no dualism of body and spirit, not even in Paul's prominent contrast between "flesh" *(sarx)* and "spirit" *(pneuma)*."[144] In Pauline thought, the body is not merely the external casing of the real, inner man, but rather the man himself considered in a certain mode of his existence.[145] Hence the exhortation of Paul to the Roman Christians: "Present your bodies as a living sacrifice, holy, acceptable to God, which is your spiritual service" (Rom.12:1). "In dealing with antinomian tendencies in Corinth that tended to dichotomise the life of the body and one's relationship to Christ, Paul reminded the Church that the body was not for immorality, but for the Lord (1Cor. 6:13). The believer serves the Lord with his entire being. Instead of being of lesser worth than the spiritual self, the body is in fact a temple of the Holy Spirit (1 Cor. 6:19), and the believer is to glorify God in his body (1 Cor. 6:20). Thus the Old Testament revelation of man's dignity as the *imago Dei* is enriched by the New Testament portrayal of the believer's body."[146]

"The Biblical concepts of the goodness of human bodily life and man's essential unity should make us very suspicious of attempts to restrict human personhood – and hence moral and legal protection – only to those among whom man's "higher," rational capacities are evident."[147]

5. Incarnation: Implications for the Personhood of the Unborn
"The incarnation of Christ carries implications for the personhood of the unborn."[148] "The inspired account of the Messiah's personal history shown in Lk 1:26-56, especially verse 31, includes the prediction not only of his birth, but also of his conception. As in other Biblical texts, conception is treated as the time at which one's personal history begins."[149] Luke (1:39,40) tells us that "in those days Mary arose and went with haste into the hill country, to a city

of Judah, and she entered the house of Zechariah and greeted Elizabeth." Several factors indicate that there was little delay between the prediction of Mary's conception (vv. 31-35) and her arrival at the house of Zechariah and Elizabeth. Elizabeth was already in her sixth month prior to Mary's visit (v. 36), and Mary stayed with Elizabeth for about three months prior to the birth of John (v. 56). If there had been a considerable delay, say a month or two between the time of the annunciation and the visit to Elizabeth, then Mary could not have spent those three months with Elizabeth prior to John's birth. Furthermore, we are told that Mary "arose and went with haste" (v.39). That puts Mary in the earliest stages of her pregnancy when she arrived at Elizabeth's house."[150] It is reasonable to assume that Jesus was probably no more than 10 days beyond his conception when Mary arrived at Elizabeth's (Lk 1: 41).

The above consideration is very significant in view of several details in the conversation between Elizabeth and Mary. It appears that the preborn John Baptist responded to the presence of the preborn Jesus in His mother Mary. When Mary's greeting reached Elizabeth, the baby John leaped in his mother's womb (vv.41, 44). John's mission in life was to bear witness to the Messiah and to prepare the people to receive him (Luke 1:17; John 1:6-8, 19-23;3:28-30). So John's response may well have been his first acknowledgment of the Messiah; John's status and role in the covenant history is found in his relationship not to Mary, but to the Messiah. This would place the focus of John's response on Jesus in the very earliest stages of the Messiah's prenatal existence. Thus the passage seems to indicate the humanity of Jesus in his embryonic state, perhaps even prior to the time of implantation in the uterus. The aforesaid five points help us to arrive at the personhood of the unborn from the moment of conception. Besides, Bible considers every pregnant woman to be with child.

Conception Means to 'Be with Child'
There is no distinction made in the value of life between the born and unborn child. Again we take the words of God to Jeremiah, 'before I formed you in the womb, I knew you (Jer. 1:5). He could not know Jeremiah in his mother's womb unless Jeremiah, the person, was present in his mother's womb.

The most important texts in this connection are the accounts of the annunciation and Mary's visit to Elizabeth, recorded in Luke 1:26-56.[151] In verse 31 Luke records the words of the angel Gabriel to Mary: "You will conceive in your womb and bear a son, and you shall call his name Jesus".

These words indicate that Jesus was recognised as a son even though Mary's pregnancy was in the earliest stages. The angel then informed Mary that her cousin Elizabeth was pregnant. The words used were: "she hath also conceived a son in her old age" Lk.1:36). Scripture makes it clear that in the pre-natal phase John the Baptist was recognised as a son even though it was three months before the time of delivery. In Lk.1: 41, 44 also John the Baptist is recognised as a "babe" before birth. That is, in the first century, and in every century, to be pregnant is to be with child, not with that which might become a child.

Commenting on Ex. 21:22, 23, John Calvin said: "The foetus, though enclosed in the womb of his mother, is already a human being, and it is a monstrous crime to rob it of life which it has not yet begun to enjoy. If it seems more horrible to kill a man in his own house than in a field, because a man's house is his place of most secure refuge, it ought surely to be deemed more atrocious to destroy a foetus in the womb before it has come to light."[152] Hence, we say that a child (born or unborn) is a person.

A Child (Born/Unborn) is a Person
The Bible consistently uses the same word for a "born" or "unborn" baby.[153] This is because the divine Author of the Bible did not recognise a material difference between the two. In Scripture, there is not some special event when a human being becomes a person. Rather, he or she is a person from the beginning who goes through growth and development both inside and outside of the womb. (As we shall see later, science also attests to this fact).

In the New Testament the Greek word *brephos* is used to describe the unborn, newborns and youth. In Luke 1:44, the word is used to mean unborn baby: "For behold, when the sound of your greeting reached my ears, the baby leaped in my womb for joy." Then, in Luke 2:12, it means a newborn: "So they came in a hurry and found their way to Mary and Joseph, and the baby as He lay in the manger." Same can be said about the newborn babies killed by Pharaoh (Acts 7:19). And in Luke 18:15, *brephos* refers to a young child: "And they were bringing even their babies to Him so that He would touch and bless them, but when the disciples saw it, they began rebuking them". To the writers of the New Testament, like the Old, whether born or unborn, a baby is simply a baby.

In the Old Testament the Hebrew word *yeled* is used in the same way as *brephos* is used in New Testament. In Exodus 21:22 it means an unborn child,

"If men struggle with each other and strike a woman with child so that she gives birth prematurely...". And yet, in other Old Testament usages, it means "youth" or even a teenager. According to The NAS Old Testament Hebrew Lexicon, the word *yeled* means boy (7 times), boys (3), child (32), child's (2) children (27) lad (2), lads (1), young (3), young men (6) and youths (5).[154] As late as the 16th century, "child" was the word used for both the born and unborn baby. Late in the game, we have developed a new word, "foetus", to describe a developing baby[155] (even this word is defined in some dictionaries as an "unborn human being")[156]. Today, we often reserve the word "child" for a person already born.

In the Bible, our worth as a human being or our "personhood" does not depend on how far along on life's journey we have come. Instead, we are beings who are made in the image of God (Gen. 1:27). Each person is valuable because God created him or her that way. It does not matter whether a person is still in his mother's womb, a newborn, a toddler, an adolescent, an adult or a senior citizen. Human life is a *continuum* from conception to birth and from there to (natural/accidental) death.

Summary of the Biblical Support that a Foetus is a Person:
1. The unborn are created by God (Ps.139/13), just as God created Adam and Eve in His image (Gen.1:26-27).

2. Man is a combination of dust and breath – dust from the ground and breath from God. God formed the dust and breathed directly into it His life giving breath which resulted in a "living being" or "soul" (Gen.2/7). The process of respiration begins at conception. Therefore the "breath of life" exists from the very moment of conception.

3. The image of God includes male and female (Gen.1:26-27), but it is a scientific fact that gender (i.e., maleness or femaleness) is determined at the moment of conception.

4. God not only formed us in the womb but established his relationship with us at that time (Ps.51/13-16; Is.49/15).

5. Unborn babies are called "children" the same word used of infants and young children (Ex.1:15-22; 21/22; Lk.1:41-44; 2:12-16; 18:15; Acts 7:19; 2 Timothy 3/15) and some times even of adults (1 Kg.3/17).

5a. The unborn are known by God in a personal way (Judges 13/3, 6-7; Ps.139/15-16; Jer.1/5).

6. Jesus Christ was human (God-man) from the time he was conceived in Mary's womb (Lk.1:26ff and Mt. 1:20-21).

6a. People were called by God prior to their birth (Ps.22/9-10; Is.49/1; Jer.1/5 Gal.1/15).

7. Jacob was given prominence over his twin Esau "before the twins were born" (Rom.9/11).

7a. The growth of the foetus is neither haphazard nor automatic but a work of divine skill. David likens God to a "potter" who "formed" his inmost being and to a "weaver" who "knit him together" in his mother's womb (Ps. 139/13).

7b. Unborn babies share a common origin with adults (Job 31/15).

8. David surveyed his life in four stages: past (Ps.139/1), present (Ps.139/2-6), future (Ps.7-12), and before birth (Ps.139/13-16). In all four these stages he refers to himself as "I".

8a. The life of the unborn is protected by the same punishment for injury or death (Ex.21/22) as that of an adult (Gen.9/6).

9. Unborn children posses personal characteristics such as sin (Ps.51/5), struggle (Genesis 25/22), and joy (Lk.1/44) that are distinctive of human persons and even spiritual characteristics such as being "filled with the Holy Spirit" (Lk.1/41).

10. Christ, in His sacrificial love, has bought man "with price" (His life) and given him an "alien dignity" which exists at the point where man is still a foetus and has no pragmatic value (Dt.7/7).[157]

Still there are some who are unwilling to recognise the personhood of those in the womb. Now we turn to the challenges they raise and try to answer those challenges.

Challenges Answered

There are a number of objections levelled against considering the unborn as persons. Some objections are directly against our reasoning based on incarnation and others are general. We see them in turn. An attempt is made to counter their reasoning.

Here we try to focus on the argument against using incarnation as a support for arriving at the personhood of the unborn. They try to show the humanity of Jesus from a different perspective and they argue that it is only a futuristic interpretation.

Against the Reasoning Based on Incarnation – Futuristic Interpretation and Jesus' Humanity as a Conceptus

It might be argued that John's response had a purely future significance. The same futuristic interpretation might be placed on the words of Elizabeth in Lk.1 verse 43: "And why is this granted me, that the mother of my Lord should come to me?"[158] But Mary is already pregnant. The process by which the angel's prediction is to become a reality is already under way. When Elizabeth, by the inspiration of the Holy Spirit, declares to Mary, "Blessed are you among women, and blessed is the fruit of your womb" (v.42), Elizabeth describes a present state of blessedness enjoyed by Mary. Elizabeth's words form a noteworthy parallelism between the blessing pronounced upon Mary and the blessing pronounced on the fruit of her womb, thereby appearing to personalise the latter, the unborn Messiah.[159]

"A second objection argues that the circumstances of Jesus' conception were so unusual that no parallels can be drawn to the normal process of human conception. While Jesus' conception was certainly unique, it does not follow that his prenatal existence offers no parallels to our own. As to his human nature, the New Testament expressly declares that he was made like his brethren in every respect (Heb. 2:14,17), sin excepted. The Last Adam (1Cor. 15:45) is the archetype of the human race. While the mode of Jesus' conception was unique, the results of that conception, as regards the integrity of the human nature, were identical to our own".[160] Now we shall consider answers for the general objections.

General Objections:

Those who argue against the personhood of the unborn question the use of philosophical definition of Personhood. They try to justify the denial of personhood on the basis of lack of conscious awareness; differences in appearance and foetal wastage. Then they assert their position saying that it is not a normal practice to apply personhood to the unborn.

Lack of Conscious Awareness – Personhood Precedes Conscious Experience

"Among other objections to the position that personhood begins in early prenatal life, is the one that says that the unborn lack conscious awareness and memory, which are usually associated with personal identity. The Cartesian dictum, "I think, therefore I am," illustrates the common tendency in much modern philosophy to identify the self with the conscious exercise of its rational capacities."[161]

"A number of considerations prevent us from reducing our sense of selfhood and personal identity to our conscious experiences. Few if any of us have distinct recollection of our lives between birth and age two; yet it would be foolish to insist that we were not persons during that time and even more outrageous to argue that the protection of the law should be withheld on such grounds. A person may suffer partial or even total amnesia, but the absence of conscious recollection is no warrant for declaring him a "nonperson" in the eyes of the law. Likewise, the lack of conscious recollections of our prenatal life does not mean we were subhuman before birth."[162]

"Personhood cannot be reduced to conscious experiences also because our ability to have conscious experiences and recollections arises out of our personhood; the basic metaphysical reality of personhood precedes the unfolding of the conscious abilities inherent in it. The fertilised human egg already possesses the capacity for becoming a conscious human being, whereas the unfertilised egg or sperm does not".[163]

At this point, some people define the term "person" according to function (we call this view, the functional view of persons). That is, they say that something qualifies as a person if it can do certain things, like think rationally. But this definition of personhood fails. First, there are clear cases in which something qualifies as a person, but cannot do the things required of the functional view of persons.[164] For example, a human person under a general anaesthesia does not qualify as a person under the functional view of persons, since a person in this situation does not have the ability to think rationally. Second, the functional view of persons does not fit certain intuitions about persons. For example, if you had a cat that could not purr, could not chase mice, and couldn't climb trees, you wouldn't say that your cat is not a feline (though you should if you define "feline" in terms of function). Instead, you would say that your cat is a cat that cannot purr, chase mice, or climb trees.[165] In the same way, if you know a human that cannot think rationally (like a foetus, or a person under a general anaesthesia), you should not say that this human is not a person, but that this is a person who (at the moment) cannot think rationally. In the light of these reasons, the functional view of persons should be rejected.

Argument Against the Philosophical Definition of Personhood

The following is the philosophical definition of personhood: a person is an individual subsistence in a human nature. An individual subsistence exists in and for itself rather than merely as part of a larger whole. Thus, for example, the human heart, while being a recognisably individualised organ of the human body, does not constitute an individual subsistence, but is part of a larger whole. The newly fertilised human ovum, on the other hand, is not merely part of the mother's body, but is a distinct, individual entity, possessing its own chromosomal identity and unique "life trajectory."[166] That is, the union of a human sperm and egg gives rise to a new individual with a biologically human nature: this is the clear witness of modern science.[167] Thus, it is proper to apply the concept of person to a human being from the time of conception.[168] "Terminology such as "subsistence" may strike some readers as being unnecessarily philosophical and abstract. In the present abortion debate, however, such "metaphysical" considerations as the exact meaning of "personhood" are at the very heart of the matter."[169] A technical, philosophical term such as 'subsistence' may help us to integrate Scriptural principles and the genetic data in a proper concept of human personhood.

Some may argue in favour of abortion on the basis of the huge differences between a foetus inside the womb and a child outside the womb. Hence we turn our attention to the argument based on the difference in appearance between the unborn and the new born.

Differences in Appearance: Inconsequential

The obvious differences in appearance between the unborn during very early pregnancy and the normal new born have led some to question the personhood of the unborn. Human beings inside the womb are smaller, less developed, and more dependent than human beings outside the womb. The lives of newborn children are protected by law. The lives of embryos and foetuses are not, at least when the context is abortion.

If you asked the average abortion-supporter why this is, why it is generally legal to kill a human being before birth but not legal to kill the same human being after birth, they would likely point you to some of the differences that exist between humans in the womb and humans out of the womb. We know that the differences between embryos and adults are differences that don't matter. Because, these are differences of degree, not differences of kind. We can all point to other people who are bigger, stronger, smarter, or less dependent than we are, but that doesn't make our life any less valuable, or any less deserving of protection.

Stephen Schwarz, in his book, *'The Moral Question of Abortion'*, notes that there are four basic ways that an embryo or foetus differs from a newborn baby. He coined the phoneme SLED to help people remember and categorise these differences. They are: Size, Level of Development, Environment, and Degree of Dependency. By looking at each of these differences in context, it is easy to see that none of them is sufficient to justify abortion, because each of them is equally applicable to many people outside the womb.

Size – the first difference is size. Embryos are smaller than foetuses who are smaller (usually) than newborns. But what does size have to do with rights of personhood? Smaller people are no more or less human than those who are bigger. Embryos and foetuses are smaller than newborns, just as newborns are smaller than infants, just as infants are smaller than toddlers, just as toddlers are smaller than adolescents, just as adolescents are smaller than teenagers, and teenagers are smaller than adults. Size does not matter. It is lawful to kill a fly and unlawful to kill a person, not because the person is bigger, but because the person is human. Trees are generally bigger than people, but while it is lawful to cut branches off of trees, it is unlawful to cut arms off of people. Why? Because humanity, not size, is what determines rights of personhood. This might seem obvious but there are people across the globe who try and justify abortion on the claim that the diminutive size of the embryo or foetus makes them nonhuman and so ethically insignificant. Since size does not determine personhood after birth, it should not be used to determine personhood before birth.

Level of Development – it is quite true that embryos and foetuses are less developed than a newborn (unless, of course, that newborn was born prematurely). But this, too, is a distinction which has no moral significance. It is a difference of degree, not of kind. Physical and/or intellectual development has nothing to do with determining personhood outside the womb. It is equally insignificant for determining personhood inside the womb. Children are generally less developed than adults. People with developmental disabilities may be less developed than some children, and those with extraordinary mental capacity are no more human than those with lesser IQs. It is humanity, not brain capacity or arm strength that determines personhood.

Environment – the third difference between an embryo or foetus and a newborn baby is their place of residence. Embryos and foetuses live inside the womb, and newborn babies live outside the womb. Just like the distinctions that have gone before, this too, is an inconsequential difference. Where someone lives has nothing to do with the essence of who that someone is. Moving from the bedroom to the kitchen, or from indoors to outdoors, or from your car to the classroom doesn't affect your personhood. Personhood stems from inclusion in the human species not from the location in which you reside. For the entire duration of pregnancy, the tiny unborn child is a human being all of its own. It is dependent upon its mother for many life-sustaining functions, but it is certainly not part of its mother's body.[170] Any attempt to disqualify unborn children from receiving their due rights of personhood because they live in a womb rather than in a room is dishonest and unjust. Location doesn't affect the personhood of those outside the womb, and it shouldn't affect the personhood of those inside the womb.

Degree of Dependency – The issue of dependency may well be the one abortion supporters turn to most in their attempt to justify abortion. "Since a foetus can't survive on its own," they argue, "it has no inherent right to life". What's the problem with this argument? In the broadest sense, it could be applied to all of us. There isn't a person alive who is radically independent from the universe we live in. We all need food, water, rest, and oxygen. We are all vulnerable to a million different bodily breakdowns. Are those who must rely on kidney machines, pace-makers or insulin shots for their survival less deserving of basic human rights than anyone else? Some of us may be less dependent than others, but if it is dependence that strips away a person's right to protection under the law, then we would all be in trouble. Embryos and foetuses who must rely on an umbilical cord in the womb are just as human as those who must rely on a feeding tube outside the womb.

Perhaps the biggest absurdity about this whole attack on dependence is the fact that dependency should merit more protection under the law, not less! After all, the younger and more dependent a child is, the more care and compassion we have for them. The US Office of Juvenile Justice and

Delinquency Prevention expresses it well when they say, "Homicides are always tragic, but our sympathies are heightened when the victim is a young child or adolescent. Thus, the deaths of juveniles raise understandable public concerns." The nation is far more outraged at violence directed towards children than at violence directed towards other adults. The reason is simple. Children are more helpless, and less capable of defending themselves. And the younger the child is, the truer this becomes. How we ever got to the place of using dependency against children rather than for children is a tragedy of staggering proportions.

These "objections assume that personhood presupposes a postnatal human form. A little reflection will show that the concept of a "human form" is a dynamic and not a static one. Each of us, during normal development, exhibits a long succession of different outward forms. The appearance of an 80-year-old adult differs greatly from that of a newborn child, and yet we speak without hesitation of both as persons. In both cases, we have learned to recognise physical appearances associated with those developmental stages as normal expressions of personhood".[171] "As more and more people become knowledgeable about prenatal development, including the appearance of the unborn in their normal growth, it will seem natural to recognise them for what they are: human beings in an early stage of development. To insist that the unborn at six weeks look like the newborn infant is no more reasonable than to expect the newborn infant to look like a teenager".[172]

"If we acknowledge as "human" a succession of outward forms after birth, there is no reason not to extend that courtesy to the unborn, since human life is a *continuum* from conception to natural death. "Human" form consists of whatever is appropriate to a particular developmental stage – whether at three weeks after conception, or at age 83, three weeks prior to death".[173]

This argument can be considered as a kind of discrimination. What we call racism, discriminates against certain classes of people whose skin colour differs from the preferred norm for social acceptability and full personhood. What we might call antifoetalism discriminates against the unborn on the basis of their physical appearance as well. This form of discrimination does not deserve any place in a humane and just society.[174]

A person is nothing more or less than a living human. Anyone who tries to narrow this general definition of personhood does so in an attempt to eliminate a certain group of people who is either getting in their way or has something they want. Creating self-defined definitions of personhood, which are uniquely crafted to eliminate certain individuals from protection under the law, has long been the method of choice for implementing all manner of genocidal atrocities. The differences that exist between a human being before birth and a human being after birth are differences that do not matter.

'Normal Usage' Argument

"Another group objects the personhood of the unborn saying that, in normal usage the term "person" is not used of the unborn, at least not in the very earliest stages of prenatal development". It is certainly true that in modern times (in some countries) "normal usage" does not apply the language of personhood to the unborn in the very earliest stages of their development. For example, in the abortion decisions of 1973 the U.S. Supreme Court asserted that the unborn were not persons in the "whole sense" until birth."[175] This does not settle the issue. One may ask: Is "normal usage" in a particular society and historical period the final court of appeal? No, because a culture's perceptions of personhood, as we know, can change."[176]

Throughout history, certain groups have felt the brunt of a system which denied their humanity, stripped their personhood, and subjected them to horrors beyond measure. In American history two specific groups of human beings – African Americans and Native Americans – were stripped of their rights of personhood as a means of justifying horrific mistreatment. For that an artificial classification was made: "human", and "non-person". This distinction was not based on an honest evaluation of the evidence, but with an eye towards justifying a specific action. In the case of Native Americans, they had land. In the case of African Americans, they had labour. Classifying them as non-persons (even property) provided a moral framework for those in power to forcefully take what they wanted without compensation. Both groups can give eloquent testimonies of the cruel realities of discriminatory definitions of personhood.

"At the time U.S. Constitution was adopted, black slaves were not considered persons in the "whole sense."[177] In the eyes of the law...the slave is not a person," (Virginia Supreme Court, 1858). "For the sake of congressional representation, the slave-holding states were allowed to count each slave as three-fifths of a person. Such was "normal usage" there, at the end of the eighteenth century. If political rights are a criterion of personhood, then American women were not considered persons in the "whole sense" well into the twentieth century".[178] Further, "the history of Nazi Germany demonstrates with terrible clarity the fatal consequences that can follow from a discriminatory definition of human personhood."[179] All these examples indicate that a culture's perceptions of personhood can change. For example, American society's "perceptions of human personhood, as we have seen, have undergone a centuries-long process of "re-education" or "consciousness raising." Classes of human beings not recognised as persons in the "whole sense" have asserted their rightful claims to human dignity, and the society, after long and often violent struggles, has altered its perceptions. These changes are consistent with the fundamental truths of the Declaration of Independence, which asserts as a self-evident truth that all men are created equal and are thus endowed by their Creator with certain inalienable rights, chief among which is the very right to life itself."[180]

Today, "unwanted," unborn children do not hold anything as tangible as land or labour, but their claims on those who would eliminate them are no less significant. They stand in the way of an unencumbered, more self-absorbed lifestyle. Once again, this notion that human beings can be classified as "nonpersons" is not built on an objective assessment of the facts, but with an eye towards justifying abortion.

While the legal framework that made such horrors possible has now been removed, it remains firmly in place for the pre-borns. During the late Middle Ages, so many children died that people did not normally identify infants as persons in the "whole sense."[181] In some countries, 'unwanted' pre-borns have no protection under the law and are being killed *en masse* every day. It is truly astounding. "The progress of medical science has given us an ever-expanding knowledge of the unborn as genuinely individual human beings, (which we shall see later) and this new scientific information needs to be recognised by law and by society's conscience."[182]

If we accept the personhood of the foetus/ embryo, how do we explain, some may ask, the enormous foetal wastage during the development in the womb?

Foetal Wastage Argument

"Another common objection is that many fertilised ova die prior to birth, as many as 30 to 50 percent. If in the eyes of God these fertilised eggs are personal beings, why does God allow so many of them to perish?"[183] Authors like Thomas W. Hilgers, question the reliability of the above statistics themselves.[184] Those figures were extrapolated from a study of only 34 human ova removed within the first 17 days of development from women who had had hysterectomies. And only a small subsection of the above study was used to support the claim that 50 percent of early embryos were lost: four of eight of the ova recovered prior to implantation were abnormal. Since all 34 ova came from women who were hospitalised for various uterine and tubal pathologies, the sample was hardly normal, and the accuracy of the results is very doubtful.[185] Based on a narrow and questionable database, the claims for "foetal wastage" ought not to be granted significant weight in assessing the morality of abortion.

"Even if these figures were accurate, they would only be an illustration of the fact that human beings can perish at any stage of the developmental process, and that prenatal life also has its hazards. The loss of many human lives in automobile accidents is no argument against taking responsible steps to reduce highway fatalities. The same preventive concern should be shown for prenatal human life. As Christians, our valuation of human life is not based on statistical norms but rather on the norm of divine revelation, which teaches the sacredness and dignity of each human life".[186]

Conclusion

Here we made an attempt to arrive at the moral worth of the human person and to establish the personhood of the unborn with the help of Scripture. The Biblical doctrine of man helped us understand the sanctity and dignity of the human person. The fact that we are created in the image and likeness of God and the life affirming ethos contributed to the understanding of the moral worth of human person.

We saw that all human beings derive their inherent worth and the right to life from being made in the image of God, standing in relation to God as their personal Creator. Every individual from fertilisation is known by God, is under His providential care, is morally accountable, and possesses the very image of God the Creator. Having such a relationship with God a human being's value and worth is constant, whether strong or weak, conscious or unconscious, healthy or disabled, socially useful or useless, wanted or unwanted, born or unborn. Then, the five kinds of Biblical texts we surveyed enabled us to arrive at the personhood of the unborn by showing that there is a *continuum* from conception to birth.

Having established the specificity of a human being as fashioned by God in His image and likeness we could conclude that the foetus is a human being and thus that human being is a human person. The Biblical teaching on personhood also came to our help to arrive at the above conclusion. After that we tried to address and respond to the various objections usually raised against the personhood of the unborn. Since human life begins at fertilisation, the full moral worth afforded to every human being is equally afforded from fertilisation onward throughout development.

So vague notions of personhood or social utility have no place in decisions regarding the worth, dignity, or rights of any human being, born/unborn. Human life, grounded in its divine origin and in the image of God, is the basis of all other human rights, natural and legal, and the foundation of civilised society. Indeed, society itself is to be judged by its protection of and the solicitude it shows for the weakest of its members (Mt.25:40; James 1:27). The unborn is the weakest of all human beings. Therefore, human being's life – born or unborn – may not be sacrificed for the economic or political welfare or convenience of other individuals or society.

7 Wyatt J., Matters of Life and Death, IVP, Leicester, 1998, p.52.

8 F.La Gard Smith, When Choice Becomes God, Harvest House Press, 1990, p.131.

9 Norman St. John Stevas, The Right to Life (Chicago: Holt, Rinehart & Winston, 1964), p.37.

10 Singer P., Rethinking Life and Death, Oxford University Press, Oxford, 1994, p.131.

11 Dworkin R., Life's Dominion, Harper Collins, London, 1995, p.239

12 Singer P., Rethinking Life and Death, Oxford University Press, Oxford, 1994, p.189

13 Singer P., Rethinking Life and Death, Oxford University Press, Oxford, 1994, p.190-200

14 'Resolution 1 14' Lambeth Conference 1998 Archives, www.lambethconference.org.

15 'Cloning, Board of Social Witness' p.4, Presbyterian Church in Ireland, www.presbyterianireland/bsw.

16 Evangelium Vitae, 38

17 Catechism of the Catholic Church, Veritas, Dublin, 1994, 2258.

18 John Jefferson Davis, Abortion and the Christian , p.20; seen at http://www.abortionfacts.com/books/abortion-and-the-christian

19 Wyatt J., Matters of Life and Death, IVP, Leicester, 1998, p.51.

20 Catechism of the Catholic Church, Veritas, Dublin, 1994, 2258.

21 Huesman J., Exodus, The Jerome Biblical Commentary, Geoffrey Chapman, London, 1970, p.57.

22 Anthony Fisher, Catholic Bioethics for New Millennium, Cambridge University Press, Cambridge, 2012, p.152.

23 However, despite the fact that according to this concept the human is created in God's image, the Creator granted the first true humans a freedom to reject a relationship with the Creator that manifested itself in estrangement from God, as the narrative of the Fall (Adam and Eve) exemplifies, thereby rejecting or repressing their spiritual and moral likeness to God. The ability and desire to love one's self and others, and therefore God, can become neglected and even opposed. The desire to repair the Imago Dei in one's life can be seen as a quest for a wholeness, or one's "essential" self, as described and exemplified in Christ's life and

teachings. According to Christian doctrine, Jesus acted to repair the relationship with the Creator and freely offers the resulting reconciliation as a gift.

24 Millard J. Erickson, Christian Theology, 2nd ed. (Grand Rapids: Baker Book House, 1998), p. 522.

25 idem

26 Gerhard Wehemeier, "Deliverance and Blessing in the Old and New Testament," Indian Journal of Theology 20 (1971): 30-42.

27 For reviews of the various interpretations Cfr. G.C. Berkouwer, Man: The Image of God, trans. Dirk Jellema (Grand Rapids: Eerdmans, 1962), pp. 67-118, and Emil Brunner, The Christian Doctrine of Creation and Redemption, trans. Olive Wyon (Philadelphia: Westminster, 1952), pp. 75-78.

28 John Jefferson Davis, Abortion and the Christian,p.21; seen at http://www.abortionfacts.com/books/abortion-and-the-christian. I am very much indebted to John Jefferson Davis' Abortion and the Christian, What Every Believer should know (Phillipsburg, NJ). Presbyterian and Reformed Publishing Co (June 1, 1984).

29 Cf. G.C. Berkouwer, Man, pp. 59, 93. See also , Millard J. Erickson, Christian Theology, (Grand Rapids, MI: Baker Book House, 1994), 498-510; Millard J. Erickson, Introducing Christian Doctrine, 2nd ed. (Grand Rapids: Baker Book House, 2001), 172-175.

30 Gerhard von Rad, commenting on Gen. 9:6, observes: "Attack on man's body is a violation of God's honour."

31 "The duties required in the sixth commandment are: all careful studies, and lawful endeavours, to preserve the life of ourselves and others, by resisting all thoughts and purposes, subduing all passions, and avoiding all occasions, temptations, and practices, which tend to be unjust taking away the life of any. . . ." Cf. Q.135 of the Westminster Larger Catechism.

32 John Jefferson Davis, Abortion and the Christian, p.21; seen at www.abortionfacts.com/books/abortion-and-the-christian

33-34 John Jefferson Davis, Abortion and the Christian, p.22; seen at www.abortionfacts.com/books/abortion-and-the-christian

35 Tracy Wilkinson and Pablo Jaramillo 'concern for the most vulnerable' ViteriContact Reporter July 5, 2015

36 John Jefferson Davis, Abortion and the Christian , p.23; seen at www.abortionfacts.com/books/abortion-and-the-christian

37 Note the suggestion of Nobel Laureate James Watson on the matter of newborn children with severe birth defects: "If a child were not declared alive until three days after birth, then all parents could be allowed the choice. . . .the doctor could allow the child to die if the parents so choose and save a lot of misery and suffering." Cited by Dr. and Mrs. J.C. Willke, Handbook on Abortion (Cincinnati: Hayes), 1975, p.113.

38-39 John Jefferson Davis, Abortion and the Christian, p.23 seen at http://www.abortionfacts.com/books/abortion-and-the-christian

40-42 John Jefferson Davis, Abortion and the Christian, p.22; seen at http://www.abortionfacts.com/books/abortion-and-the-christian

43 1Cor. 1:26-29

44 See the second part of this book.

45 Gen 2:7; Ps 139:14-16; Is 42:5; Jer 1:5, 10:23; Rom 14:9

46 Gen 1:26, 27; 9:6

47 John 3:16

48 This is attested to by the whole of the Decalogue (not only the Sixth Commandment; Fifth Commandment in the Catholic and Lutheran traditions) and by the incarnation

49 Gen 4:1; Ps 127:3

50 "Nephesh"

51 Some Christians hold that Scripture describes human beings as composed of distinct parts, either body and soul (dichotomy), or body, soul, and spirit (trichotomy). CMDA is aware of this viewpoint but feels that the issue in clinical medicine should be approached viewing a human being as a functional unity. The body soul distinction could provide a rationale to those who would disrespect human life as the "higher" (implying soul) functions of "personhood" or "rationality" are not present

52 Job 10:8-11; Jer 1:5; Ps 139:13-16 (*"golem"* meaning "embryo," i.e., first few weeks of gestation)

53 Is 7:14

54 Ps 51:5; Ps 119:13-16

55 Apostolic, Nicean-Constantinopolitan, and Athanasian

56 Nicea (325 AD), Constantinople (381 AD), Ephesus (431 AD), and Chalcedon (451 AD)

57 see The Beginning of Human Life, Addendum II: Conception and Fertilization: Defining Ethically Relevant Terms.

58 Luke 1:31; Matt 1:20 (where the term "gennao" stands unambiguously for conception)

59 Heb 2:17

60 G. Hardin, "Abortion or Compulsory Pregnancy?", in Journal of Marriage and Family, May, 1968, cited by R.F.R Gardener, Abortion: The Personal Dilemma, (Grand Rapids, Michigan: Eerdmans), 1972, p.25.

61 D. Callahan, Abortion: Law, Choice and Morality, (New York and London: Collier Macmillan), 1970; cited in R.F.R Gardener, Abortion: The Personal Dilemma, (Grand Rapids, Michigan: Eerdmans), 1972, p.125.

62 D. Callahan, Abortion: Law, Choice and Morality, (New York and London: Collier Macmillan), 1970; cited in R.F.R Gardener, Abortion: The Personal Dilemma, (Grand Rapids, Michigan: Eerdmans), 1972, p.125.

63 See, R.H. Gundry, 'Soma' in Biblical Theology with Emphasis on Pauline Anthropology, (London: New York: Cambridge University), 1976.

64 H.W. Wolff, Anthropology of the Old Testament, (Philadelphia: Fortress), 1974, p.59.

65 If man's physical being is in the image of God we should immediately wonder what, if any organs, God possesses. Does he have sexual organs, and if so which? The very absurdity that God is a sexual being renders this interpretation highly

66 R.F.R Gardener, Abortion: The Personal Dilemma, (Grand Rapids, Michigan: Eerdmans), 1972, p.116.

67 F.A. Schaeffer, The God Who is There, (Chicago: Inter-Varsity), 1968, p.87.

68 B.K. Waltke, "Reflections from the Old testament on abortion", in Journal of the Evangelical Theological Society, 19, no. 1 (1976): pp.3-13, p.9.

69 See, Bernard Ramm, A Handbook of Contemporary Theology, (Grand Rapids, Michigan: Eerdmans) 1966, pp.61-64

70 H.W. Wolff, Anthropology of the Old Testament, (Philadelphia: Fortress), 1974, p.55.

71 See, R. Brow, in D. P. Alexander, eds. Eerdman's Hand Book to the Bible, (Grand Rapids: Eerdmans), 1973, pp.24f.

72 We have elaborated on the ensuing texts and so some sort of repetition is unavoidable

73 See, C.S. Lewis, "Dogma and the Universe", in W. Hooper, ed., God in the Dock, (Grand Rapids, Michigan: Eerdmans), 1970, pp.38-47.

74 Quoted by H. Thielicke, How the World Began?, trans. by J.W. Doberstein, (Philadelphia: Muehlenberg), 1961, p.82.

75 F. Brown, S.R. Driver and C.A Briggs, A Hebrew and English Lexicon, (Oxford: Clarendon), 1907, p.409.

76 E.R. Dalglish, Psalm Fifty-One in the Light of Near Eastern Patternism, (Leiden: E,J Brill), 1962, p.121.

77 E.R. Dalglish, Psalm Fifty-One in the Light of Near Eastern Patternism, (Leiden: E,J Brill), 1962, p.124.

78 For this point I am indebted to Christina M.H. Powell, Ph.D., medical writer, and research scientist trained at Harvard Medical School and Harvard University. She addresses faith and science issues at http://www.questionyourdoubts.com.

79 Sagan, Carl, The Dragons of Eden: Speculations on the Evolution of Human Intelligence, New York: Random House, 1977, 196.

80 Wyatt J., Matters of Life and Death, IVP, Leicester, 1998, p.142.

81 "For you created my inmost being, you knit me together in my mother's womb. I praise you because I am fearfully wonderfully made."

82 Stott J., Issues Facing Christians Today, 4th edn. (Zondervan, Michigan), 2006, p.400.

83 Wyatt J., Matters of Life and Death, IVP, Leicester, 1998, pp.145-146. 42

84 John Jefferson Davis, Abortion and the Christian , p.23; seen at http://www.abortionfacts.com/books/abortion-and-the-christian

85 John Jefferson Davis, Abortion and the Christian ,p.24; seen at http://www.abortionfacts.com/books/abortion-and-the-christian

86 John Jefferson Davis, Abortion and the Christian , p.24; seen at http://www.abortionfacts.com/books/abortion-and-the-christian

87 John Jefferson Davis, Abortion and the Christian , p.24; seen at http://www.abortionfacts.com/books/abortion-and-the-christian

88 As we have already seen, according to Professor E.R. Dalglish, the psalmist is relating his sinfulness to the very inception of life; he traces his development beyond his birth to the genesis of his being in his mother's womb – even to the very hour of conception. See, Edward R. Dalglish, Psalm Fifty-One in the Light of Ancient Near Eastern Patternism (Leiden:E.J. Brill, 1962), p. 121.

89 John Jefferson Davis, Abortion and the Christian, p.24; seen at http://www.abortionfacts.com/books/abortion-and-the-christian

90-91 John Jefferson Davis, Abortion and the Christian, p.27; seen at www.abortionfacts.com/books/abortion-and-the-christian

92 John Jefferson Davis, Abortion and the Christia , p.24; seen at http://www.abortionfacts.com/books/abortion-and-the-christian

93 Waltke, "Reflections from the Old Testament on Abortion," Journal of the Evangelical Theological Society 19, no. 1 (1976): 13; Dalglish, Psalm Fifty-One, pp.123, 124.

94 John Jefferson Davis, Abortion and the Christian , pp.24-25; seen at www.abortionfacts.com/books/abortion-and-the-christian

95 Dalglish, Psalm Fifty-One, p.57.

96 Ibid., p. 124. Dalglish points out that the notion of the moral law as a natural endowment is found elsewhere in Rom.2:15, where Paul says of the Gentiles that "What the law requires is written on their hearts." Though the Gentiles do not have the law, on occasion they "do by nature what the law requires" (Rom.2:14). There the idea is clearly that man's moral sense is not merely the product of postnatal socialisation, but is in some sense innate. Dalglish also points to an interesting Talmudic text, Nidda 30b, which is closely related to the proposed rendering of Ps. 51:6: "[The embryo] is also taught all the Torah from the beginning to end. . . . As soon as it sees the light, an angel approaches, slaps it on its mouth and causes it to forget all the Torah completely." (p.125).

97 John Jefferson Davis, Abortion and the Christian, p.25 seen at www.abortionfacts.com/books/abortion-and-the-christian.

98 John Jefferson Davis, Abortion and the Christian, p.27 seen at http://www.abortionfacts.com/books/abortion-and-the-christian

99 John Jefferson Davis, Abortion and the Christian, p.25; seen at http://www.abortionfacts.com/books/abortion-and-the-christian

100 John Jefferson Davis, Abortion and the Christian, pp.25-26; seen at www.abortionfacts.com/books/abortion-and-the-christian

101 See part II.

102 Albert W. Liley, "The foetus in Control of His Environment," in Hilgers and Horan, eds., Abortion and Social Justice (New York: Sheed and Ward, 1972), p.29.

103-104 John Jefferson Davis, Abortion and the Christian, p.26; seen at www.abortionfacts.com/books/abortion-and-the-christian

105 F. Delitzsch, Biblical Commentary on the Book of Job, trans. F. Bolton (Grand Rapids: Eerdmans, n.d.), 1:166.

106 Donald Shoemaker, Abortion, The Bible and Christian, (Grand rapids: Bake Book House, 1976).

107 A.B. Davidson, cited by H.H. Rowley, ed., Job: The New Century Bible (London: Nelson, 1970), p.102.

108 John Jefferson Davis, Abortion and the Christian, p.26; seen at www.abortionfacts.com/books/abortion-and-the-christian.

109 Norman Habel, The Book of Job (Cambridge: Cambridge University Press, 1975), p.59.

110 E.M. Good, "Love in the Old Testament," Interpreter's Dictionary of the Bible (New York: Abingdon, 1962), 3:167.

111 John Jefferson Davis, Abortion and the Christian, p.27; seen at www.abortionfacts.com/books/abortion-and-the-christian.

112 John Jefferson Davis, Abortion and the Christian, p.27; seen at www.abortionfacts.com/books/abortion-and-the-christian.

113 John Jefferson Davis, Abortion and the Christian, p.27; seen at www.abortionfacts.com/books/abortion-and-the-christian.

114 John Jefferson Davis, Abortion and the Christian, p.27-28; seen at www.abortionfacts.com/books/abortion-and-the-christian.

115 John Jefferson Davis, Abortion and the Christian, p.28; seen at www.abortionfacts.com/books/abortion-and-the-christian.

116 John Jefferson Davis, Abortion and the Christian, p.28; seen at www.abortionfacts.com/books/abortion-and-the-christian.

117-120 John Jefferson Davis, Abortion and the Christian, p.28; seen at www.abortionfacts.com/books/abortion-and-the-christian.

121 Meredith G. Kline, "Lex Talionis and the Human Foetus," Journal of the Evangelical Theological Society 20, no.3 (1977): 193-202.

122-123 John Jefferson Davis, Abortion and the Christian, p.29-30; www.abortionfacts.com/books/abortion-and-the-christian.

124 Position 1, the "miscarriage" interpretation, is followed by the Latin Vulgate, Martin Luther's German Bible, the RSV, the NEB, and by modern interpreters such as J.C. Rylaarsdaam and Bruce Waltke (Rylaarsdaam, The Interpreter's Bible, ed. George Buttrick [New York: Abingdon, 1952], 1:999-1000; Waltke, "Old Testament on Abortion," p.3, n.3). Waltke, however, pointing to the accidental nature of the alleged miscarriage, does not draw the conclusion that the unborn child is less than a human being on the basis of the nonimposition of the capital penalty. He argues in fact that the imago Dei is present from conception.

125 John Jefferson Davis, Abortion and the Christian, p.30; seen at www.abortionfacts.com/books/abortion-and-the-christian.

126 Cf. Calvin, Commentaries on the Last Four Books of Moses, trans. C. Bingham (reprinted Grand Rapids: Eerdmans, 1847), 3:41-42; Keil and Delitzsch, Biblical Commentary on the Old Testament: Volume 2, 1866. The Pentateuch, trans. J. Martin (Grand Rapids: Eerdmans, 2012), pp. 134, 135): U. Cassuto, Commentary on Exodus, trans. I. Abrahams(Jerusalem: Magnes, 1967), pp. 273-77; Harold Brown, "What the Supreme Court Didn't Know," Human Life Review 1, no.2 (1975):8-11; Donald Shoemaker, Abortion, the Bible, and the Christian (Cincinnati: Hayes, 1976), pp. 37-39; Jack Cottrell, "Abortion and the Mosaic Law," Christianity Today, March 16, 1973, pp. 6-9; C.C. Ryrie, "The Question of Abortion," in You Mean the Bible Teaches That. . . (Chicago: Moody, 1974), pp. 86-88; John Frame et al., "Report of the Committee to Study the Matter of Abortion," Agenda: 38th General Assembly, Orthodox Presbyterian Church (1971), pp. 94-98. Bernard Jackson, "The Problem of Exod. 21:22-5," Vetus Testamentum 23 (1973: 273-304), holds that v. 22 originally referred to a premature live birth, but that through a long process of redaction the meaning of the entire passage has been substantially changed.

127 C.F Keil and F. Delitzch, Commentary on the Old Testament, Vol.I (Grand Rapids: Eerdmans, 1983), pp.134-135.

128 John Jefferson Davis, Abortion and the Christian (Phillipsburg, New Jersey; Presbyterian and Reformed, 1984), p.52.

129 The meanings of 'nagaph' and 'ason' give further support to the view that the death of the child by induced miscarriage is not in view in Ex. 21:22.

130 Gen. 25:25-26; 35:11; 38:28-30; Exod. 1:5; Deut. 28:57; 2 Sam. 16:11; 1 Chron. 1:12; Job 1:21; 3:11; Eccles. 5:15; Jer. 20:18. Num. 12:12 indicates the birth of a stillborn child.

131 Lawrence O. Richards, Expository Dictionary of Bible Words, (Grand Rapids, Mic: Zondervan Publishing House, 1985), pp. 156-157. For different meanings of 'yeled' see, our foot note 76.

132 More recently, Meredith G. Kline has offered an exegesis of Exodus 21:22-25, which we may designate "Position III." (Lex Talionis, Kline) While Kline's exegesis agrees with Position II that the life of the unborn child is granted a legal status equal to the mother's, the exegetical route by which he establishes that conclusion differs from that of Position II. In Kline's view, Case A refers to the following circumstances: The child is born prematurely, but alive and uninjured; the woman experiences a fatal injury. In such a case the assailant must render a monetary compensation in the amount demanded by the husband. In Case B, if the child suffers calamitous injury or death, the penalty must be a just monetary compensation. Thus Position III holds that Case A refers to injuries to the mother alone, and Case B to injuries to the child alone. In either case, the law treats a fatal injury as a case of negligent manslaughter, for which monetary compensation may be rendered as a substitute for the forfeiture of life.

133 James Hoffmeier, (ed.) Abortion: A Christian Understanding and Response, (Grand Rapids), 1987, p.62.

134 John Jefferson Davis, Abortion and the Christian, p.31; seen at http://www.abortionfacts.com/books/abortion-and-the-christian.

135 Berkouwer and Williams have helpful discussions on the questions of ensoulment and the creationist-traducianist debate. See G.C. Berkouwer, Man; H. Wheeler Robinson, The Christian Doctrine of Man, 3rd ed. (Edinburgh: T.& T. Clark, 1926); John A.T. Robinson, The Body: A Study in Pauline Anthropology (London: SCM, 1952); Edmond Jacob, "Psyche," Theological Dictionary of the New Testament (1974), 9:608-31; N. W. Porteous, "Soul," Interpreter's Dictionary of the Bible IV (1962), 4:428-29; George H. Williams, "Religious Residues and Presuppositions in the American Debate on Abortion," Theological Studies 31, no. 1 (1970): 10-75. John Jefferson Davis, "Abortion and the Christian", p.32; www.abortionfacts.com/books/abortion-and-the-christian.

136 For a survey of the various positions, and a helpful philosophical analysis of the concept of personhood, see Gabriel Pastrana, "Personhood and the Beginning of Human Life." Thomist 41, no. 2 (1977):247-94. .John Jefferson Davis, "Abortion and the Christian", p.32; http://www.abortionfacts.com/books/abortion-and-the-christian.

137 John Jefferson Davis, "Abortion and the Christian", p.32; www.abortionfacts.com/books/abortion-and-the-christian.

138 J. A. T. Robinson, The Body: A Study in Pauline Anthropology (London: SCM, 1952); p. 14. Robinson cites in this connection the famous statement of H. Wheeler Robinson: "The Hebrew idea of the personality is an animated body, and not an incarnated soul."

139 Edmond Jacob, "Psuche," Theological Dictionary of the New Testament (1974), 9:608-31; p.631.

140 John Jefferson Davis, "Abortion and the Christian", p.32; http://www.abortionfacts.com/books/abortion-and-the-christian.

141 Gerhard von Rad, Old Testament Theology, trans. D. Stalker (New York: Harper and Row, 1962), 1:145. Cf. Berkouwer, Man, p.75: "It is very noteworthy . . . that there has been an increasing reluctance to exclude man's body from the image of God – and exclusion generally supported previously, when theologians sought the content of the image in man's 'higher' qualities, in contrast to the 'lower' bodily qualities which should not be considered in connection with the image." John Jefferson Davis, "Abortion and the Christian , p.32; www.abortionfacts.com/books/abortion-and-the-christian.

142 John Jefferson Davis, "Abortion and the Christian" , p.32; http://www.abortionfacts.com/books/abortion-and-the-christian. Such a view provides an adequate framework for understanding a text like Genesis 5:3, which describes the seminal transmission of the image from Adam to his son Seth. If the imago were restricted to man's conscious mental capacities, it would be difficult to understand how such a statement could be meaningful.

143 http://www.abortionfacts.com/books/abortion-and-the-christian, p.33.

144 That is made clear by such texts as Romans 8:6, where Paul speaks of the mind of the flesh; 1 Corinthians 3:3, where carnality is associated with jealousy and envy; and Galatians 5:19ff., where the "works of the flesh" include idolatry, sorcery, and envy. Berkouwer, Man, p.205.

145 Herman Ridderbox, Paul: An Outline of His Theology, trans. J. de Witt (Grand Rapids: Eerdmans 1975), p.116.

146-148 http://www.abortionfacts.com/books/abortion-and-the-christian, p.33.

149 The mention of human conception some forty times in the Scripture indicates in itself the significance of this event in God's dealings with his people.

150 http://www.abortionfacts.com/books/abortion-and-the-christian, p.33-34.

151 For details see the article by Graham A.D. Scott, "Abortion and the Incarnation," Journal of the Evangelical Theological Society 17 (1974):29-44.

152 John Calvin, Commentaries on the Four Last Books of Moses, trans. Charles William Bingham, 4 Vols. (Grand rapids: Wm. B., Eerdmans Publishing Co.1950), 3:41-42.

153 Alcorn, Randy, Abortion in the Bible and Church History, www.epm.org/articles/aborhistory.html, accessed 8-25-06.

154 Brown, Driver, Briggs and Gesenius, "Hebrew Lexicon entry for Yeled", The NAS Old Testament Hebrew Lexicon.

155 Origin of "foetus", http://www.wordwizard.com/, accessed 5-27-04.

156 Cambridge International Dictionary of English, for example.

157 Lars Wilhelmsson, Abortion Eclipse of Morality, p. 37-38 seen at www.vitalchristianity.org/docs/abortion.

158 Calvin comments on these words as follows: "She calls Mary the mother of her Lord. This denotes a unity of person in the two natures of Christ; as if she had said, that he who has begotten a mortal man in the womb of Mary is, at the same time, the eternal God," (Calvin, Commentary on a Harmony of the Evangelists [Grand Rapids: Associated Publishers, n.d.], p.23).

159 http://www.abortionfacts.com/books/abortion-and-the-christian, p.34.

160 His human nature, in the language of Chalcedon, is "consubstantial" with our own. www.abortionfacts.com/books/abortion-and-the-christian, p.34.

161 http://www.abortionfacts.com/books/abortion-and-the-christian, p.34-35.

162 http://www.abortionfacts.com/books/abortion-and-the-christian, p.35.

163 http://www.abortionfacts.com/books/abortion-and-the-christian, p.35.

164 See Beckwith, "The Explanatory Power of the Substance View of Persons." In Christian Bioethics, 2004 January- April, 10(1), pp. 33-54.

165 See Beckwith, "The Explanatory Power of the Substance View of Persons."

166 See, http://www.abortionfacts.com/books/abortion-and-the-christian, p.35.

167 Carlson, Bruce, Human Embryology and Development Biology, St, Louis, MO: Mosby, 1994, chs. 2-4; Gilbert, Scott, Developmental Biology, 7th edn. Sunderland, MA, Sinnauer Associates, 2003, pp, 183-220, 363-390; Larson, William J., Human Embryology, 3rd edn. New York, Churchill Livingstone, 2001, chs. 1-2; Moore, Keith and Persaud, T, V, N., The Developing Human, Clinically Oriented Embryology 7th edn., New York, 2003; W. B., Saunders,2003, chs. 1-6; Muller Werner A., Developmental Biology, New York Springer Verlag, 1997, chs. 1-2; O'Rahily, Ronan and Mueller Fabiola, Human Embryology and Teratology, 3rd edn., New York, John Wiley & Sons, 2000, chs.3-4.

168 The definition of person proposed above, however, is framed in light of the general case, rather than the exception like identical twins. For a detailed analysis of the philosophical use of the term "person," see Gabriel Pastrana, "Personhood and the Beginning of Human Life," Thomist 41, no. 2 (1977):247-94.

169 http://www.abortionfacts.com/books/abortion-and-the-christian, p.35.

170 See Part II, 3, C of this book, 'Unborn' is not Part of Mother's Body.

171 http://www.abortionfacts.com/books/abortion-and-the-christian, p.35.

172 http://www.abortionfacts.com/books/abortion-and-the-christian, p.36.

173 http://www.abortionfacts.com/books/abortion-and-the-christian, p.36.

174 http://www.abortionfacts.com/books/abortion-and-the-christian, p.36.

175 http://www.abortionfacts.com/books/abortion-and-the-christian, p.36.

176 http://www.abortionfacts.com/books/abortion-and-the-christian, p.36.

177, 179-180 See http://www.abortionfacts.com/books/abortion-and-the-christian, p.36.

178 Lynn Hunt, Inventing Human Rights – A History, w.w Norton & Company/New York London, 2007, pp.167-175; see also, www.abortionfacts.com/books/abortion-and-the-christian, p.36.

181 Philippe Aries, Centuries of Childhood, trans. R. Baldick (New York: 1965), pp. 38-39, cited by James M. Humber, "The Case Against Abortion," Thomist, 39, no. 1 (1975):75.

182-183 See http://www.abortionfacts.com/books/abortion-and-the-christian, pp.36-37

184 Thomas W. Hilgers, M.D., "Human Reproduction," Theological Studies 38, no. 1 (1977): 136-52.

185 Ibid., p. 148; see also, http://www.abortionfacts.com/books/abortion-and-the-christian, p.37.

186 http://www.abortionfacts.com/books/abortion-and-the-christian, p.37.

PART TWO
The Unborn Child is a Human Person: Science

How complex and mind – boggling is our physical construction! Chemically, the body is unequalled for complexity. Each one of man's 30 trillion cells is a mini chemical factory that performs about 10,000 chemical functions. With its 206 bones, 639 muscles, 4 million pain sensors in the skin, 750 million air sacs in the lungs, 16 million nerve cells and 30 trillion cells in total, the human body is remarkably designed for life. And the brain! The human brain with the nervous system is the most complex arrangement of matter anywhere in the universe. One scientist estimated that our brain, on the average, processes over 10,000 thoughts and concepts each day. Three billion DNA pairs in a fertilized egg control all human activities, 30,000 genes making 90,000 proteins in the body….
So, "one who is a fan of science will also be a fan of human life – at all its stages."

The Need for Scientific Fact

The process of eroding the old ethic and substituting the new has already begun. It is seen most clearly in changing attitudes toward human abortion. In defiance of the long held Western ethic of intrinsic and equal value for every human life regardless of its stage, condition, or status, abortion is becoming acceptable by society as moral, right, and even necessary. Since the old ethic has not been fully displaced it has been necessary to separate the idea of abortion from the idea of killing, which continues to be socially abhorrent. The result has been a curious avoidance of the scientific fact, which everyone really knows, that human life begins at conception and is continuous whether intra- or extra-uterine until death. The very considerable semantic gymnastics which are required to rationalise abortion as anything but the taking of a human life would be ludicrous if they were not often put forth under socially impeccable auspices. It is suggested that this schizophrenic sort of subterfuge is necessary because while a new ethic is being accepted the old one has not yet been rejected.[1]

The distortions caused by passion and prejudice make it all the more imperative to keep the scientific facts clearly in focus. *'When Did I begin? 'Conception of Human Individual in History, Philosophy and Science'* by Norman M. Ford,[2] is a rich collection of biological information about early human development. In this work he aimed to solve the debate on "how far we can trace back our own personal identity as the same continuing individual living body, being or entity". He concluded that there is no human individual or soul present until two or three weeks after fertilisation. His book effectively undermined the case for any absolute prohibition on abortion. Later Ford had repudiated his position. "Most of the scientists conclude that fertilisation in mammals normally represents the beginning of life for a new individual".[3]

It is commonly claimed in pro-abortion arguments that one cannot determine when human life begins. Does science address the beginning of human life? If so, what does it say? Does science have anything to say about abortion? Those who have taken embryology know very well the answer to this question. If you examine pro-choice arguments for abortion, you will find the proponents using such terms as "tissue" and "grams of material" (a weight). What they do not like to discuss is what that "tissue" consists of. In fact, the preborn human foetus is genetically a fully human being at the point of conception. As you will learn below, the aborted foetus is not just a "blob of tissue."

The beginning of human life is seen differently by different individuals, groups, cultures, and religions. Embryonic and foetal life are a *continuum*, within which are time sequences and points – birth of a newborn, viability, neuromaturation, implantation, and conception – that may be declared as the beginning of human life. For each of these there are ethical and legal implications and considerations.

Abortion laws reflect the interests of a given society at a given time. We have witnessed a change in some of the countries from virtual denial of the right to abortion to acceptance for certain reasons. And so abortion laws remain ambiguous. Fundamental to productive debate and reconciliation between minority and majority groups, is an understanding of the ill-defined concept of "the beginning of human life."

Pro-lifers are often criticised for their position that a new, human life begins at conception. Many incorrectly think that this belief is based on some blind religious dogma, a scripture passage somewhere, or some stubborn need to tell women what to do with their bodies. All the while, this same opposition likes to pretend that they are the scientific, logical ones – obviously not blinded by religion or some judgmental God.

Of course, this is exactly opposite to reality. The entire basis for a new, human life beginning at conception stems from well documented, universally recognised scientific fact. The only ones who deny this are those blinded by their own religious dogma of so-called "choice" who have a stubborn need to deny scientific fact in order to stay faithful to their own ideology.

If science had proven that human life actually began at implantation or at nine weeks or whenever, then that's precisely when the Catholics and any other reasonable belief system would believe that human life began. And, logically, it would be from that moment when this human being should be treated with the rights and dignities that come with being a human being.

But that's not what science has told us. Science has quite clearly and decidedly proven that a new, human life begins at conception (i.e. fertilisation – the moment sperm and ovum meet and form an entirely new, self-directing living organism of the human species with its own individual DNA distinct from both mother and father).

Biology and Personhood
Do facts of biology have any bearing on the definition of personhood? Now we are going to watch the drama of life through another pane of the window, that is 'science'. Can we argue that the question of when human life begins is a biological question? And hence, can anyone claim that to speak of a human being with biological life being a person with rights is an unwarranted leap from science to moral judgment since such a statement is based solely on biological facts? There is a tremendous consensus in the scientific community about when life begins. To begin with we shall see how do scientists distinguish between ' life' and 'non-life'?

Life: General Description
To understand what it means to be human, let us start with defining what constitutes life. Science defines life as the possession of self-sustaining biological processes. This definition distinguishes the living from the dead (those whose self-sustaining processes have ceased) and from the inanimate (objects who lack such processes). Self-sustaining biological processes include homeostasis, organization, metabolism, growth, development, adaptation, response to stimuli, and reproduction.

Homeostasis refers to the ability of a cell, or the entire body, to maintain a state of internal balance by adjusting its physiological processes.

Organisation means the functional unity of a living organism that creates integration and control between all the parts of the organism.

Metabolism involves the consumption of food and the production of waste.

Biology defines life at the cellular level. The cell is the smallest unit of life. Every living thing is comprised of cells. An organism made up of only one cell, such as an amoeba, is alive as much as an organism made up of an estimated 10 trillion cells, such as a human being. Infectious agents such as viruses – which cause diseases such as the common cold, the flu, polio, and AIDS – and prions – which cause diseases such as kuru and Creutzfeldt-Jakob Disease – fall short of the definition of life. Viruses and prions cannot undergo reproduction or metabolism without help from the cells they are infecting.

Criteria of Living Things
A scientific textbook called *Basics of Biology* gives five characteristics of living things; these five criteria are found in all modern elementary scientific textbooks too.
1. Living things are highly organised.
2. All living things have an ability to acquire materials and energy.
3. All living things have an ability to respond to their environment.
4. All living things have an ability to adapt.
5. All living things have an ability to reproduce.

According to this elementary explanation of life, life begins at fertilisation, when a sperm unites with an oocyte. From this moment, the being is highly organized, has the ability to acquire materials and energy, has the ability to respond to his or her environment, has the ability to adapt, and has the ability to reproduce (the cells divide, then divide again, etc., and barring pathology and pending reproductive maturity has the potential to reproduce other members of the species). Non-living things do not do these things. Even before the mother is aware that she is pregnant, a distinct, unique life has begun his or her existence inside her.

Human Life
The life of the unborn is unquestionably human because a human being is a member of the species *homo sapiens*. Human beings are products of conception, which is when a human male sperm unites with a human female oocyte (egg). When humans procreate, they do not make non-humans like slugs, monkeys, cactuses, bacteria, or any such thing. Emperically-verifiable proof is as close as our nearest abortion clinic: send a sample of an aborted foetus to a laboratory and have them test the DNA to see if it is human or not. Genetically, a new human being comes into existence from the earliest moment of conception.

Human Life: Beginnings

"By all the criteria of modern molecular biology, life is present from the moment of conception."[4] The life of a human being begins at the moment of fertilisation.[5] "Conception" is a term used for the beginning of biological human life and has been variously defined in the medical and scientific literature as the moment of fertilisation, syngamy (the last crossing-over of the maternal and paternal chromosomes at the end of fertilisation), full embryonic gene expression between the fourth and eighth cellular division,[6] implantation, or development of the primitive streak. There has been an argument that life is present in the embryo, not when it was conceived but at the time of quickening. It is weak an argument. Today, and for a considerable period of time, this distinction has been shown to be a totally false one since it has been accepted by biologists that there is no qualitative difference between the embryo at the moment of conception and at the moment of quickening. Life is fully present from the time of conception. It seems to follow that soul too must be present from the time of conception.[7]

Jason M. Steffens writes: There is, in fact, no doubt from a scientific standpoint that an unborn child is a life from the moment of conception. Not only is it a life, but, 'by its intrinsic biological nature,' it is a human life from the moment of conception, for 'it can be nothing else.' This is because 'to be a human being is decided for an organism at the moment of fertilisation of the ovum.' By the end of the eighth week of its existence, an unborn child 'has features that are distinctly human,' confirming the child's humanness.[8] French geneticist Dr. Jerome L. LeJeune testified before a United States Senate subcommittee in 1981: "To accept the fact that after fertilisation has taken place a new human being has come into being is no longer a matter of taste or opinion. The human nature of the human being from conception to old age is not metaphysical contention, it is plain experimental evidence."[9]

Scientifically and Biblically, conception is most appropriately defined as fertilisation. The activation of an egg by the penetration of a sperm[10] triggers the transition to active organismal existence. It is artificial and arbitrary to use other proposed biological "markers" (such as implantation, development of a primitive streak, absence of potential for twinning, brain activity, heartbeat, quickening, viability, or birth and beyond) to define the beginning of human life. A biological view of human life beginning at fertilisation[11] is, therefore, consistent with the Biblical view of human life.

Human Being: Definition

As it is clear from the above discussion, a single cell is alive. A cell is human if the genetic blueprint of the cell is human DNA. Techniques of cellular biology make it possible to take cells from human organs and grow them indefinitely in laboratory culture. The cells are alive and they are human. An organism refers to an entire living entity. Some organisms, such as bacteria, consist of only one cell. Other organisms, such as humans, start as one cell but develop to become multi-cellular, with many specialised cells all working together to maintain the life processes of the whole organism. So scientists do not consider human cancer cells taken from a cervical tumour that grow in a laboratory dish human organism because they are only one small part of an entire human organism.

Scientists do, however, consider a human embryo that has been growing for three days in a laboratory dish and is now comprised of approximately eight cells, a human organism. These eight cells of a human embryo three days after fertilisation possess organisation and function as a unit capable of further development. These cells represent the entire human organism, not just a part of an organism like the human cancer cells in laboratory culture. Although these eight cells are not yet differentiated into the specialised cells that are present in a fully developed human, these cells have the capacity to give rise to every specialised cell that will be needed as development progresses; they are said to be pluripotent.

Five days after fertilisation, the human embryo will be shaped like a hollow sphere and contains from 70 to 100 cells. The term for the human embryo at this stage of development is a blastocyst. The blastocyst is the stage of human development when the embryo attaches to the wall of the uterus, a process scientists call implantation. This typically occurs seven to 10 days after fertilisation. This adhesion to the wall of the uterus allows the developing embryo to receive oxygen and nutrients from the mother to allow further growth and development. Modern foetology has brought new insight on the growth of the foetus in the mother's womb which foetologists call their second "patient." An embryo in the earliest stages of development is a living, multi-cellular organism with a genetic code unique from the genetic code of its mother and father. An embryo that develops from the fertilisation of a human egg and a human sperm is a human embryo. So, an embryo is a human life, with the right conditions for further development, a healthy communication, and relationship with God, other human beings, and the environment.

Thus, a human being, despite the expression of different and more mature secondary characteristics, has genetic and ontological identity and continuity throughout all stages of development from fertilisation until death. The human embryo will develop the secondary characteristics of self-awareness, rationality, and capacity for language that collectively distinguish human beings from other living organisms. A human embryo is not a potential human being, but a human being with potential.

Hence, we define a human being as follows: A living human being is a self-directed,[12] integrated organism[13] that possesses the genetic endowment of the species *homo sapiens*[14] who has the inherent active biological disposition (active capacity and potency)[15] for ordered growth and[16] in a continuous and seamless maturation process, with the potential to express secondary characteristics such as rationality and self-awareness.

Modern Molecular Biology and Philosophy: A Century of Transition
Scientific advances, theological discussions, and magisterial directives of a doctrinal nature co-operated together to make the 19th century a century of transition. By the beginning of the 20th century the living voice of the Church was speaking a rather clear message of God's truth. To understand how this developed we must look at what transpired before and into the 19th century.

It was not until toward the end of the 17th century, when the microscope began to be developed into an efficient instrument, that the early stages of the embryo could be studied effectively. Arantius had already shown in the 16th century that the maternal and foetal blood circulation were separate, neither continuous nor contiguous. Ovarian follicles were first described by de Graaf in 1672 when the true significance of the sperm and the ovum was not understood. Spallanzani and Wolf demonstrated in the 18th century that both the female ovum and the male sperm were necessary for the initiation of human development, which occurred through progressive growth and differentiation. In the 1820s Von Baer's work established the foundation for the biologist's knowledge of the germ layers in embryos. In the 1830s Schleiden and Schwann formulated the cell theory. This knowledge that the adult body is composed entirely of cells and cell products paved the way for a realisation that the body of the new individual is developed from a single cell, the cell formed by the union in fertilisation of a germ cell contributed by the male parent and with a germ cell contributed by the female parent. This knowledge was somewhat crystallised in Wilhelm His's work *The Anatomy of Human Embryos*, published in 1880.[17]

As a result of these advances in the science of biology, it became more and more apparent that Aristotle's judgement of the 40th day of gestation for the hominisation of the male and the 80th day for the hominisation of the female was arbitrary and unscientific.[18] As the true significance of the earlier stages of foetal development became better understood, it became more apparent also that hominisation might well occur earlier, perhaps even at the moment of conception.

Modern molecular biology has not been able to remove all the mystery from the process of each individual's origin. Is the precise moment of conception, the precise moment of each human person's entrance as man into this world? Modern science (genetics) inclines to give an affirmative answer to this question. Conception is the process of union by which the parental cells (sperm and ovum) unite to become the first cell of a new individual. The action of uniting is not strictly instantaneous. It is rather a process. When we speak of 'the moment of conception', we mean the precise time when the process is completed. The sperm and the ovum normally meet in the fallopian tube. The ovum has been prepared and is pushed along the tube toward the uterus. The sperm that reaches it is one of the few that survive the trip through the oviduct from the vagina. Millions of sperm must start the trip. Many sperm go right by, un-attracted to the ovum. When a sperm is attracted to the ovum, a complex chemical interaction occurs. The ovum reacts by surrounding the sperm and helping it to come in.

The genetic material brought by the sperm and the genetic material present in the ovum are in two individual packets. These move toward each other and unite, so that the full number of 46 chromosomes is restored, 23 from the mother's ovum and 23 from the father's sperm. The cell which results is in a full sense a fertilized ovum, but it is no longer merely an ovum. It is now called the zygote (bound together). This is now an entirely new individual. Already it has the typical, unique set of chromosomes that belongs to each cell of the new, unique human body. Having derived half of its genetic make-up from each parent, the human zygote is unlike any cell that belongs to either the father or mother. A totally new genetic package has been produced.

But when does the new individual begin to exist? With the help of science, we can say, it is the moment when the two individual genetic packets from the ovum and the sperm have completed the process of uniting with each other to form one whole, a totally new genetic package.

This most momentous moment in the order of creation for any human being is the moment when he is called to be a unique person 'in the image and likeness of God'. We will be really convinced that the most miraculous moment is the moment of conception, if we understand what the scientists are telling us about ourselves and the evolving continuity of the process as one stage flows smoothly into the next from conception through cleavage, morula, blastocyst, embryo, foetus, to infant, to child. It seems that this is the moment. The zygote differs vastly from the female ovum and the male sperm, especially in their chromosomal content. Besides, the ovum and sperm will inevitably die very soon, unless they are combined together in the process of fertilisation. Separately, these two do not have the power to reproduce themselves. Human zygote does have the power to reproduce itself.

Within the past 40 years' molecular biology has made tremendous advances demonstrating that this newly formed zygote is not just a glob of human stuff but a complex, highly organised, dynamic and unique individual entity. It is an already developing individual. It is already evolving into that adult human person it will one day be. In the understanding that hominisation takes place immediately in the fertilised ovum, along with the human person the human body is also actually present, but only in an embryonic stage. It would also be accurate to say that the human body is actually present; the fully formed adult human body is virtually present.

The zygote has been called a dynamic blueprint of what the adult human person, resulting from this cell, will be. It is not just a static blueprint of an object, that must be constructed by others from external material. Rather, it is a dynamic blueprint which, if it receives the proper nourishment and suitable environment, grows and develops from the inside. The following scientific conclusion of the report from a Conference on Abortion, sponsored by the Harvard Divinity School and the Joseph P. Kennedy Jr., Foundation, September 6-7, 1967, clarifies this: "The potential for future development is as great in the fertilised egg as in the blastocyst, as in the embryo, as in the foetus, as in the premature, as in the infant, as in the child."[19]

Today, the molecular scientists tell us that there is no qualitative difference between life at conception and at other stages of development including the birth of the newly–born infant. Paul Ramsey writes: "In a remarkable way, modern genetics also teaches that there are 'formal causes', immanent principles, or constitutive elements long before there is any shape or motion or discernible size. These minute formal elements are already determining the organic life to be the uniquely individual human being it is to be. According to this present-day scientific equivalent of the doctrine that the soul is the 'form' or immanent entelechy of the body, it can now be asserted for the first time in the history of 'scientific' speculation upon this question that who one is and is to be, is present from the moment the ovum is fertilised."[20]

Helmut Thielicke sees the possibility of a conflict that can arise within the order of creation itself, that is one side of its meaning and purpose – namely, the calling into personal, responsible relationship with the Creator, which is granted only to man – can come into conflict with another side of its meaning and purpose – namely, the created relationship between wedlock and parenthood. There can be no argument here about the fact of this conflict – at least in the simple form here described. For "once impregnation has taken place it is no longer a question of whether the persons concerned have responsibility for a possible parenthood; they have become parents."[21]

We can presume that had Thomas Aquinas been aware of the biological advances that we have now today – that the fertilized ovum is biologically a living organism of the human species with the intrinsic capability of developing into a mature human person – he would not have recommended the Aristotelian theory of mediate or delayed animation. Rudolph Joseph Gerber arrived at the same conclusion: "Genetic DNA (deoxyribonucleic acid) might be considered as a strong indication of immediate animation. These chemical patterns perform a unique role in cellular economy which St. Thomas and his contemporaries could not have discovered. As the chief functional unit of genetic material, DNA determines the basic architecture of every cell, the nature and life of all cells, the specific protein syntheses, enzyme formation, self-reproduction, and directly or indirectly, the nature of the developing individual. It would be interesting to see how Aristotle, Thomas and Avicenna would react to learning that the egg is not a mass of homogeneous menstrual blood but a precise blueprint of the later human adult. "Had they been provided with the discoveries of the past several years, it is not unthinkable that they would have altered their stand on the succession of lower forms and seen good reason to believe that, in normal cases the substantial form of rationality, the human soul, would be present in the zygote from the very first moment of fertilisation."[22]

It seems reasonable to consider that the human zygote, as we understand it today, with DNA and RNA (ribonucleic acid), would in Thomas' understanding satisfy as having the organised matter required for the infusion of a human spiritual soul. We can say that what Thomas saw as present in the embryo of 40 days is present in the zygote as we understand it in the light of modern advances in molecular biology. From what we have seen so far, it becomes clear that the newly formed ovum is highly organised, dynamic and complex. It needs only the proper nourishment and environment to develop into a fully developed human being. In the first few days of its existence the human zygote provides its own nourishment. There is no qualitative difference, as we said earlier, between the human zygote and the human embryo at the 40 day or 80-day stage. Based on recent scientific advances, we can hold that the human zygote is a sufficiently organised unit to be a human person with a human body that is in the process of continuous evolutionary development from the inside toward full development. So we can legitimately call it an actual human person with a body whose full development is already in dynamic process.

In the case of identical twins, we cannot rule out the possibility that the animation of the second twin results from the immediate creation of his human soul just at the moment of division into two identical twins. Rudolph Joseph Gerber explains it as follows: "Identical twins spring from one ovum, fecundated by one sperm, and the ensuing zygote for some unknown reason splits into two distinct entities. (Nevertheless) some believe that it is relatively easy to explain the origin of the second soul. The individual rational soul, assuming it to be present from the first, remains in one of the separated parts, though it is not possible to determine in which. When the other part of the egg is fully separated from information by the first soul, a new soul is created and infused instantaneously for this second twin. There is no disproportion between form and matter in either case, because the division of the embryo into two parts implies that each part is equally formed and equally able to develop into a human person. It appears, then, that the argument from didymology is no absolute indication that the rational soul cannot be infused at the moment of fertilisation."[23]

Reviewing the literature available from the modern molecular biology and from the philosophical discussion that have taken place over the many centuries of developing Christian thought and guided by the understanding of developing Christian theology, one can say that normally the human certainly exists in the human zygote from the first moment of conception. We should be able to appreciate one who is in a state of doubt about the precise moment when the new individual begins to exist as a human person. It is difficult to understand how one can be certain that the human person normally does not exist in the human zygote from the first moment of conception. On the basis of evidence and reasoning we have already presented, we shall consider that the opinion which maintains the new human person is to be present in the human zygote from the first moment of conception is solidly true. So, anybody deliberately and directly causes an abortion in self or in another is choosing an action involving danger of taking an innocent human life.

A Unique Genotype
It is a well-established fact that a genetically distinct human being is brought into existence at conception. "The human foetus is a living tissue with a unique genetic makeup, destined to become a fully developed human organism. The embryo contains all the essential biological material and genetic information required for complete cellular maturation, human tissue and organ development. Of all the tissues of the body, it alone has a fixed genetic makeup different from that of the body in which it is lodged. A woman cannot say of foetal tissue, "this is mine," in the sense that she can say of kidney tissue, "this is mine." She cannot keep it any more than she can give it to someone else; she must surrender it in birth – or die".[24]

'Biology tells that during intercourse, some 300,000,000 sperm are deposited in the vagina and begin a journey upwards through the uterus and into the fallopian tube leading from the uterus toward the ovary. If an ovum has been released from the ovary, it passes from the ovary down the fallopian tube towards the uterus. The survival time of the unfertilised egg is thought to be approximately 24 hours. Both sperm and egg will die if fertilisation does not occur within that time period. Once fertilisation has taken place, the zygote is its own entity, genetically distinct from both mother and father. The newly fertilized egg contains a staggering amount of genetic information, sufficient to control the individual's growth and self-directed development. That is, it contains the hereditary characteristics of both mother and father, one half from each, derived from the DNA material, the genetic thread of life.'[25]

Surveying the latest embryology, Maureen Condic says: "Following the binding of sperm and egg to each other, the membranes of these two cells fuse, creating in this instant a single hybrid cell: the zygote or one-cell embryo. Cell fusion is a well studied and a very rapid event, occurring in less than a second .... Subsequent to sperm –egg fusion, events rapidly occur in the zygote that do not normally occur in either sperm or egg. The contents of what was previously the sperm, including its nucleus, enter the cytoplasm of the newly formed zygote."[26] Condic details the rapid development of this zygote as the maternally derived nucleus completes its final round of meiotic division within 30 minutes of sperm-egg fusion and the maternally and paternally derived nuclei undergo rapid structural and chemical changes. The DNA of both pro-nuclei is demethylated, the nuclei replicate their DNA in anticipation of the first round of cell division, transcription begins in both halves of the genome and the two pro-nuclei move towards the centre of the cell, in preparation for the first cell division (i.e., *mitosis*) of the zygote. Syngamy, she explains, is a rather minor moment in this drama, as the nuclear membranes that separate the two pro-nuclei break down and the maternally and paternally derived chromosomes are co-located in the same general region of the cytoplasm.

Based on the factual description of the events following sperm-egg binding, 'we can confidently conclude that a new cell, the zygote, comes into existence at the 'moment' of sperm-egg fusion, an event that occurs in less than a second. At the point of fusion sperm and egg are physically united – i.e. they cease to exist as gametes, and they form a new entity that is materially distinct from either sperm or egg. The behaviour of this new cell also differs radically from that of either sperm or egg: the developmental pathway entered into by the zygote is distinct from both gametes. Within minutes of membrane fusion, the zygote initiates changes in its ionic composition that will, over the next 30 minutes, result in chemical modifications of the *zona pellucida*, an acellular structure surrounding the zygote'.[27] These modifications block sperm binding to the cell surface and prevent further intrusion of additional spermatozoa on the unfolding process of development.

Thus, the zygote acts immediately and specifically to antagonise the function of the gametes from which it is derived; while the 'goal' of both sperm and egg is to find each other and to fuse, the first act of the zygote is immediately to prevent any further binding of sperm to the cell surface. Clearly, then, the prior trajectories of sperm and egg have been abandoned, and a new developmental trajectory – that of the zygote – has taken their place.[28] Thus, sperm-egg fusion is indeed a scientifically well defined 'instant' in which the zygote (a new cell with unique genetic composition, molecular composition, and behaviour) is formed.[29]

"In the 1960s the genetic code was unravelled. We now know that from the moment the ovum is fertilised by the penetration of the sperm, the zygote has a unique genotype distinct from both parents. The 23 pairs of chromosomes are complete. The sex, size, and shape, the colour of skin, hair, and eyes, the intelligence and temperament of the child are already determined."[30] As said before, "each human being begins as a single fertilised cell while an adult has about thirty million cells. Between these periods (from fusion to maturity) 45 generations of cell division are necessary. Of the 45 generations of cell division, however, 41 occur before birth."[31] The DNA code formed shortly after conception will remain unchanged through the life of the foetus, and after birth. Scientists see, in this event, the start of the human organism of human life. 'A single thread of DNA from a human cell contains information equivalent to a library of one thousand volumes, or six hundred thousand printed pages with five hundred words on a page. According to R. Houwink, the genetic information stored in the new individual at conception is the equivalent of 50 times the amount of information contained in the Encyclopaedia Britannica.'[32]

Summing up we can say, rather than a long drawn-out process, as Ford believed,[33] fertilisation is now known to be very speedy. The fusion of sperm and ovum is a more or less 'momentary' event. The sperm immediately ceases to exist and the ovum, too, changes radically. The new entity has all the organization – the biological self-directness – of an organism. The subsequent lining up of the DNA from each gamete is merely one of the series of changes within the organism that follows because it is already a distinct organism. It is simply untrue that the unborn child is merely "part of the mother's body.[34] In addition to being genetically distinct from the time of conception, the unborn possesses separate circulatory, nervous, and endocrine systems".[35]

"Likewise, it is misleading to speak about the newly conceived as "potential" human life. Prior to conception the sperm and egg represent only the potentiality of a new human life, but once fertilisation has taken place, an actual human life has begun. More accurately, the newly conceived individual is an actual life with great potential".[36]

Womb with a Window: The Unborn is a Human Person
Hippocrates made it clear saying: "I will neither give a deadly drug to anybody if asked for it, nor will I make a suggestion to this effect. Similarly, I will not give to a woman an abortive remedy."[37] Do you know why? He was aware of the fact that a foetus is a human being.

At the average time when a woman is aware that she is pregnant (the fifth to sixth week after conception), the pre-born human being living inside her is metabolizing nutrition, excreting waste, moving, sucking his or her thumb, growing, and doing many other things that non-living things just do not do.

As early as 21 days after conception, the baby's heart has begun to beat his or her own unique blood-type, often different than the mother's.[38] At 40 days after conception, brainwaves can be read on an EEG, (electro-encephalogram). The pre-born human being may be dependent upon the mother for nutrition, however, this does not diminish his or her humanity, but proves it. Moreover, dependence upon a parent for survival is not a capital crime. So it is false to claim that no one knows when life begins and dishonest to argue that abortion does not kill a human being. Let us see what biology tells us about it.

Stages of Development
"To see personhood beginning at conception is to erect a psychological ladder which supports such a view: at conception a human being is called a zygote; at implantation, an embryo; at two months' gestation, a foetus; at birth, a baby; at fifteen years, a teenager or juvenile; and at twenty-one years, an adult. Zygote, embryo, foetus, baby, juvenile, adult are mere descriptions of a human being at different stages of his development".[39]

Time Line of Prenatal Development
The new genetic program is achieved when the two parent pronuclei come to lie side by side within the egg for perhaps a day, as their contents combine in the ultimate biological union of male and female. In the instant when the union is consummated, the whole egg substance divides into two entirely new cells, identical to one another. These are the first two cells of the baby-to-be. So begins the first day of the first nine months of life.[40]

Fertilisation/Conception
At the moment of fertilisation, a new and unique human being comes into existence with its own distinct genetic code. Twenty-three chromosomes from the mother and twenty-three chromosomes from the father combine to result in a brand-new and totally unique genetic combination. Whereas the heart, lungs, and hair of a woman all share the same genetic code, her unborn child, from the moment of fertilisation, has a separate genetic code that is all its own. There is enough information in this tiny zygote to control human growth and development for the rest of its life. Until implanting into the lining of the uterus, each cell lives off stored energy; at this stage in development the zygote is receiving no direct sustenance from the parents. In the hours of conception every aspect of the genetic inheritance for a new individual will be determined once and for all: to be a boy or girl, with brown, or with blue eyes, fair or dark, tall or short; all the rich detail of physical attributes from head to toes.

Implantation

Renowned scientific author, Barry Werth, calls implantation (which he describes as "the joining of two lives") the "second great challenge of pregnancy, after fertilisation."[41] This blastocyst emits chemical substances which weaken the woman's immune system within the uterus so that this tiny foreign body is not rejected by the woman's body."[42] Were this tiny embryo simply "part of the woman's body" there would be no need to locally disable the woman's immunities.

Gastrulation

A few days after implantation, gastrulation begins. Gastrulation is the process by which the embryo is transformed from a simple ball of cells into a multi-layered organism. By folding in on itself, the basic body begins to take shape as cells differentiate into specialised cell types. Cells that will become muscles, skeleton and gut begin on the outside, but during this migration will soon find their permanent home in the body's interior. Developmental biologist, professor and author, Lewis Wolpert, once said, "It is not birth, death or marriage, but gastrulation that is truly the most important time in your life."[43]

"The human immune system is programmed to distinguish between molecules that are 'self' and 'non-self' and to destroy the latter. The blastocyst, measuring less than one-hundredth of an inch– a barely visible dot – behaves like a parasite, burrowing into the lining. Yet the uterus, after initially swelling to engulf the embryo and marshalling white blood cells to dispose of it, suddenly turns receptive, even acquiescent. Its blood vessels engorge with food and oxygen-bearing blood, and its tissues cordon off an area for the invader. Then, as the embryo bores through the small maternal blood vessels in its path, rupturing them, the haemorrhaging uterine tissues respond by releasing a starch that becomes its first meal. At once the embryo gorges itself and starts to grow at astonishing speed – doubling daily in size. Before the expectant mother knows she is pregnant, the basic relationship between mother and child is forged."[44]

There was a time when it was believed that the mental development of a baby began at birth. But now we know that birth is a relatively insignificant event in developmental terms. This will unveil to us the drama of life through different stages: actualisation (first month which includes fertilisation and implantation), development (second month), movement (third month), growth (fourth/fifth months), viability (sixth/seventh/eighth months) and birth (ninth month on). We shall see them in detail.

Actualisation (First Month)

One to nine days: Sperm joins with ovum (egg) to form ONE cell – smaller than a grain of salt! The new life has inherited 23 chromosomes from each parent. This one cell contains the complex genetic blueprint for all physical development, i.e. from skin colour to sex. The fertilised egg travels down the fallopian tube into the uterus, where the lining has been prepared for implantation. She still implants or "nests" in her mother's uterus (one week).

"After two weeks of development the name of the new human life is changed from zygote to embryo. Blood cells are formed by 17 days, and a rudimentary heart as early as 18 days. The development of the nervous system also begins at approximately the 18th day".[45] Three weeks from fertilisation, the developing embryo signals its presence through placental chemicals and hormones, preventing the mother from menstruating. When this occurs the nourishment required can begin. All her human characteristics are present at conception.

"By the 21st day the foundations of the child's brain, spinal cord, nerves, and sense organs are completely formed".[46] By this time of pregnancy, "approximately 21 days after fertilisation and eight days after first taking shape, the heart starts beating. Over the next four days, the heart will settle into its regular rhythm and will start pumping blood throughout the embryo's newly formed blood vessels".[47] It will continue to do so for an entire lifetime and will have beat roughly 54 million times before the baby is even born. The kidneys, at this point, are preparing for urine production, eye "bulges" become visible, and the brain begins dividing into three primary sections: forebrain, midbrain, and hindbrain. The arms and legs are also taking shape. Around day 26, arm buds are visible. By the 28th day, it is possible to distinguish between the upper and lower arm. The embryo is now surrounded and protected by the amniotic sac and is actually starting to produce the necessary cells for producing the eggs or sperm necessary for their own reproductive future.

"[The first month of life] will bring a marvellous transformation, the greatest developmental change of a lifetime. The hundreds of cells turn into many thousands and together they become ten thousand times larger than the early cluster had been. The wonder of it is that these myriad cells organise themselves into a human body with the beginnings of all its exquisitely specialised components, all in their right places and some already practising their functions."[48]

Development (Second Month)

A month after fertilisation, brain development rapidly speeds up'.[49] In just two days' time (between day 31 and 33), the brain's size increases by 25 percent. It is estimated that during the course of prenatal development an average of one million neurons (impulse-conducting cells that make up the nervous system) are produced every minute. Hand formation begins around day 31. Two days later, the feet begin taking shape, the retina of the eyes gain pigment, and the nose starts to elevate. She has grown 10,000 times to 6-7 mm. long. Her heart muscle pulsates (3 to 3 1/2 weeks). Blood flows in her veins (but stays separate from the mother's blood. The blood of the mother circulates to the foetus from which she gets nutrition, etc. as well as various diseases).[50]

The fifth week will see the embryo more than double in size, growing from approximately 5mm in length (0.19in) to 10mm. Permanent kidneys appear during the fifth week, and the external portions of the ear begin to differentiate.

"[At] five weeks old, [the embryo] is well past the stage when it looks like a formless clump of cells. The skin layers are still barely developed, and the tiny body is quite transparent. The head and tail can be distinguished, as well as the heart, the vertebrae of the spinal column, and the beginnings of a tiny hand."[51] By the sixth week, "the nervous system is so well developed that it controls the movements of the child's muscles, though the woman may not yet even be aware that she is pregnant".[52] The embryo responds reflexively to stimulus and may be able to feel pain. By now, "all the internal signs of the unborn child are present, though yet in a rudimentary form. The brain is sending out impulses, which coordinate the functions of the other bodily organs. Reflex responses are present at 42 days, and brain waves have been noted at 43 days. The blood vessels leading from the heart are fully deployed and continue to grow in size. The stomach is producing digestive juices, and the kidneys are beginning to function by extracting uric acid from the child's blood".[53]

Lars Hemberger, Professor and Chairman of the Department of Obstetrics and Gynaecology at Sweden's Gothenburg University notes that, "even this early in pregnancy, the embryo is extremely lively, in constant motion, sleeping for only brief periods."[54] Bone ossification has begun, lips have appeared, all 20 teeth buds are in the gums, the diaphragm has formed, the kidneys are producing urine and the stomach is producing gastric juices. "By six weeks, the cerebral hemispheres are growing disproportionately faster than other sections of the brain. The embryo begins to make spontaneous and reflexive movements. Such movement is necessary to promote normal neuromuscular development. A touch to the mouth area causes the embryo to reflexively withdraw its head."[55]

Distinct leg movements can be seen after seven weeks; hiccups have also been observed. Female ovaries are identifiable and the 4-chambered heart has reached completion. Fingers and toes are distinctly separated, knee joints are present, and the embryo develops the ability to smell. The placenta forms a unique barrier that keeps the mothers blood separate while allowing food and oxygen to pass through to the embryo. The brain waves can be detected and recorded. The brain begins to control movement of muscles and organs – the liver is now taking over the production of blood cells. "By the end of the seventh week, the child will flex his neck if the mouth and nose are tickled with a hair. By this time the ears are also formed and may show the specific features of a family pattern. By now the fingers and toes are fully recognizable. Lines in the hands and fingerprints begin to appear at eight weeks and remain a distinctive characteristic of the individual".[56]

"Day 49 has been elected to be the final day of the scientifically recorded day-to-day diary of development. On this day, the embryo is considered to be essentially complete. The creative enterprise of prolific cell division, differentiation, streaming migrations, establishment of new cell communities, and specialization: these come to rest when the foundations for all the working parts of the body are in place."[57]

In the words of Norman Geisler: her eyes, nose, ears, and toes are formed more fully. Her heart beats and blood flows (her own type). Her skeleton develops. Every limb begins to appear. She is sensitive to touch on her lips and has reflexes. All her bodily systems are present and functioning. She is a well-proportioned, small scale baby (3cm) sitting up and one gram in weight.[58]

At eight weeks the key distinction lies in the formation of the first real bone cells that begin to replace the cartilage. By this time of pregnancy, every organ is present and in place. The embryonic period is now over. Ninety percent of the structures found in an adult human being can be found in this tiny embryo (now called a foetus, Latin for "offspring" or "young one")[59] which is only about an inch and a half long. The brain, at this point, accounts for almost half of the body's total weight, and 75% of 8-week foetuses demonstrate right-hand dominance. Intermittent breathing motions (though there is no air present in the uterus) occur, and male testes are releasing testosterone. As the skin thickens, it loses much of its transparency.

"Measuring 1.25" from crown to rump and weighing about one-thirtieth of an ounce, the (56-day-old) embryo is now all but fully formed. All body systems are in place and elaborated. Architecturally, the organism is more or less whole... Though the energy output is about one-fifth that of an adult, the heart is functionally complete... A great passage has been made."[60]

Movement (Third Month)
"The baby becomes very lively [during the third month of pregnancy]. In the freedom of the watery pool the tiny being moves gracefully and with ease and progresses to outdo any newborn in acrobatic feats."[61]

Nine weeks from fertilisation: The eyelids close at this point, and foetuses are now capable of sucking their thumb, swallowing amniotic fluid, grasping objects, responding to touch and even doing backward and forward somersaults. The uterus can be recognised in female foetuses and external genitalia become more recognisable.

Rapid growth between nine and 10 weeks increases body weight by 75 percent. Fingernails, toenails and unique fingerprints all appear at this time. "Between the ninth and tenth weeks local reflexes such as swallowing, squinting, and tongue retraction begin to appear. If the child's forehead is touched, he may turn his head away and pucker up and frown. By now the child can bend the wrist and elbow independently and has the full use of his arms. By this time the entire body is sensitive to touch and is also capable of spontaneous movement."[62] The mother provides the shelter and the basics: food, water and oxygen, but the real star of the show is the foetus herself, building, dividing and growing according to an intricate set of plans created at the moment of conception.[63]

Thumb sucking has been observed by the eleventh week, and x-rays will disclose clear details of the skeleton. "By the twelfth week, the child is swallowing regularly and can move his thumb in opposition to his fingers. The child, three and one half inches long by the end of the twelfth week, will have a complete brain structure, which will of course continue to grow".[64] "By this time, the child is active and the reflexes are more pronounced."[65] At this time, as Arnold Gesell has stated, the unborn child "is a sentient moving being. We need not pause to speculate as to the nature of his psychic attributes, but we may assert that the organization of his psychosomatic self is now well under way."[66]

"Over the course of the first trimester or first three months, the single egg will begin to transform itself into a fully formed baby. But all the features of the human body, nerves, organs, muscles, are mapped out in the fragile first weeks."[67]

Growth (Fourth/Fifth Month)

By 13-18 weeks she can feel organic pain. She can alter her position, respond to pain, noise, and light. The embryo is completely organised.[68] "Muscular response is no longer mechanical and irregular, but now graceful and fluid. This motion is present prior to "quickening," when the mother first notices the child's movements, which generally occurs between weeks 12 and 16, although some women feel very little movement as late as 20 weeks."[69]

It should be clearly understood that the time of "quickening," long considered important in the law, represents a mother's subjective perception, and not an objective point at which "animation" occurs or the first "signs of life" appear.[70] As Dr. Albert W. Liley, a widely recognised authority in foetal medicine, has stated: Historically, "quickening" was supposed to delineate the time when the foetus became an independent human being possessed of a soul. Now, however, we know that while he may have been too small to make his motions felt, the unborn baby is active and independent long before his mother feels him. Quickening is a maternal sensitivity and depends on the mother's own fat, the position of the placenta and the size and strength of the unborn child. Quickening is hardly an objective basis for making a decision about the existence or the value of the life of the unborn child.[71]

Though the foetus has long been in almost perpetual motion, by 16-20 weeks from fertilisation, the body is large enough for the mother to start feeling the kicks. Eyelids have now completely covered the eyes, and fine hairs have begun to cover the entire body. Her skin, hair, and nails develop by fifth month. She dreams (e. g. has rapid eye movement, REM).[72] She can cry (if air is present). She responds to sounds in frequencies too high or too low for adults to hear. The foetus now sleeps, awakens and exercises its muscles energetically – turning its head, curling its toes and opening and closing its mouth. The palm, when stroked, will make a tight fist. The foetus breathes amniotic fluid to help develop its respiratory system. Sexual differentiation has become apparent. At the end of this period, the foetus is eight to ten inches long, its weight increases six times (to 1/2 birth weight). By the end of the fifth month, the child weighs approximately one pound and will be about 12 inches long.[73] It can hear its mother's voice.[74] "Fine baby hair has begun to grow on his head and a fringe of eyelashes is beginning to appear. The skeleton is hardening. The mother can feel the child's head, arms, and legs".[75]

After the 20th week it is customary to speak of a premature delivery rather than of a spontaneous abortion. "At some point between the sixteenth and twentieth week it becomes possible to hear the child's heartbeat with a simple stethoscope, as well as by the refined ECG apparatus."[76] "The little foetus moves more and more every day, and the jerky body motions during the embryonic stage are now replaced by slower and apparently more goal-oriented movements. The hands often find their way to the mouth, ultrasound scanning shows, and the arms and legs are stretched and bent. The occasional breathing movement also appears; the foetus can be seen to yawn or hiccough now and then and seldom lies perfectly still for any length of time."[77]

Viability (Sixth, Seventh, Eighth Months)
Where modern medical services exist 24-weeks gestational age is generally considered the beginning of viability outside the womb. At this point in pregnancy (barely halfway through a full term), the odds of long-term survival are still relatively slim, but new medical advances continue to increase the likelihood of survival and decrease the age of viability. The foetus may 'jump' in response to external sounds and oil and sweat glands begin to function.

According to Dr. Andre Hellegers of Georgetown University, 10 percent of children born between 20 and 24 weeks' gestation will survive.[78] "The development of an artificial placenta would push the date of viability back into the earliest stages of gestation. Modern techniques of intensive therapy are able to save premature babies that would have been considered non-viable only a few years ago".[79] Fine hair grows on its eyebrows and head. Eyelash fringe appears. Weight is about 640g (1lb. 6oz.) and height 23cm (9in).[80]

By the seventh month we can notice the presence of eyes and teeth. Its eyelids open and close, and eyes look around. Its hands grip strongly. Its mother's voice is recognised.[81] By now, "the child weighs slightly over two pounds, and some definitions of "viability" are fixed at this point. This, however, is only an approximation".[82] By the eighth month its weight increases by 1kg. (over 2lb.) and its quarters get cramped.[83]

Birth (Ninth Month)
Most babies (85-95%) are born between 266 and 294 days weighing six to nine pounds in most cases. The foetus initiates labour[84] by stimulating the

adrenal cortex to secrete a hormone that induces the mother's uterus to begin contracting. All these show that the unborn baby is not the part of mother's body. In the womb, babies of all nationalities look roughly the same. It is only towards the end of pregnancy that colour variations become apparent. A baby's skin often appears pink when it is first born because the blood vessels are so close to the skin's surface. Final formation of skin, hair, and eye pigmentation requires exposure to light, something the baby doesn't have much access to in the womb.

Now we can conclude: "Where once it seemed that the mental development of a baby began at birth, now it appears that birth could be a relatively insignificant event in developmental terms."[85] There has long been a common misperception that most abortions occur before the embryo or foetus is recognisably human. Day after day, thousands of aborting women wrongly believe that they're simply eliminating some undifferentiated human cell tissue. Because the general ignorance of prenatal development is so convenient to the abortion industry, it's not hard to guess why 'Planned Parenthood' does so little to accurately educate their clients.

Of course, even if human embryos didn't become so recognisably human in such a short amount of time, would that somehow change the ethics of abortion? After all, isn't it the height of injustice to abuse another member of the human community simply because they don't look the way we expect them to? Abortion is not the mere removal of cell tissue; it is the death of living, growing human person. Medical science already refers to a spontaneous heart rhythm and the presence of brain waves to determine whether someone is alive at the other spectrum of human existence. In simplistic terms, if an organ donor is in an automobile accident and is on life support in a hospital, the physician cannot "pull the plug" and donate the patient's organs to others unless the patient is "brain dead" and his heart is not beating on its own. If the medical community maintained consistency with this generally-accepted medical definition of human life, then we would condemn every abortion after the time when the average woman discovers she is pregnant.

"Pregnancy involves the medical care of two patients, not one. The unborn child is not a passive partner, but rather in many ways controls the dynamics of the pregnancy. This new perception of the unborn child has led to the development of a whole new medical specialty called perinatology, which cares for its patients from conception to about one year of postnatal existence.

For the modern physician, human life begins at conception, and medical care and observation must start at the earliest period of life".[86]

So we can say that contrary to what many non-scientists believe, human beings are not constructed in the womb – they develop. In fact, all the major organ systems are initiated within the first few weeks after conception. The process of embryonic development is a continuous process, with no obvious point at which the foetus magically becomes a "person." In fact, the development process continues well after birth, including many characteristics that determine our personality or personhood. What are the stages in human embryonic development? Science tells us that the heart of the human foetus begins to form 18 days after conception.[87] There is a measurable heart beat 21-24 days after conception.[88] This is only 7-10 days after a woman would expect to begin her menses. Since most women have cycles that can vary by this amount, they do not discover they are pregnant until after this point. Therefore, all abortions stop a beating heart, even "early" abortions. However, most abortions do not occur until 4-6 weeks after the foetus begins to form. The human brain begins to form on day 23,[89] is formed enough to produce brain waves by six weeks.

Seeing is Believing: The Interacting Foetuses
Developing human beings begin responding to and interacting with their environment long before they are born. Even though we do not qualify or disqualify something as a person on the basis of what it can or can't do, it's still worth noting that foetuses display aspects of their personal nature while still in the womb. That is, foetuses can do things that you would only expect of more fully developed persons. How responsive and active the baby is, in the womb, is beyond our imagination!! As we have already seen it can breathe, feel, complain, respond to people and elicit loving care; it is in a position to recognise its mother's voice;[90] it tastes and smells; it can make polished movements. In addition, it can dream, sense light and even play together, in the event of twins!!

The following are visual evidences such as the foetuses displaying aspects of their personal nature while still in the womb. These testimonies highlight the remarkable social interactions taking place inside the womb. "The foetus behaves in a much more complex way than previously imagined... During its odyssey in the womb it will smile, recognise its mother's voice and maybe even dream."[91] We have similar testimony from L. Nilsson: "By mid pregnancy the foetus has begun to explore its own body and environment using its hands. It often holds on to the umbilical cord, and when a thumb approaches its mouth, it will turn and begin to make sucking motions with its lips... The foetus is also using its sense of hearing for orientation. Its most familiar sounds are surely the noises of the mother's digestive system and the swishing from her major blood vessels, but gradually the foetus also begins to perceive the sounds of the mother's world, such as music and the father's voice. The eyes of the foetus are sensitive to light, even though the eyelids are still shut tight... We have no way of knowing whether the foetus tastes the slight salinity of the amniotic fluid. Still, we have indirect evidence that the foetus tastes and smells, since a newborn immediately reacts positively or negatively to tastes that are sweet, salty, or bitter."[92]

The following testimonies again, highlight the remarkable social interactions taking place inside the womb: "The womb is not a quiet, isolated place; life within it offers abundant and varied experiences that prepare the baby for the world she will meet when she moves out. We are learning to recognise how sensitive, able and already experienced a newly born baby is. She is able to breathe and feed, and occasionally can complain loudly. She is also able, in quiet and subtle ways, to respond to people and is so endearing in her actions that she can elicit the loving care she needs. Her competence has developed gradually. New means of observation have made it possible to discover how responsive and active the baby already is in the months preceding birth. Certainly she does not simply lie there curled up in the legendary foetal position."[93]

Dr Bernard Nathanson M.D makes a convincing statement: I have put Mozart in a tape player and held it against a womb at, say, seven months, and the baby moved a little, but when I put Van Halen on, the baby was jumping all over the place.[94]

The use of ultra sound revealed much more. "Until healthy babies were first observed by ultra sound in extensive studies in the 1980s while the mothers were resting quietly, it was not known that babies have such a diverse repertoire of movements at this early time, and perform these so smoothly and so frequently. It was a revelation that movements are polished almost from their first appearance and do not start in a clumsy and poorly coordinated way... The system is innately fine-tuned from the start and by exercise it is maintained in working order."[95]

The use of endoscopes revealed the foetus can sense light as early as the third month of pregnancy. Lennart Nilsson and Lars Hamberger, explain like this: "Does a foetus see anything? It is known that the eye can sense light as early as the third month of pregnancy."[96] "Sometimes when an endoscope is inserted into the amniotic sac, a foetus tries to protect its eyes from the light on the instrument, either by turning away or by using its hands and fingers."[97]

National Geographic, in their video, *In the Womb: Multiples*, goes so far as to say, as identical twins grow bigger, they're almost always in contact, touching hands, faces, feet and gradually becoming more aware of themselves and each other. "Twins, and other multiples, are known for a particular characteristic in utero. Scientists have even witnessed them playing games together... Scientists think their prenatal behaviour [carries] over into early childhood."[98] We have an amazing photograph, by Michael Clancy, photojournalist, of a surgery being performed on a 21 week-old foetus named Samuel Armas. The picture was taken on August 19, 1999, at Vanderbilt University Medical Centre in Nashville Tn., during an incredible procedure to correct spina bifida on an unborn child.[99] In the photograph, the unconscious boy's hand is poking through the surgical incision in the uterus and is resting on the finger of the surgeon. This picture paints a thousand words that mere words cannot match, but allow me to draw attention to the obvious fact that the surgeon is performing surgery on one living human being who is residing in the womb of another living human being.

The revelation by the 4D scans were very telling: "One of the many things revealed by the 4D scans is the fact that babies have rapid eye movement sleep. This is a period of sleep when the eyes slicker around behind the eyelids. Later in life, this is an indication of dreaming. This gentle flicker of an eye could be a sign that the foetus, still with a month to go before being born is already dreaming."[100] The above said evidences and illustrations lead us to the conclusion that the unborn child is a person.

Other Visual Evidence

Prenatal medical photography has disclosed the wonders of foetal development even further in recent years. The strikingly beautiful pictures by Swedish photographer Lennart Nilsson in his book *A Child is Born* dispels visually the arguments that a foetus is something other or less than a human being. Apart from the above scientific evidences we are endowed with some other visual evidences too. Lennart Nilsson in his photo essay, *Drama of Life Before Birth*, in the April 30, 1965 edition of *Life Magazine* has again captured the amazing development of foetuses. A long time before the abortion controversy became common, Nilsson wrote dispassionately: "The birth of a human life really occurs at the moment the mother's egg cell is fertilised by one of the father's sperm cells."[101]

Nilsson's photo of a 3½ week-old embryo is accompanied by this surprising caption: "This embryo is so tiny—about a tenth of an inch long—that the mother may not even know she is pregnant. Yet there is already impressive internal development, not visible here. This embryo has the beginnings of eyes, spinal cord, nervous system, thyroid gland, lungs, stomach, kidney and intestines. Its primitive heart, which began beating haltingly on the 18th day, is now pumping more confidently. On the bulge of the chest, the tiny buds of arms – not yet visible – are forming."[102] At 6½ weeks, shortly before the embryo (meaning "to swell") is called a foetus (meaning "young one"), Nilsson shows us a "baby in miniature" though at this point it is lacking the sharp features of what we would recognise as a new born infant.

Nilsson comments: "Though the embryo now weighs only 1/30 of an ounce, it has all the internal organs of the adult in various stages of development. It already has a little mouth with lips, and early tongue and buds for 20 milk teeth. Its sex and reproductive organs have begun to sprout."[103] The 11-week-old foetus is nothing less than a "tiny teenager" exercising newfound independence and letting his presence be known: "Bones, including the ribs, are now rapidly forming. The body wall has grown from the spine forward and is joined at the front – like a coat being buttoned. All the body systems are now working. Nerves and muscles are synchronising with the young bones so that the arms and legs can make their first movements. Soon the foetus gets more cramped, and as it gains steadily in strength, the mother will begin to feel the sharp kick and thrust of a foot, knee, and elbow."[104] By this point in time, the largest number of abortions will already have taken place. The awesome developing life described by Nilsson – far from being the "blob of cells" that many of us once thought – has been killed either by menstrual extraction (up to five or six weeks) or by vacuum aspiration (between six and twelve weeks). If the foetus is allowed to live to the 16th week (fourth month), "the body has filled out fantastically, quite recognisable now as a baby. The eyes are still closed, but the nose, lips, and ears finally look like nose, lips and ears."[105] At 18 weeks, "the foetus is clearly sucking its thumb. This pre-natal practice prepares the baby to feed spontaneously as soon as it is born. It can go through the motions of crying, too."[106]

Many foetuses are aborted each year even at this advanced stage. Although relatively few (when compare with the vast majority of typically six-to-ten-week abortions) are aborted at this stage, the overall numbers still reach into many hundreds of the more advanced foetuses.

A shocking report from England on 24th March 2014 has provoked alarm and outrage worldwide. The report indicates that the remains of as many as 15,000 aborted babies were incinerated by British hospital as a heating source. The report of babies burned to heat UK hospitals is a shocking reminder of the callous way human life was treated by the Nazi regime. According to the report in the *London Telegraph* newspaper, the aborted babies were incinerated as "clinical waste" in "waste to energy" plants at British hospitals.[107]

In light of such information, is picturing a thumb-sucking, crying foetus just a phony phenotype argument or soppy sentimentalism? Or is it a reminder that "what we naturally associate with the newborn babies outside the womb – whom we regard as a person – is already associated with unborn babies inside the womb."[108] Finally, Nilsson brings us to the 28th week: "Here the development of the foetus is virtually completed, and some premature babies are born no older than this one. [20 years on from this assessment, some premature babies are now surviving from 21-22 weeks.] The extra time in the womb gives it added strength and health and time to acquire from its mother precious, though short-term, immunity to a number of diseases."[109]

Nilsson's words not only describe the biological development of the foetus, but his pictures tell the real story of what it means to terminate a pregnancy. It is no more possible for a foetus to be just a little bit human than it is for a woman to be just a little bit pregnant. It seems that our "old-fashioned" parents and grandparents knew what they were talking about when they referred to a woman as being not just pregnant, but *as being with child*. There is *The Making of Me* film shown in the *Wonders of Life Pavilion* at Disney's Epcot Centre which is written and directed by Glenn Caron, creator of the

Moonlighting television series which includes many of these and other startling photographs of foetal development by Lennart Nilsson.

In contrast, it is much easier to ignore what we can't see. Dr. Paul Rockwell, a physician in New York, shares his observation for consideration: "Eleven years ago while giving an anaesthetic for a ruptured ectopic pregnancy (at two months' gestation) I was handed what I believe was the smallest living human ever seen. The embryo sac was intact and transparent. Within the sac was a tiny human male swimming extremely vigorously in the amniotic fluid, while attached to the wall by the umbilical cord. This tiny human was perfectly developed, with long, tapering fingers, feet and toes. It was almost transparent, as regards the skin and the delicate arteries and veins were prominent to the ends of the fingers. The baby was extremely alive and swam about the sac approximately one time per second, with a natural swimmer's stroke. This tiny human did not look at all like the photos and drawings and models of 'embryos' I have been able to observe since then, obviously because this one was alive! When the sac was opened, the tiny human immediately lost its life and took on the appearance of what is accepted as the appearance of an embryo at this stage (blunt extremities, etc). It is my opinion that if the lawmakers and people realised that very vigorous life is present, it is possible that abortion would be found more objectionable than euthanasia."[110]

Why do pro-"choice" people become so indignant when opponents display photographs of the well-formed feet and hands of a nine-week-old foetus? Why do they avoid accurate photographs of aborted foetuses? How can anyone look with his eyes upon what is being aborted and not recognise it as being more than a "mass of cells," but a living organism, with every appearance of a child who struggles and resists his own death? Most of us have found it to be true: "Seeing is Believing." We know also that a picture is worth a thousand words! Although visual evidence can be misleading, we still tend to rely on what we can see with our own two eyes.

When it comes to deciding the point at which human life begins we tend to rely on what we can physically see for ourselves. That is one reason why, in the Western world, a person's life is counted from the day he comes out of the womb. Not every society is limited to visual confirmation, however. Paradoxical as it is in light of their widespread practice of abortion, even the Chinese (overestimating by three months) have traditionally counted a child one-year-old at birth in recognition of the continual active life that has already taken place in the womb.[111]

All these lead us to the conclusion that a new human being comes into existence during the process of fertilisation. We have still more evidences for that. Even many prominent defenders of abortion, admit that abortion kills human beings.

Other Evidences

Sincere defenders of abortion do not claim that the unborn is not human, though they argue that there is nothing immoral in abortion. Having seen their sincere opinion about the nature of the unborn, we will hear what the experts in this field have to say. Then we will take a perusal through the standard, authoritative embryology texts. These testimonies will help us to arrive at the conclusion that the unborn is human.

Pro-Death Defenders

Every new life begins at conception. This is an established scientific fact[112]. It is true for animals and for humans. When considered alongside the law of biogenesis – that every species reproduces after its own kind – we can draw only one conclusion in regard to abortion: No matter what the circumstances of conception, no matter how far along in the pregnancy, abortion always ends the life of an individual human being. Every honest abortion advocate concedes this fact.[113] They will readily admit that abortion is the killing of a living being. Here are a few examples: "We know that it is killing, but the states permit killing under certain circumstances." Dr. Neville Sender, founder of *Metropolitan Medical Service*, an abortion clinic in Milwaukee, Wisconsin.

"If I see a case...after twenty weeks, where it frankly is a child to me, I really agonize over it because the potential is so imminently there...On the other hand, I have another position, which I think is superior in the hierarchy of questions, and that is "who owns this child?" It's got to be the mother." Dr. James MacMahon, who performs D&C (also known as Partial Birth) abortions.

"When you do a D&C most of the tissue is removed by the Olden forceps or ring clamp and you actually get gross parts of the foetus out. So you can see a miniature person so to speak, and even now I occasionally feel a little peculiar about it because as a physician I'm trained to conserve life and here I am destroying life."[114]

Faye Wattleton, the longest reigning president of the largest abortion provider in the world – Planned Parenthood – argued as far back as 1997 that everyone already knows that abortion kills. She proclaims the following in an interview with *Ms. Magazine*: I think we have deluded ourselves into believing that people don't know that abortion is killing. So any pretence that abortion is not killing is a signal of our ambivalence, a signal that we cannot say yes, it kills a foetus.

Naomi Wolf, a prominent feminist author and abortion supporter, makes a similar concession when she writes: Clinging to a rhetoric about abortion in which there is no life and no death, we entangle our beliefs in a series of self-delusions, fibs and evasions. And we risk becoming precisely what our critics charge us with being: callous, selfish and casually destructive men and women who share a cheapened view of human life...we need to contextualize the fight to defend abortion rights within a moral framework that admits that the death of a foetus is a real death.

David Boonin, in his book, *A Defense of Abortion*, makes this startling admission: In the top drawer of my desk, I keep [a picture of my son]. This picture was taken on September 7, 1993, 24 weeks before he was born. The sonogram image is murky, but it reveals clearly enough a small head tilted back slightly, and an arm raised up and bent, with the hand pointing back toward the face and the thumb extended out toward the mouth. There is no doubt in my mind that this picture, too, shows [my son] at a very early stage in his physical development. And there is no question that the position I defend in this book entails that it would have been morally permissible to end his life at this point.[115]

In a congress in which scientific experts from around the world attended, they testified as to the beginning of an individual life. Senator Max Baucus (D. Montana), a pro-death member of the separation of powers subcommittee, had been invited by the staff to submit a list of pro-death witnesses who would testify that life begins at some time other than fertilisation. In the first round of hearings Senator Baucus failed to produce a single witness. However, he finally produced Professor Leon Rosenberg as the lone pro-death witness at the hearings who dismissed the question as a religious and metaphysical issue.

According to Professor Rosenberg's logic, if the question of when life begins is not a scientific question, but a religious one which must be answered by theologian, not by scientists then, how come legal experts (Supreme Court justices) opened up *carte blanche* killing of the unborn? Furthermore, if this is so, why have some of the scientists been the proponents of the pro-death movement if they are not even qualified to make such a decision according to Rosenberg? Although the issue of when human life begins is a religious question, it is also a scientific question. In the Christian religion faith is not believing that which is contrary to factual evidence. While faith may transcend reason, it does not contradict it. Although Christian faith is supra-rational, it is not irrational.

So, what do doctors find when they do abortions? A lump of tissue? An amorphous blob? Below is a description of what the abortionist must look for to make sure that he has removed the entire foetus: Dr. David Brewer, a former abortionist described his first encounter with abortion, while training at a clinic. He recalled going to a clinic "to learn about abortion. After all, abortion was just applying the technique of a D&C to a woman who was in a little different stage – she was pregnant."

And so the young resident did as he was told: He watched the material come down the plastic tube and emptied the reddish contents of the little bag onto a blue towel – to make sure the doctor had gotten it all: "I opened the sock up and I put it on the towel and there were parts of a person. I'd taken anatomy; I was a medical student. I knew what I was looking at. There was a little scapula [shoulder blade] and there was an arm, and I saw some ribs and a chest, and I saw a little tiny head, and I saw a piece of a leg, and I saw a tiny hand. ... I checked it out and there were two arms and two legs and one head, etc., and I turned and said, I guess you got it all ... It was pretty awful that first time... it was like somebody put a hot poker into me."

If women (and their male sexual partners) had to examine the results of their abortions, their approach to abortion will be different. See the following evidence: "I had a quick sonogram and then received a shot of methrotrexate. This is a drug that is used for cancer treatment, it stops cell growth. After the shot, I came home... I went to bed that evening around 9pm. I used the suppositories as soon as I went to bed. I remember feeling the contractions start about half an hour later. In the beginning, they were mild, but within an hour the pain was severe. I continued contracting and bleeding most of the night. Around three in the morning, I went to the bathroom. I had been passing a lot of clots most of the evening. I assumed that the pain and pressure I was feeling was from more clots. When I stood up, I noticed that the pain and the pressure was not from clots, but from passing the placenta. When I looked in the commode, I saw laying in the centre of the placenta my baby. I saw the baby's perfectly formed hands, the little fingers. I remember the scream that came from my mouth... [from a seven-week abortion] (I used to be Pro-choice...But...)" As long as the foetus is just a blob of tissue abortion will continue to be widely practiced. This is why abortion advocates oppose any attempts to provide women with scientific, unbiased information on foetal development. Ignorance is bliss. Foeticide is legal.

Peter Singer, contemporary philosopher and public abortion advocate, joins the chorus in his book, *Practical Ethics*. He writes: "It is possible to give 'human being' a precise meaning. We can use it as equivalent to 'member of the species *Homo Sapiens*'. Whether a being is a member of a given species is something that can be determined scientifically, by an examination of the nature of the chromosomes in the cells of living organisms. In this sense there is no doubt that from the first moments of its existence an embryo conceived from human sperm and eggs is a human being".[116]

Don't miss the significance of these acknowledgements. Prominent defenders of abortion rights publicly admit that abortion kills human beings. They are not saying that abortion is morally defensible because it doesn't kill a distinct human entity. They are admitting that abortion does kill a distinct human entity, but argue it is morally defensible anyway. We will not go to their arguments now; but the point here is this: There is simply no debate among honest, informed people that abortion kills distinct human beings. That is, the unborn is a human being. Individual human life begins at fertilisation, and there are all sorts of authoritative, public resources to prove this. Consider the evidences below.

General Testimonies
Biologically speaking, every abortion at every point in the pregnancy ends the life of a genetically-distinct human being. The American Medical Association (AMA) declared as far back as 1857 that "the independent and actual existence of the child before birth, as a living being" is a matter of objective science. They deplored the "popular ignorance...that the foetus is not alive till after the period of quickening."

The landmark verdict in the *Roe vs. Wade* case (1973) legalised abortion in the US. It is actually built on the claim that there's no way to say for certain whether or not abortion kills because no one can say for certain when life begins. Justice Harry Blackmun, who authored the majority opinion wrote: "The judiciary, at this point in the development of man's knowledge, is not in a position to... resolve the difficult question of when life begins... since those trained in the respective disciplines of medicine, philosophy, and theology are unable to arrive at any consensus."[117]

In 1981, a United States Senate Judiciary Subcommittee received the following testimony from a collection of medical experts (Subcommittee on Separation of Powers to Senate Judiciary Committee S-158, Report, 97th Congress, 1st Session, 1981) : "It is incorrect to say that biological data cannot be decisive...It is scientifically correct to say that an individual human life begins at conception."[118] Hence, Justice Blackmun's assertion is a ridiculous one, at least as it applies to the field of medicine. In biological terms, life's beginning is a settled fact. The Official Senate Report reached this conclusion: "Physicians, biologists, and other scientists agree that conception marks the beginning of the life of a human being – a being that is alive and is a member of the human species. There is overwhelming agreement on this point in countless medical, biological, and scientific writings."

On April 23 and 24, 1981, US Congress held hearings on "the question of when human life begins." Dr. Eugene Diamond, a medical school professor, said: "either the justices were fed a backwoods biology or they were pretending ignorance about a scientific certainty."[119] It is difficult to believe that the justices did not know the scientific facts. If they did not, they should have, especially when one considers the horrendous ramifications of their decision.

However, pick up any embryology book today and you will find that every person's life began at fertilisation. "Almost all higher animals start their lives from a single cell, the fertilised ovum (zygote)... The time of fertilisation represents the starting point in the life history, or ontogeny, of the individual."[120] "Every baby begins life within the tiny globe of the mother's egg... It is beautifully translucent and fragile and it encompasses the vital links in which life is carried from one generation to the next. Within this tiny sphere great events take place. When one of the father's sperm cells, like the ones gathered here around the egg, succeeds in penetrating the egg and becomes united with it, a new life can begin."[121]

"Fertilisation is a sequence of events that begins with the contact of a sperm (spermatozoon) with a secondary oocyte (ovum) and ends with the fusion of their pro-nuclei (the *haploid nuclei* of the sperm and ovum) and the mingling of their chromosomes to form a new cell. This fertilised ovum, known as a zygote, is a large *diploid* cell that is the beginning, or *primordium*, of a human being."[122] The common expression fertilized ovum refers to the "zygote." This is a definition of the word "zygote" from the book on *Embryology and Birth Defects*.[123] Having had recourse to the word zygote, Keith Moore & T.V. Persaud wrote: Zygote. This cell, formed by the union of an ovum and a sperm (Gr. zyg tos, yoked together), represents the beginning of a human being. "[The zygote], formed by the union of an oocyte and a sperm, is the beginning of a new human being."[124]

T.W. Sadler, too observes: "The development of a human being begins with fertilisation, a process by which two highly specialised cells, the spermatozoon from the male and the oocyte from the female, unite to give rise to a new organism, the zygote."[125]

Dianne Irving writes: "To begin with, scientifically something very radical occurs between the processes of gameto-genesis and fertilisation – the change from a simple part of one human being (i.e., a sperm) and a simple part of another human being (i.e., an oocyte – usually referred to as an 'ovum' or 'egg'), which simply possess 'human life', to a new, genetically unique, newly existing, individual, whole living human being (an embryonic single-cell human zygote). That is, upon fertilisation, parts of human beings have actually been transformed into something very different from what they were before; they have been changed into a single, whole human being. During the process of fertilisation, the sperm and the oocyte cease to exist as such, and a new human being is produced."[126]

The following references illustrate the fact that a new human embryo, the starting point for a human life, comes into existence with the formation of the one-celled zygote. Animal biologists use the term embryo to describe the single cell stage, the two-cell stage, and all subsequent stages up until a time when recognisable humanlike limbs and facial features begin to appear between six to eight weeks after fertilisation. "Embryo: An organism in the earliest stage of development; in a man, from the time of conception to the end of the second month in the uterus."[127]

According to *England, Marjorie A*, development of the embryo "begins at Stage 1 when a sperm fertilizes an oocyte and together they form a zygote."[128] That is, "Human development begins after the union of male and female gametes or germ cells during a process known as fertilisation (conception). *Larsen, William J.* joins with these experts when he says: "The chromosomes of the oocyte and sperm are...respectively enclosed within female and male pro-nuclei. These pro-nuclei fuse with each other to produce the single, diploid, 2N nucleus of the fertilised zygote. This moment of zygote formation may be taken as the beginning or zero-time point of embryonic development."[129]

Floare Farcas wrote: "Each of us has a very precise starting moment. This is when all the necessary and sufficient genetic information is gathered inside one cell, the fertilised egg. This is the moment of conception. There is no difference between the early person you were at conception and the late person you are now! You were and are a human being! Consequently, unborn babies must be protected and guaranteed their 'right to life'."[130]

Jon, E. Dougherty, of *WorldNet Daily.com* writes that humans are never 'fully developed.' We're not born 'complete.' We grow, change, mature and age constantly, which means we're always 'developing,' and we develop though the first nine months of our lives attached to a 'host' – our mothers. So, "the fact that the first nine months of our developmental life is *in utero* is of no consequence to our overall lifespan; it is just the first stage. There are many developmental stages – early, middle and late. But life has to begin somewhere. We don't go from 'nothing' to adulthood.... It begins when it begins – at the moment a human being is biologically 'under construction'."[131]

O'Rahilly, Ronan and Müller Fabiola consider fertilisation as a critical landmark in the life of a person. Their position is clarified in the following statement: "Although life is a continuous process, fertilisation is a critical landmark because, under ordinary circumstances, a new, genetically distinct human organism is thereby formed.... The combination of 23 chromosomes present in each pronucleus results in 46 chromosomes in the zygote. Thus the diploid number is restored and the embryonic genome is formed. The embryo now exists as a genetic unity."[132]

Dr. John Eppig, a Senior Staff Scientist, of *Jackson Laboratory* (Bar Harbor, Maine) and a Member of the *NIH Human Embryo Research Panel*, agrees with other scientists in saying: "the word 'embryo' includes the time from after fertilisation..."[133] Jonathan Van Blerkom of *University of Colorado*, expert witness on human embryology before the *NIH Human Embryo Research Panel* tried to explain the term embryo. "The question came up of what is an embryo, when does an embryo exist, when does it occur. I think, as you know, that in development, life is a *continuum*.... But I think one of the useful definitions that has come out, especially from Germany, has been the stage at which these two nuclei [from sperm and egg] come together and the membranes between the two break down."[134]

We have further evidences regarding embryo: "Embryo: the developing organism from the time of fertilisation until significant differentiation has occurred, when the organism becomes known as a foetus."[135] "Embryo: The developing individual between the union of the germ cells and the completion of the organs which characterize its body when it becomes a separate organism.... At the moment the sperm cell of the human male meets the ovum of the female and the union results in a fertilised ovum (zygote), a new life has begun.... The term embryo covers the several stages of early development from conception to the ninth or tenth week of life."[136] "Embryo: The early developing fertilised egg that is growing into another individual of the species. In man the term 'embryo' is usually restricted to the period of development from fertilisation until the end of the eighth week of pregnancy."[137]

[A] number of specialists working in the field of human reproduction have suggested that we stop using the word embryo to describe the developing entity that exists for the first two weeks after fertilisation. In its place, they proposed the term pre-embryo. I'll let you in on a secret. The term pre-embryo has been embraced wholeheartedly by *in vitro* fertilisation (IVF) practitioners for reasons that are political, not scientific. The new term is used to provide the illusion that there is something profoundly different between what we still call a six-day-old embryo and what we and everyone else call a sixteen-day-old embryo.

Silver, Lee M. warns us about the danger involved in using the term pre-embryo. "The term pre-embryo is useful in the political arena – where decisions are made about whether to allow early embryo (now called pre-embryo) experimentation – as well as in the confines of a doctor's office, where it can be used to allay moral concerns that might be expressed by IVF patients. 'Don't worry,' a doctor might say, 'it's only pre-embryos that we're manipulating or freezing. They won't turn into real human embryos until after we've put them back into your body.'"[138]

The zygote ... is a unicellular embryo... "The ill-defined and inaccurate term pre-embryo, which includes the embryonic disc, is said either to end with the appearance of the primitive streak or ... to include neurulation. The term is not used in the book *Human Embryology & Teratology* by O'Rahilly, R. and F. Muller (1996).

Now we turn our attention to what the authoritative embryology text books have to say about the beginning of life.

Textual Testimonies

What do embryology books have to say about human development? Clark Edward Corliss, in his work *Patten's Human Embryology: Elements of Clinical Development* observed: "It is the penetration of the ovum by a spermatozoan and resultant mingling of the nuclear material each brings to the union that constitutes the culmination of the process of fertilisation and marks the initiation of the life of a new individual."[139]

We have a good explanation of the term 'conception', in the book *Biological Principles and Modern Practice of Obstetrics*, co-authored by J.P. Greenhill and E.A. Friedman. The term 'conception', according to them, refers to the union of the male and female pronuclear elements of procreation from which a new living being develops." "The zygote thus formed represents the beginning of a new life."[140]

"Zygote: this cell results from the union of an oocyte and a sperm. A zygote is the beginning of a new human being (i.e., an embryo). Human development begins at fertilisation, the process during which a male gamete or sperm ... unites with a female gamete or oocyte ... to form a single cell called a zygote. This highly specialised, totipotent cell marks the beginning of each of us as a unique individual."[141]

In the *Essentials of Human Embryology*, the author Larsen William J says that he begins his description of the developing human "with the formation and differentiation of the male and female sex cells or gametes, which will unite at fertilisation to initiate the embryonic development of a new individual. ... Fertilisation takes place in the oviduct ... resulting in the formation of a zygote containing a single diploid nucleus. Embryonic development is considered to begin at this point... This moment of zygote formation may be taken as the beginning or zero-time point of embryonic development."[142]

In *Human Embryology & Teratology* we read: "Fertilisation is an important landmark because, under ordinary circumstances, a new, genetically distinct human organism is thereby formed... Fertilisation is the procession of events that begins when a spermatozoon makes contact with a secondary oocyte or its investments."[143] According to Keith L. Moore, "A zygote is the beginning of a new human being (i.e., an embryo)."[144] In another book *Before We Are*

Born: Essentials of Embryology, the same author repeats: "[The zygote], formed by the union of an oocyte and a sperm, is the beginning of a new human being."[145]

In their book *Pathology of the Foetus and the Infant*, E.L. Potter and J.M. Craig, make it clear that a life started by the union of sperm and ovum will continue to live unless otherwise destroyed. "Every time a sperm cell and ovum unite a new being is created which is alive and will continue to live unless its death is brought about by some specific condition."[146]

To sum up: Human development begins at fertilisation, the process during which a male gamete or sperm (spermatozoan) unites with a female gamete or oocyte (ovum) to form a single cell called a zygote. We can see our beginning as a unique individual in this highly specialised, totipotent cell. Besides, we have testimonies from experts in this field.

Geneticists and other Experts

The following are excerpts from the testimony of leading geneticists, before the Senate Subcommittee on Separation of Powers.[147] Dr. Jerome LeJeune, the father of modern genetics, professor of fundamental genetics at the University of Descarte, Paris, France and the discoverer of the Down Syndrome chromosome, asked: "When does a person begin?" Then he said: "I will try to give the most precise answer to that question actually available to sciences. Modern biology teaches us that ancestors are united to their progeny by a continuous material link, for it is from the fertilisation of the female cell (the ovum) by the male cell (the spermatozoa) that a new member of the species will emerge. Life has a very, very long history but each individual has a very neat beginning the moment of its conception. To accept that fact that after fertilisation has taken place, a new human has come into being, is no longer a matter of taste or of opinion".[148] According to him, the human nature of the human being from conception to old age is not a metaphysical contention, it is plain experimental evidence. He wrote: "...each of us has a unique beginning, the moment of conception...when the information carried by the sperm and by the ovum have encountered each other, then a new human being is defined because its own personal and human constitution is entirely spelled out."

"The information which is inside the first cell obviously tells this cell all the tricks of the trade to build himself as the individual this cell is already....to build that particular individual which we will call later Margaret or Paul or Peter, it's already there, but it's so small we cannot see it ...It's what life is, the formula is there; ....if you allow the formula to be expanded by itself, just giving shelter and nurture, then you have the development of the full person."[149] He puts it very clearly: "Science has a very simple conception of man; as soon as he has been conceived, a man is a man."[150] Jason M. Steffens too quotes him.

Dr. Micheline Matthews-Roth, principal research associate of the Harvard University Medical School asserts: "In biology and in medicine, it is an accepted fact that the life of any individual organism reproducing by sexual reproduction begins at conception (fertilisation), the time when the egg cell from the female and the sperm cell from the male join to form a single new cell, the zygote; this zygote is the starting cell of the new organism . . ." [Dr. Matthews-Roth proceeded to quote from eight biology text-books which stated that life begins at conception.] He continues: "You will notice that I have been using the words fertilisation and conception interchangeably. It is very important that in drafting the statute the word 'conception' be specifically defined as meaning the time of the fusion of the egg cell and the sperm cell. This is important because there seems to be a tendency in some medical circles to define conception as being the time of the implantation of the developing embryo in the wall of the uterus rather than the time of fertilisation of the egg by the sperm. It is crucial to remember, since implantation occurs about 6 to 10 days after fertilisation, that the zygote is already well on its way in the process of development by the time implantation occurs. In summary, then, it is incorrect to say that biological data cannot be decisive . . . so, therefore, it is scientifically correct to say that an individual human life begins at conception, when the egg and sperm join to form the zygote, and that this developing human always is a member of our species in all stages of its life. Our laws, one function of which is to help preserve the lives of our people, should be based on accurate scientific data."[151]

Professor Hymie Gordon, chairman of the Department of Medical Genetics at the Mayo Clinic observes: "Thus from the moment of conception the organism contains many complex molecules; it synthesizes new intricate structures from simple raw materials; and replicates itself. By all the criteria of modern molecular biology, life is present from the moment of conception."[152] "When fertilisation is complete, a unique genetic human entity exists."[153] That is the opinion of C. Christopher Hook, M.D, Oncologist, Mayo Clinic, Director of Ethics Education, Mayo Graduate School of Medicine.
Dr. Alfred M. Bogiovanni, currently a member of the University of Pennsylvania Medical School faculty arrives at the same conclusion: "I have

learned since my earliest medical education that human life begins at the time of conception. The standard textbooks which were used in the courses I took, many of them in continuous use until today, so state it...I am no more prepared to say that these early stages represent an incomplete human being that I would be to say that the child prior to the dramatic events of puberty which I have outlined is not a human being. This is human life at every stage albeit incomplete until late adolescence."[154] Hence, he submits that the human life is present throughout this entire sequence from conception to adulthood and any interruption at any point throughout this time constitutes a termination of human life.

Dr. Jasper Williams, of the Williams Clinic in Chicago, and past president of the National Medical Association observes as follows: "Human life's singular characteristic is mental behaviour associated with development of genetically influenced bodily characteristics . . . This process begins when the sperm fertilises the ovum . . . The work of Edwards and his associates in England with test tube babies has repeatedly proved that human life begins when after the ovum is fertilised the new cell mass begins to divide."[155]

Dr. Watson A. Bowes, Jr., of the University of Medical School, makes an assertion similar to the one made by Pro. Jerome Lejeune, M.D., Ph. D: "But one thing is clear. Following fertilisation there is an inexorable series of events that unfolds with cells dividing, moving, pausing, differentiating, and aggregating with a baffling precision and purpose. In the early hours, days, and weeks of this development a hypothetical observer, if able to witness this microscopic drama, would find it impossible to identify precisely when major qualitative changes have occurred just as parents observing daily their child's growth and development cannot say precisely when he or she stopped being a child and became an adult . . . Thus the beginning of a single human life is from a biological point of view a simple and straightforward matter—the beginning is conception. In conclusion, the beginning of a human life from a biological point of view is at the time of conception. This straightforward biological fact should not be distorted to serve sociological, political, or economic goals."[156]

Dr. Harold W. Manner, Chairman of the Department of Biology at Loyola University of Chicago, summarised it: "When a human sperm fertilises a human egg, the result is a human being—from the moment of conception. The killing of this living human being must be considered homicide."[157] Dr. Landrum Shettles, pioneer in sperm biology, fertility and sterility, discoverer of male – and female- producing sperm asserts: "I oppose abortion. I do so, first, I accept what is biologically manifest – that human life commences at the time of conception and second, because I believe it is wrong to take innocent human life under any circumstances."

Dr. Walker Percy, who is a famous novelist as well as doctor, noted that it is common-place of modern biology that the life of an organism begins "when the chromosomes of the sperm fuse with the chromosomes of the ovum to form a new DNA complex that thenceforth directs the ontogenesis of the organism," producing the undeniable "*continuum* that exists in the life of every individual from the moment of fertilisation of a single cell."[158] He then adds: "The onset of individual life is not a dogma of the Church but a fact of science. How much more convenient if we lived in the thirteenth century, when no one knew anything about microbiology and arguments about the onset of life were legitimate. . ... Nowadays it is not some misguided ecclesiastical who are trying to suppress an embarrassing scientific fact. It is the secular-journalistic establishment."[159]

In the *Journal of California Medicine* in 1970 the issue was clearly laid out as: "The result has been a curious avoidance of the scientific fact which everyone really knows that human life begins at conception and is continuous whether intra- or extra-uterine until death. The very considerable semantic gymnastics which are required to rationalise abortion as anything but taking a human life would be ludicrous if they were not often put forth under socially impeccable auspices."[160] Quality of life outside the womb cannot be divorced from quality of life inside the womb where there are foetuses who possess the same human "qualities" as we do on the outside. It is as true in the first trimester as in the third, or else third trimester foetuses would never have developed from the first trimester embryos. Eight-month-old babies in the womb do not suddenly appear from nonhuman embryos. Only our inability to appreciate the uniqueness of human life itself permits us the foolishness of asking when life begins.

These are the testimonies of some of the world's leading geneticists and other experts in the field. In biology and in medicine, it is an accepted fact that the life of any individual organism resulting from sexual reproduction begins at conception or fertilisation. Until *Roe vs. Wade* in the USA this was taught in all science textbooks. Thus the question of when life begins is no longer a question for theological or philosophical dispute. It is an established scientific fact. While theologians and philosophers may debate the meaning or purpose of life, it is an established fact that all life, including human life, begins at the moment of conception.

The teaching texts and so many medical experts come to this same conclusion. Why, you know? Because there are simple ways to measure whether something is alive and whether something is human. In spite of the information circulated by Planned Parenthood and the rest of the abortion-rights community, everyone already knows that abortion kills a human being. The abortion section of the Planned Parenthood website explains abortion this way: "Abortion ends a pregnancy before birth." They just assume that the method for ending the pregnancy is so obvious (killing the human being living in the womb) that it hardly bears mentioning. More likely, Planned Parenthood is simply accommodating the general ignorance which believes abortion to be the mere removal of potential human life, rather than the actual killing of existing human life.

The science of embryology tells us that human beings develop rapidly after fertilisation of the egg. In fact, since the heart of the foetus begins to beat by 24 days, virtually all abortions (other than "emergency contraception") stop a beating heart. In fact, since most abortion occur between 4-6 weeks, they also destroy a functioning brain. Even modern embryology textbooks agree that human life begins at conception. Since abortion ends human life, one must ask the question whether abortion is justifiable homicide or murder.

At this point one may object saying even if an embryo is technically alive at fertilisation, it's still just a clump of microscopic cells. Until the heart is beating or the brain is functioning, women should be free to have an abortion. As a reply to this objection we will say that growth in the womb is a rapid process; all systems are in place by week eight and so the foetus in the womb is not simply part of mother's body. An accurate understanding of prenatal development makes it impossible to argue that abortion is the mere removal of undifferentiated cell tissue or that the developing embryo is simply a part of the mother's body.

'Unborn' is not Part of Mother's Body
The pro-abortion people excuse themselves saying that the foetus is only a part of the mother's body and the mother can do with it as she wishes. Again they maintain that, it can be difficult to feel much emotional attachment to something that so little resembles a baby. In truth, a human blastocyst (five days after fertilisation) looks exactly as a human being should look.

Biologically, from the moment of conception the new human being is not a part of the mother's body.[161] As we understand, the foetus has its own autonomous life. Medical advances have eliminated the artificial distinction between prenatal and postnatal human life. Dr. H.M. Liley explains: "In assessing foetal health, the doctor now watches changes in maternal function very carefully, for he has learned that it is actually the mother who is a passive carrier, while the foetus is very largely in charge of the pregnancy."[162]

It is the newly conceived individual, rather than the mother, that takes the initiative in effecting crucial physiological changes. "After fertilisation the zygote divides first into two cells, then four, then eight, and so on, at a rate of almost one division per day. It is during this earliest stage of development the mass of cells may divide into identical parts forming identical twins."[163]

Within minutes of membrane fusion, the zygote initiates changes in its ionic composition that will, over the next 30 minutes, result in chemical modifications of the zona pellucida, an acellular structure surrounding the zygote.[164] These modifications block sperm binding to the cell surface and prevent further intrusion of additional spermatozoa on the unfolding process of development. Thus, the zygote acts immediately and specifically to antagonize the function of the gametes from which it is derived; that is, while the 'goal' of both sperm and egg is to find each other and to fuse, the first act of the zygote is immediately to prevent any further binding of sperm to the cell surface.

After the first six or seven days of cell division, which takes place in the fallopian tube, the new human life enters the uterus and implants itself in the uterine lining. Renowned scientific author, Barry Werth, calls implantation (which he describes as "the joining of two lives") the "second great challenge of pregnancy, after fertilisation."[165] "This is often called the "blastocyst" stage. One pole of the growing sphere of cells, called the trophoblast, penetrates the uterine lining and develops into the placenta. The other pole develops as the embryonic human being. It is worth noting here that the placenta is an extension of the child's body, not of the mother. The part of the developing blastocyst that becomes the placenta produces hormones, which enter the mother's bloodstream and prevent the onset of menstruation. This hormonal signal sent to the mother's body from the newly conceived life is essential for its survival, since otherwise the new life would be sloughed away by the menstrual flow."[166] If this tiny embryo were simply "part of the woman's body" there would be no need to locally disable the woman's immunities. The mother provides an environment for the unborn child, but the child's hormonal system has an active influence on changes in that environment[167], and so the real star of the show is the foetus herself, building, dividing and growing according to an intricate set of plans created at the moment of conception.[168]

Hence we assert that those who would claim that the foetus is just another part of the mother's body ignore the biological facts known for centuries: namely, that the foetus has its own brain, its own heart, its own blood type, its own circulatory system, its own fingerprints, its own nervous system and internal organs etc. It is an elementary fact of biology that the foetus is a completely separate individual from the mother with his/her own genetic code. It feels his/her own pain, can be healthy while the mother is ill, be ill when the mother is healthy and can have diseases which are not present in the mother and vice versa. The foetus can be awake while his/her mother is asleep and asleep while she's awake. "The embryo can die while the mother continues to live, and for a limited period of time in which the child can be kept alive, the opposite is also possible. Just as both organisms have their own possibilities of living or dying so each of them also, as we have seen, can have their own illnesses in which the other does not participate."[169]

As we learn from the timeline prenatal development, it is the foetus who takes initiatives for the labour by stimulating the adrenal cortex to secrete hormone that induces the mother's uterus to contract. Thus, it is the foetus who determines when it is time for birth.

Furthermore, about half the time the baby is of a different sex than the mother. Since when, does a mother's body have male genitals, two brains, four kidneys? Since it is impossible for a normal human body to be both male and female at the same time, how else can you explain such a fact other than that there are two bodies, two human beings? All these show that the unborn baby is not a part of mother's body.

The unborn child is no mere "mass of tissue," but a distinctly individualised human being with a characteristic pattern of behaviour. So, "(P)regnancy involves the medical care of two patients, not one. The unborn child is not a passive partner, but rather in many ways controls the dynamics of the pregnancy. This new perception of the unborn child has led to the development of a whole new medical specialty called perinatology, which cares for its patients from conception to about one year of postnatal existence. For the modern physician, human life begins at conception, and medical care and observation must start at the earliest period of life."[170] The human embryo being a separate person,[171] and not simply the part of mother's body, has to be given the protection due to a human person from the moment of conception.

The Unborn is A Person

At this point in the debate, some try and introduce a separate distinction and the question of "personhood." There is a difference, they will argue, between being alive and being a person. Abortion may kill a living human being, but it doesn't kill a person. Because according to the "pro-choicers" "it is not a person?" However, the progress of prenatal medicine has made it increasingly clear that the unborn child possesses a distinct individuality. As Dr. Arnold Gesell has noted: "Our own repeated observation of a large group of foetal infants. . . left us with no doubt that psychologically they were individuals. Just as no two looked alike, so no two behaved precisely alike. . . These were genuine individual differences, already prophetic of the diversity which distinguishes the human family."[172]

The developing human takes on very quickly the characteristics that are so familiar to us in human beings outside the womb. It goes un-noticed by many people.The rate of growth, as we have seen, is astonishing. In fact, during the several days following implantation, the embryo doubles in size every day. In just six weeks' time, the human embryo goes from looking like a "bunch of cells" to looking like a baby – though only a half inch tall!

By definition, humanity and personhood go hand in hand. Developing humans in the womb have an intrinsically personal nature and even demonstrate "personality" in many of the same ways that newborn babies do. I beg to be allowed to repeat the definition of a 'person'. According to Webster's Seventh New Collegiate Dictionary, a person is "a human being". A person, simply put, is a human being. This fact should be enough. The humanity of unborn children, by definition, makes them persons, and should, therefore, guarantee their protection under the law.

We've already established that there is no debate on the question of the humanity of the unborn. As we have seen, it is a matter of plain, objective science.[173] Embryos and foetuses are fully and individually human from fertilisation on. If this were not true, if unborn children were not genetically-distinct human beings, there would be no need to even talk about rights of personhood. "Removing a foetus" would be the moral equivalent of pulling a tooth. This, however, is not the case, and so the debate must enter the political arena.

Dr. Robert George, a professor of jurisprudence at Princeton and a member of the President's Council on Bioethics wrote an article outlining this whole topic in more detail.[174] To reach a secular and sceptical public, Dr. Robert

George and Christopher Tollefsen, a philosopher at the University of South Carolina avoided religion and staked their case on science. George and Tollefsen, located humanity not in a soul but in a biological program. "To be a complete human organism," they write, "an entity must possess a developmental programme (including both its DNA and epigenetic factors) oriented toward developing a brain and central nervous system." The programme begins at conception; therefore, so does personhood. In his words: "That is, in human reproduction, when sperm joins ovum, these two individual cells cease to be, and their union generates a new and distinct organism. This organism is a whole, though in the beginning developmentally immature, member of the human species."[175]

Should humans be recognised as persons under the law? Yes, because humans are persons. Something is a person if it has a personal nature.[176] "Human embryos, whether formed by fertilisation (natural or *in vitro*) or by successful somatic-cell nuclear transfer (SCNT – i.e., cloning), do have the internal resources and active disposition to develop themselves to the mature stage of a human organism, requiring only a suitable environment and nutrition. In fact, scientists distinguish embryos from other cells or clusters of cells precisely by their self-directed, integral functioning – their organismal behaviour. Thus, human embryos are what the embryology textbooks say they are, namely, human organisms – living individuals of the human species – at the earliest developmental stage." – Dr. Robert George. What he means by that is that, human embryos only need a suitable environment and nutrition to become more mature human beings. But despite our maturity, biological or otherwise, we are "whole" members of the human species – human beings, and so human persons and hence with inherent dignity and right to life.

In other words, something is a person if, by nature, it has the capacity to develop the ability to think rationally, express emotion, make decisions, etc. This capacity is something that a person has as soon as he begins to exist, since it is part of his nature (in other words, if he exists, he has it). Since humans have a personal nature, humans are persons. As for the foetus, since it is a human (something with a personal nature), it is a person.[177]

In order to exclude some people, some define the term "person" according to function (call this view the functional view of persons). That is, they say that something qualifies as a person if it can do certain things, like thinking rationally. But this definition of personhood fails. First, there are clear cases in which something qualifies as a person, but cannot do the things required of the functional view of persons.[178] For example, a human person under a general anaesthesia does not qualify as a person under the functional view of persons, since a person in this situation does not have the ability to think rationally. Second, the functional view of persons does not fit certain intuitions about persons. For example, if you had a cat that could not purr, could not chase mice, and could not climb trees, you would not say that your cat is not a feline (though you should if you define "feline" in terms of function). Instead, you would say that your cat is a cat that cannot purr, chase mice, or climb trees.[179] In the same way, if you know a human that cannot think rationally (like a foetus, or a person under a general anaesthesia), you should not say that this human is not a person, but that this is a person who (at the moment) cannot think rationally. In light of these reasons, the functional view of persons should be rejected.

Pope John Paul II once wrote "Some try to justify abortion by claiming that the product of conception, at least until a certain number of days, cannot yet be considered a personal human life.... In reality from the moment in which the ovum is fertilised, a new life begins which is not that of the father or of the mother but of a new human being which develops of its own accord. It would never be made human if it were not human already.... This has always been clear, and modern genetic science offers clear confirmation."[180]

Francis Beckwith writes: "...not only is the conceptus human insofar as being caused by humans, it is a unique human individual, just as each of us is. ...It has its own unique genetic code (with forty-six chromosomes), which is neither the mother's nor the father's. From this point until death, no new genetic information is needed to make the unborn entity a unique individual human.... Although sharing the same nature with all human beings, the unborn individual, like each one of us, is unlike any that has been conceived before and unlike any that will ever be conceived again."[181] So, it is impossible for a foetus to not be a person.[182]

The state of California, which is one of the states with liberalised abortion laws in its courts, recognises that at least sometime before birth the infant is considered a human person.[183] Dr. McCarthy De Mere, lawyer and practicing physician, and law professor at the University of Tennessee says that: "from the medical standpoint there are mountains of documents to show that the human embryo is a separate person, biologically distinct from the mother. From both the legal and medical standpoint, there is absolutely no question in my mind and I feel in the minds of most individuals who have given serious thought to this question, the exact moment of the beginning [of] personhood and of the human body is at the moment of conception."[184]

Conclusion

Eric Versluys, a senior in mechanical engineering at Colorado State University implied his belief that personhood starts at conception. He wrote in a letter to the editor of *The Rocky Mountain Collegian*: "The world has been in the dark about a terrible breach of human rights that has been going on for more than 30 years. For the past 33 years, about 48.6 million people have been brutally murdered. Still going on today, approximately 3,500 people lose their lives every day at the hands of trained killers. It isn't going on in the bush of Africa or the sands of the Middle East, but down the block from where you live."[185]

Many of the questions that arise from the abortion controversy are directly related to the scientific knowledge regarding the beginning of human life which means that it is primarily a scientific issue. So we need to have recourse to scientific facts.[186] Hence, a sound approach to the ethics of abortion must be grounded in the scientific and medical facts. The unborn child, after all, is the central figure in the abortion controversy. His or her moral and legal status depends on a careful examination of the process of prenatal development.[187] So the facts of prenatal development are indispensable for determining when human life begins. When those facts are known, it remains for the ethicist, the physician, the legislator, the pastor and society at large to interpret their moral and legal implications. Any discussion of abortion that ignores the facts of prenatal development is incomplete.

Personhood holds the key to filling the Blackmun Hole, a startling admission in the *Roe vs. Wade* majority opinion: "The appellee and certain amici argue that the foetus is a 'person' within the language and meaning of the Fourteenth Amendment. In support of this, they outline at length and in detail the well-known facts of foetal development. If this suggestion of personhood is established, the appellant's case, of course, collapses, for the foetus' right to life would then be guaranteed specifically by the (Fourtcenth) Amendment." (Justice Harry Blackmun, *Roe vs. Wade*). In 1973, the science of foetology was not able to prove, as it can now, that a living, fully human, and unique individual exists at the moment of fertilisation and continues to grow through various stages of development in a *continuum* until death. However, now as we have seen, science has well advanced in this area. One of the great powers of science is that it is able to help clarify moral issues like personhood of the unborn. It's a powerful tool. Science is clear on this point.

If you are a fan of science, then consider also being a fan of human life – at all of its stages. A sound approach to the ethics of abortion must be grounded in the scientific and medical facts. From our study above, we understand that an embryo is a complete human life. It is an individual, unique, self-directing organism. All it needs is food and suitable shelter (just like the rest of us) and it will grow into an adult human being. It is most unfortunate that scientific facts known for decades or longer have been quietly ignored by many proponents of abortion.[188]

Arguments that the unborn child is simply "part of the woman's body," or that human life does not begin at conception, as we have seen, do not accord with the well-established scientific facts. Even medical authorities personally sympathetic to abortion, acknowledge that. An editorial in *California Medicine*, the official journal of the California Medical Association, makes this clear.[189]

1 California Medicine 113, no.3 (1970), reprinted in The Human Life Review 1, no.1 (1975): 103-4.

2 Other works by Ford are 'Moral Issues that arise in experimentation on human embryos' Australian Catholic Record, 62 (1986), 3-20; 'Reply to Michael Coughlan,' Bioethics 3 (1989) 342-6; 'When Did I Begin?' A Reply to Nocholas Tonti- Filppini, LQ 57 (1990) 59-66; Ethics, Science and Embryos: Weighing the Evidence' The Tablet 46 (1990) 141-2 and 584; The Prenatal Person: Ethics From Conception to Birth, (Oxford: Blackwell 2002; Stem Cell: Science, Medicine, Law and Ethics, with M. Herbert (Sydney: StPaul's, 2003); The Moral Significance of the Human Foetus', in R. Aschcroft, H. Draper, A. Dawson and J. McMillan (eds.), Principles of Health Care Ethics, Chichester: Wiley, 2007, pp.387- 92.

3 This is the opening sentence of R. Yanagimachi, 'Mammalian Fertilization' in Knobil et.al. (eds.), The Physiology of Reproduction, (New York: Raven, 1988), p.135.

4 Dr. Hymie Gordon, Chairman, Department of Genetics at the Mayo Clinic.

5 Some scientists and theologians note that it is only at the end of the process of fertilization (the joining of the male and female chromosomes at syngamy) that a substantive change has taken place resulting in a new, unique, living, individual human person. According to this view, the substantive change inherent in the human diploid single-cell zygote is not yet present at the moment of fertilisation (union or fusion of sperm and egg) or during the pronuclear stage of fertilization. However, these cells do contain within themselves the organizing principle for the self-development and self-maintenance of the full human organism.

6 Up until this stage maternal mRNAs support all or most of the biosynthetic activities of the early embryo.

7 It has been accepted by biologists that there is no qualitative difference between the embryo at the moment of conceptionand at the moment of quickening. Life is fully present from the time of conception. It seems to follow that if there is a soul, it too, must be present from the time of conception. See Lars Wilhelmsson, Abortion Eclipse of Morality, seen at www.vitalchristianity.org/docs/abortion, p.16.

8 See, James M. Steffens, "The Peculiar Being: The Rights of Unborn Children Iowa," 88 IOWA L. REV. 217 (1998). Online at: http://www.june24.net.

9 See, James M. Steffens, "The Peculiar Being: The Rights of Unborn Children Iowa," 88 IOWA L. REV. 217 (1998). Online at: http://www.june24.net.

10 Or the equivalent event in nuclear transfer/cloning.

11 See Lars Wilhelmsson, Abortion Eclipse of Morality, p. seen at www.vitalchristianity.org/docs/abortion, p.16.

12 Early zygote dependence on maternal genetic material does not argue against this, since the role and integration of this information into the organism's development are determined by the organism itself.

13 The term "organism" is a biological concept that refers to the functional unity of the organism, specifically the functions of integration, control, and behaviour (and in this . case, development) of the organism as a whole, whether single cellular, multi-cellular, multi-tissue, or multi-organ. Implicit in this concept is the primacy of the functional unity of the organism as a whole and not merely the sum of the function of its parts. This definition is also univocal and can be applied to all forms of living organisms.

14 The term "organism" is a biological concept that refers to the functional unity of the organism, specifically the functions of integration, control, and behaviour (and in this . case, development) of the organism as a whole, whether single cellular, multi-cellular, multi-tissue, or multi-organ. Implicit in this concept is the primacy of the functional unity of the organism as a whole and not merely the sum of the function of its parts. This definition is also univocal and can be applied to all forms of living organisms.

15 Both human genetic identity and active potential and capacity (an inherent disposition for development) define a unique human being. While somatic cells have genetic identity to human beings (they have a latent potency and capacity such as exists in all raw materials), they do not possess an inherent active biological disposition (active potency and capacity) for further development into a unique human being. Somatic cell nuclear transfer (cloning) artificially confers such an active potency and capacity on a cell with genetic identity resulting in a unique human being.

16 Hydatiform moles (the result of abnormal fusions between egg and sperm) and teratomas (arising from the abnormal parthenogenic division of germ cells) lack ordered growth and development.

17 For the historical data on embryology, cf. Bradley M. Patten, Human Embryology, New York, 1953, pp.1-5.

18 There seemed to be no scientific reason for distinguishing between the male and female as far as hominization is concerned, and no scientific reason for choosing precisely the 40th or 80th day for the hominization of a new individual.

19 Report of 'Conference on Abortion', sponsored by the Harvard Divinity School and the Joseph P. Kennedy Jr., Foundation, September 6-7, 1967, p.39.

20 Paul Ramsey, "The Morality of Abortion," in Life or Death: The Ethics and Options, Seattle, 1968, p.69.

21 Helmut Thielicke , The Ethics of Sex, New York, 1964, pp226-227.

22 Rudolph Joseph Gerber, "When is the Human Soul Infused?", Laval theologique et philosophique, 22 (1966) 234- 247, p.247. See also, Vincent C. Punzo, Reflective Naturalism, New York, 1969, pp.218-222.

23 Rudolph Joseph Gerber, "When is the Human Soul Infused?", Laval theologique et philosophique, 22 (1966) 234- 247, p.242

24 Lars Wilhelmsson, Abortion Eclipse of Morality, seen at www.vitalchristianity.org/docs/abortion, p.13.

25 See John Jefferson Davis, Abortion and the Christian , p.14; seen at http://www.abortionfacts.com/books/abortion-and-the-christian

26 See M. Condic, When Does Human Life Begin? A Scientific Perspective, (Thornwood, NY: Westchester Institute, 2008).

27 Rather than, being extra-embryonic tissues as Ford believed, zona pellucida is an essential organ of the zygote, normally functioning to maintain the embryo's unity and unicity, preserving its characteristic cleavage pattern, protecting it during its 'journey to the womb' and preventing fusions with other zygotes. Thus, biologists such as Moore (upon whom Ford normally relies) are convinced that the zona and the placenta are organs of the developing organism.

28 See, M. Condic, When Does Human Life Begin? A Scientific Perspective, (Thornwood, NY: Westchester Institute, 2008).

29 See, M. Condic, When Does Human Life Begin? A Scientific Perspective, (Thornwood, NY: Westchester Institute, 2008).

30-31 Lars Wilhelmsson, Abortion Eclipse of Morality, p. seen at www.vitalchristianity.org/docs/abortion,p.14.

32 R. Houwink, Data: Mirrors of Science, Elsevier Pub. Com. (1970), pp. 104-90, cited by Heffernan, "Early Biography of Everyman,"in Abortion and Social Justice, 1974, p.4. student for life. Org.

33 Norman M. Ford, 'When Did I begin?'Conception of human individual in history, philosophy and science', Camebridge University Press, 1988, pp.102-8, 119, 211-212.

34 See, Part II, 3, C; 'Unborn' is not Part of Mother's Body.

35 John Jefferson Davis, Abortion and the Christian , p.15; seen at http://www.abortionfacts.com/books/abortion-and-the-christian

36 John Jefferson Davis, Abortion and the Christian , p.15; seen at http://www.abortionfacts.com/books/abortion-and-the-christian

37 Hippocrates, 400 B.C., Greece.

38 Moore & Persaud, The Developing Human, p.310; L.Nilsson & L.Hamberger, A Child is Born, 2003, p.86; R. Rugh & L.B. Shettles, From Conception to Birth, 1973, p.217.

39 HBVS Person, The Image of God (imago Dei) How We View Ourselves,p. seen at http://www.vitalchristianity.org/docs/Image, p.9.

40 Geraldine Lux Flanagan, Beginning Life. New York: DK, 1996. pp. 14, 23.

41 Alexander Tsiaras and Barry Werth, From Conception to Birth, (New York: Doubleday, 2002), p.58.

42 John Jefferson Davis, Abortion and the Christian , p.15; seen at http://www.abortionfacts.com/books/abortion-and-the-christian.

43 Anjana Ahuja, "Lewis Wolport gives the miracle of life the hard cell," The Sunday Times (UK), March 28, 2009, par. 1.

44 Barry Werth, From Conception to Birth. New York, NY: Doubleday, 2002. p7.

45 John Jefferson Davis, Abortion and the Christian , p.15; seen at http://www.abortionfacts.com/books/abortion-and-the-christian.

46 John Jefferson Davis, Abortion and the Christian , p.16; seen at http://www.abortionfacts.com/books/abortion-and-the-christian.

47 Lars Wilhelmsson, Abortion Eclipse of Morality, p. seen at www.vitalchristianity.org/docs/abortion, p.14.

48 Geraldine Lux Flanagan, Beginning Life. New York: DK, 1996. p. 37.

49 Lars Wilhelmsson, Abortion Eclipse of Morality, seen at www.vitalchristianity.org/docs/abortion, p.14. This book has helped me a lot in writing this part.

50 Norman Geisler, "The Natural Right," In Search of a National Morality (Grand Rapids: Baker Book House, 1992), p.120.

51 Lennart Nilsson and Lars Hamberger, A Child is Born, 4th edition. New York: Bantum Dell, 2003. p.98.

52 John Jefferson Davis, Abortion and the Christian, p.16; seen at http://www.abortionfacts.com/books/abortion-and-the-christian.

53 John Jefferson Davis, Abortion and the Christian , p.16; seen at http://www.abortionfacts.com/books/abortion-and-the-christian.

54 Lennart Nilsson and Lars Hamberger, A Child is Born, (New York: Bantam Dell, 2003), p.101.

55 See, The Biology of Prenatal Develpment, National Geographic, 2006.

56 John Jefferson Davis, Abortion and the Christian, p.16; seen at http://www.abortionfacts.com/books/abortion-and-the-christian

57 Geraldine Lux Flanagan, Beginning Life. New York: DK, 1996. pp. 55, 56.

58 Norman Geisler, "The Natural Right," In Search of a National Morality (Grand Rapids: Baker Book House, 1992), p. 120.

59 This Latin term is used in medicine to refer to the unborn child from approximately eight weeks until birth. Since it has tended to depersonalize the unborn in the abortion debate, many prefer to use the terminology "unborn child," which more accurately communicates the real genetic and physiological continuity of prenatal and postnatal human life.

60 Alexander Tsiaras, From Conception to Birth. New York, NY: Doubleday, 2002. p. 183.

61 Geraldine Lux Flanagan, Beginning Life. New York: DK, 1996. p. 59.

62 John Jefferson Davis, Abortion and the Christian , p.16; seen at http://www.abortionfacts.com/books/abortion-and-the-christian.

63 See, In the Womb, National Geographic, 2005.

64 John Jefferson Davis, Abortion and the Christian, p.16; seen at http://www.abortionfacts.com/books/abortion-and-the-christian.

65 John Jefferson Davis, Abortion and the Christian, p.16; seen at http://www.abortionfacts.com/books/abortion-and-the-christian.

66 Cited by Bart T. Heffernan, "Early Biography of Everyman," p.15. See also C. Everett Koop, "The Other Human Rights Issue", Eternity, October, 1978, p.40.

67 See, In the Womb, National Geographic, 2005.

68 Norman Geisler, "The Natural Right," In Search of a National Morality (Grand Rapids: Baker Book House, 1992), 120.

69 John Jefferson Davis, Abortion and the Christian, p.16; seen at http://www.abortionfacts.com/books/abortion-and-the-christian.

70 John Jefferson Davis, Abortion and the Christian, p.16; seen at http://www.abortionfacts.com/books/abortion-and-the-christian.

71 Cited by Heffernan, "Early Biography of Everyman," p.15.

72 Lars Wilhelmsson, Abortion Eclipse of Morality, seen at www.vitalchristianity.org/docs/abortion, p.15.

73 John Jefferson Davis, Abortion and the Christian , p.17; seen at http://www.abortionfacts.com/books/abortion-and-the-christian.

74 Norman Geisler, "The Natural Right," In Search of a National Morality (Grand Rapids: Baker Book House, 1992), p.120.

75 John Jefferson Davis, Abortion and the Christian , p.17; seen at http://www.abortionfacts.com/books/abortion-and-the-christian.

76 John Jefferson Davis, Abortion and the Christian , p.17; seen at http://www.abortionfacts.com/books/abortion-and-the-christian.

77 Lennart Nilsson and Lars Hamberger, A Child is Born, 4th edition. New York: Bantum Dell, 2003. p.122.

78 Cited by Heffernan, "Early Biography of Everyman," p.17.

79 John Jefferson Davis, Abortion and the Christian, p.17; seen at http://www.abortionfacts.com/books/abortion-and-the-christian.

80 Norman Geisler, "The Natural Right," In Search of a National Morality (Grand Rapids: Baker Book House, 1992), 120.

81 Norman Geisler, "The Natural Right," In Search of a National Morality (Grand Rapids: Baker Book House, 1992), 120.

82 John Jefferson Davis, Abortion and the Christian, p.17; seen at http://www.abortionfacts.com/books/abortion-and-the-christian.

83 Norman Geisler, "The Natural Right," In Search of a National Morality (Grand Rapids: Baker Book House, 1992), 120.

84 Norman Geisler, "The Natural Right," In Search of a National Morality (Grand Rapids: Baker Book House, 1992), 120.

85 See, in the Womb, National Geographic, 2005.

86 John Jefferson Davis, Abortion and the Christian, p.17; seen at http://www.abortionfacts.com/books/abortion-and-the-christian

87 Heart Development at the Loyola University Chicago website.

88 "Life Before Birth" Life Magazine Educational Reprint 27, April 30, 1965, page 6 and Week 4 at the Loyola University Chicago website.

89 Brain development slideshow at Temple University.

90 Lars Wilhelmsson, Abortion Eclipse of Morality, seen at www.vitalchristianity.org/docs/abortion, p.15.

91 See, In the Womb: Multiples, National Geographic, 2005.

92 Lennart Nilsson and Lars Hamberger, A Child is Born, 4th edition. New York: Bantum Dell, 2003. p.141.

93 Geraldine Lux Flanagan, Beginning Life. New York: DK, 1996. p.9.

94 Bernard N. Nathanson, The Hand of God (Washington, DC: Regnery Publishing, 1996, 130.

95 Geraldine Lux Flanagan, Beginning Life. New York: DK, 1996. p.62.

96 Lars Wilhelmsson, Abortion Eclipse of Morality, p. seen at www.vitalchristianity.org/docs/abortion, p.15.

97 Lennart Nilsson and Lars Hamberger, A Child is Born, 4th edition. New York: Bantum Dell, 2003. p.146.

98 See, In the Womb: Multiples, National Geographic, 2005.

99 One can see the photo at http://www.michaelclancy.com/

100 See, In the Womb: Multiples, National Geographic, 2005

101 L. Nilsson, "Drama of Life Before Birth," Life, 1965, p.127.

102 L. Nilsson, "Drama of Life Before Birth," Life, p.127.

103 Nilsson, "Drama of Life Before Birth," Life, 127.

104 Smith, When Choice Becomes God, 129.

105 Smith, When Choice Becomes God, 129.

106 L. Nilsson, "Drama of Life Before Birth," Life, 127.

107 Any way it is consoling to hear that The Department of Health has reportedly issued a ban on the practice, prohibiting the hospitals from exploiting the bodies of babies victimized by abortion any further.

108 Smith, When Choice Becomes God, 129.

109 L. Nilsson, "Drama of Life Before Birth," Life (April 30, 1965) cited in F. LaGard Smith, 127.

110 See, Paul E. Rockwell, "Month 2" When You Were Formed in Secret by Gary Bergel, 1980.

111 Lennart Nilsson, "Drama of Life Before Birth," Life (April 30, 1965) cited in F. LaGard Smith, 127.

112 Lars Wilhelmsson, Abortion Eclipse of Morality, p. 16 seen at www.vitalchristianity.org/docs/abortion. See also, John Jefferson Davis, Abortion and the Christian , p.14; seen at http://www.abortionfacts.com/books/abortion-and-the-christian.

113 John Jefferson Davis, Abortion and the Christian , p.14; seen at http://www.abortionfacts.com/books/abortion-and-the-christian.

114 Dr. Benjamin Kalish, abortionist Abortion Providers Quotes on Whether Abortion is Killing from www.clinicquotes.com.

115 David Boonin, A Defense of Abortion, U.K. 2003, p.xiv.

116 Peter Singer, Practical Ethics, Cambridge, Uni. Press, 1979, pp.85-86. 102.

117 See, Alexandra Desanctis, National Review, January 23, 2017: Justice Harry Blackmun invented the 'trimester' framework and admitted that it was arbitrary.

118 Micheline Matthews-Roth, Harvard University Medical School; "When a human sperm fertilizes a human egg, the result is a human being – from the moment of conception. The killing of this living human being must be considered homicide." JohnPowel, Abortion; The Silent Holocaust (Allen, TX: Argus Communications, 1981), p.74.

119 See, John Powell, Abortion: The Silent Holocaust (Allen, Texas: Argus Communications, 1981), pp.68, 69

120 Carlson, M. Patten's Foundations of Embryology. 6th edition. New York: McGraw-Hill, 1996, p.3.

121 Geraldine Lux Flanagan, Beginning Life. New York: DK, 1996. p.13.

122 Moore, Keith L. Essentials of Human Embryology. Toronto: B.C. Decker Inc, 1988, p.2.

123 Moore Keith L. & T.V. Persaud, "Before We Are Born: Essentials of Embryology and Birth Defects." 4th edition, W.B. Saunders Company, (1993), Page 1.

124 Keith L. Moore in The Developing Human: Clinically Oriented Embryology, 7th edition. Philadelphia, PA: Saunders, 2003. pp.16, 2.

125 Sadler, T.W. Langman's Medical Embryology. 7th edition. Baltimore: Williams & Wilkins 1995, p.3; see also, Sadler T.W, Langman's Medical Embryology, 10th edition. Philadelphia, PA: Lippincott Williams & Wilkins, 2006. p.11.

126 Dianne N. Irving, "When Do Human Beings Begin? 'Scientific' Myths and Scientific Facts," Libertarians for Life, (1999), at: http://www.l4l.org/

127 Dox, Ida G. et al. The Harper Collins Illustrated Medical Dictionary. New York: Harper Perennial, 1993, p.146.

128 England, Marjorie A. Life Before Birth. 2nd ed. England: Mosby-Wolfe, 1996, p.31.

129 Larsen, William J. Human Embryology. 2nd edition. New York: Churchill Livingstone, 1997, p17.

130 Floare Farcas, 'Life Begins at Conception', "The Peak", Simon Fraser University, (1996) at http://www.peak.sfu.ca/

131 Jon E. Dougherty, "Life Begins at Conception," Catholic Educator's Resource Center, (2001) at www.catholiceducation.org

132 O'Rahilly, Ronan and Müller, Fabiola, Human Embryology & Teratology. 2nd edition. New York: Wiley-Liss, 1996, pp. 8, 29. This textbook lists "pre-embryo" among "discarded and replaced terms" in modern embryology, describing it as "ill-defined and inaccurate" (p. 12)., See also the third edition of the same, 2001, p.8.

133 Dr. John Eppig, Senior Staff Scientist, Jackson Laboratory (Bar Harbor, Maine) and Member of the NIH Human Embryo Research Panel – Panel Transcript, February 2, 1994, p. 31.

134 Jonathan Van Blerkom of University of Colorado, expert witness on human embryology before the NIH Human Embryo Research Panel – Panel Transcript, February 2, 1994, p. 63.

135 Cloning Human Beings. Report and Recommendations of the National Bioethics Advisory Commission. Rockville, MD: GPO, 1997, Appendix-2.

136 Considine, Douglas (ed.). Van Nostrand's Scientific Encyclopedia. 5th edition. New York: Van Nostrand Reinhold Company, 1976, p. 943.

137 Walters, William and Singer, Peter (eds.). Test-Tube Babies. Melbourne: Oxford University Press, 1982, p.160.

138 Silver, Lee M. Remaking Eden: Cloning and Beyond in a Brave New World. New York: Avon Books, 1997, p.39.

139 Clark Edward Corliss, Patten's Human Embryology: Elements of Clinical Development. New York: McGraw Hill, 1976. p30.

140 J.P. Greenhill and E.A. Friedman, Biological Principles and Modern Practice of Obstetrics. Philadelphia: W.B. Saunders, 1974. pp. 17, 23.

141 Moore, K. and T.V.N. Persaud. The Developing Human: Clinically Oriented Embryology (4th ed.), W.B. Saunders Company, Philadelphia, 1998, pp2-18.

142 Larsen, W.J. Essentials of Human Embryology, Churchill Livingstone, New York. 1998, pp. 1-17.

143 O'Rahilly, R. and F. Muller, Human Embryology & Teratology, Wiley-Liss, New York . 1996, pp. 5-55, p.55

144 Keith L. Moore, The Developing Human: Clinically Oriented Embryology, 7th edition. Philadelphia, PA: Saunders, 2003. pp.16, 2.

145 Keith L. Moore, Before We Are Born: Essentials of Embryology, 7th edition. Philadelphia, PA: Saunders, 2008. p. 2.

146 E.L. Potter and J.M. Craig, Pathology of the Foetus and the Infant, 3rd edition. Chicago: Year Book Medical Publishers, 1975. p. vii.

147 These were experts such as Dr. Eugene Diamond, a medical school professor, Dr Jerome LeJeune, professor of fundamental genetics at the University of Descarte, Paris, France, Dr Micheline Matthews-Roths, principal research associate of the Harvard University Medical School: Professor Hymie Gordon, chairman of the Department of Medical Genetics at the

Mayo Clinic, Dr McCarthy DeMere, lawyer and practising physician, and law professor at the University of Tennessee, Dr Alfred Bogiovanni, formerly chairman of paediatrics at the University of life in Nigeria and a member of the University of Pennsylvania Medical School faculty, Dr Jasper Williams,of the Williams Clinic and Dr. Watson A. Bowes, Jr., of the University of Colorado Medical School.

148 See, John Powell, Abortion: The Silent Holocaust (Allen, Texas: Argus Communications, 1981), 70.

149 See, Jerome Lejeune, M.D., Ph.D. The Concentration Can , Ignatius Press, (1992).

150 Quoted by Jason M. Steffens, in 'The Peculiar Being: The Rights of an Unborn Child in Iowa,' 88 IOWA L. REV. 217 (1988). Online at: http://www.june24.net/

151 See, John Powell, Abortion: The Silent Holocaust (Allen, Texas: Argus Communications, 1981), pp. 70,71

152 See, John Powell, Abortion: The Silent Holocaust (Allen, Texas: Argus Communications, 1981), p.71.

153 C. Christopher Hook, Oncologist, Mayo Clinic, Director of Ethics Education, Mayo Graduate School of Medicine

154 See, John Powell, Abortion: The Silent Holocaust (Allen, Texas: Argus Communications, 1981), 72.

155 See, John Powell, Abortion: The Silent Holocaust (Allen, Texas: Argus Communications, 1981), 72.

156 See, John Powell, Abortion: The Silent Holocaust (Allen, Texas: Argus Communications, 1981), 74.

157 See, John Powell, Abortion: The Silent Holocaust (Allen, Texas: Argus Communications, 1981), 74.

158 See, George F. Will, "The Case of the Unborn Patient," The Washington Post, 92.

159 See, George F. Will, "The Case of the Unborn Patient," The Washington Post, 92.

160 C. Everett Koop, "The Right to Live," The Zero People, ed. by Jeff Lane Hensley (Ann Arbor: Servant Books, 1983), p.59.

161 John Jefferson Davis, Abortion and the Christian, p.14; seen at http://www.abortionfacts.com/books/abortion-and-the-christian.

162 H.M. Liley, Modern Motherhood, cited by Heffernan, "Early Biography of Everyman," (1969), p.18; see also "Foetus in Control", by he same author, pp.27-36. John Jefferson Davis, Abortion and the Christian, p.17; seen at http://www.abortionfacts.com/books/abortion-and-the-christian.

163 John Jefferson Davis, Abortion and the Christian , p.15; seen at http://www.abortionfacts.com/books/abortion-and-the-christian.

164 Rather than, being extra-embryonic tissues as Ford believed, zona pellucida is an essential organ of the zygote, normally functioning to maintain the embryo's unity and unicity, preserving its characteristic cleavage pattern, protecting it during its 'journey to the womb' and preventing fusions with other zygotes. Thus, biologists such as Moore (upon whom Ford normally relies) are convinced that the zona and the placenta are organs of the developing organism.

165 Alexander Tsiaras and Barry Werth, From Conception to Birth, (New York: Doubleday, 2002), p.58.

166 John Jefferson Davis, Abortion and the Christian , p.15; seen at http://www.abortionfacts.com/books/abortion-and-the-christian.

167 The active nature of the unborn child is detailed in Liley, "Foetus in Control." pp. 27-36.

168 See, In the Womb, National Geographic, 2005.

169 Lars Wilhelmsson, Abortion Eclipse of Morality, p.14, seen at www.vitalchristianity.org/docs/abortion.

170 John Jefferson Davis, Abortion and the Christian , p.17; seen at http://www.abortionfacts.com/books/abortion-and-the-christian.

171 See, John Powell, Abortion: The Silent Holocaust (Allen, Texas: Argus Communications, 1981),72.

172 A.Gesell, The Embryology of Behavior, cited by Heffernan, "Early Biography of Everyman," (1945), pp. 17, 18

173 Lars Wilhelmsson, Abortion Eclipse of Morality, p.16, seen at www.vitalchristianity.org/docs/abortion

174 And if you want to really learn, about this pick up the excellent book entitled Embryo, by Dr. Robert George.

175 Robert P. George and Christopher Tollefsen EMBRYO: A Defense of Human Life., Doubleday, 2008

176 Greg Koukl, "Are Humans Persons?" Accessed June 3, 2009; Available from www.str.org/site/News2?page=NewsArticle&id=5117

177 Robert George and Christopher Tollefsen, Embryo: A Defense of Human Life (New York: Doubleday Broadway Publishing Group, 2008), 58. It is recommended to consult any of the standard human-embryology texts, such as Moore and Persaud's 'The Developing Human', Larsen's 'Human Embryology', Carlson's 'Human Embryology & Developmental Biology', and O'Rahilly and Mueller's 'Human Embryology & Teratology' and the like.

178 Francis Beckwith, "The Explanatory Power of the Substance View of Persons," Christian Bioethics 10 (2004):pp 33-54.

179 Beckwith, "The Explanatory Power of the Substance View of Persons."

180 See, Eric Versluys, "South Dakota law is clear," The Rocky Mountain Collegian, Colorado State University, 2006-MAR-09, at: http://www.collegian.com/

181 Francis Beckwith, "Is the unborn human less than human?," ChristianAnswers.net, at:http://www.christiananswers.net/

182 Francis Beckwith, "The Explanatory Power of the Substance View of Persons," Christian Bioethics 10 (2004): 33-54.

183 Viability was defined as: "given normal development through the first seven months of intrauterine life, a premature infant is expected to live." Davenport Catholic Messenger, Sept. 25, 1969.

184 See, John Powell, Abortion: The Silent Holocaust (Allen, Texas: Argus Communications, 1981), p.72.

185 Eric Versluys, "South Dakota law is clear," The Rocky Mountain Collegina, 2006-MAR-09, at:http://www.collegian.com/

186 See for example, Andre Hellegers, "Fetal Development," Theological Studies 31 (1970): 3-9; C.R. Austin, "The Egg and Fertilization," Science Journal 6 (1970):37-42; E.C. Amoroso, "Development of the Early Embryo,"Science Journal 6 (1970): 59-64; Bart T. Heffernan, "The Early Biography of Everyman," and Albert W. Liley, "The Foetus in Control of His Environment," in Hilgers and Horan, eds., Abortion and Social Justice (New York: Sheed and Ward, 1972), pp. 3-36.

187 For the information in this section I am indebted to Andre Hellegers, "Fetal Development," Theological Studies 31 (1970): 3-9; C.R. Austin, "The Egg and Fertilization," Science Journal 6 (1970):37-42; E.C. Amoroso, "Development of the Early Embryo," Science Journal 6 (1970): 59-64; Bart T. Heffernan, "The Early Biography of Everyman," and Albert W. Liley, "The Foetus in Control of His Environment," in Hilgers and Horan, eds., Abortion and Social Justice (New York: Sheed and Ward, 1972), pp. 3-36.

188 Dr. Edwin Vieira, Jr., "A False Assumption," Libertarians for Life, (1999) at:http://www.l4l.org/

189 From Catholic Bioethics for New Millennium, Anthony Fischer, Cambridge, 2012, pp.101-130.

PART III
Ethical Reflections on the Personhood of the Unborn

*His life was gentle, and the elements, Somix'd in him
that Nature might standup, And say to all the world,
"This was a man!"*

Shakespeare, c1599

Personhood[1]

Dr. Leon R. Kass, Professor of the Liberal Arts of Human Biology, University of Chicago made a striking observation: "We have paid some high prices for the technological conquest of nature, but none perhaps so high as the intellectual and spiritual costs of seeing nature as mere material for our manipulation, exploitation and transformation. With the powers for biological [genetic] engineering now gathering, there will be splendid new opportunities for a similar degradation in our view of man. Indeed, we are already witnessing the erosion of our idea of man as something splendid or divine, as a creature with freedom and dignity. And clearly, if we come to see ourselves as meat, then meat we shall become."[2]

Ethics and morality refer to the norms by which moral agents live and treat each other.[3] Human personhood is the central issue of ethics, for any theory that purports to explain how man should act towards his fellow man must begin with what man is. The term personhood denotes the idea that human beings are members of a moral community, that they have moral rights and privileges as a result, and that there is an inherent value to this status.[4]

Greek Dualism

"Since the time of Plato, Western society has viewed man in a dualistic way. Greek dualism, not Hebrew unity, has ruled our society's concept of man. For Plato, the body was the prison house of the soul, the unfit bearer of the soul. Thus, Aristotle defined man as a rational animal in which the rational soul was infused in the body at the fortieth day for males and the 80th day for females".[5]

"Such thinking paved the way for Gnosticism. This heresy, bifurcated the world of the mind and the spirit as good and the world of the material and earthly as evil. This means, the physical body is evil since it belongs to the material, the earthly, and it sees the material world ultimately as an illusion. Redemption meant man being set free from the evil body as it will one day be discarded. This dualistic distinction is prevalent in the mindset of the pro-abortion movement. Joseph Fletcher, the father of situation ethics, identifies rationality as the central criterion of personhood and argues that we cannot adequately understand the issue of abortion unless we are able to separate biological life from personhood."[6]

The Judeo-Christian understanding is not that man is a soul or spirit and has a body, but that man is spirit, soul and body or soul and body – animated body. "Biological life is an essential part of a person's being. Even though the soul and the body are not synonymous, there is not the radical separation that Greek thinking purports. The body is an integral part of man rather than an accidental and temporary place of being".[7]

Human Being versus Human Person
If the developing foetus is shown to be a human being there is no need for a specific command against foeticide (abortion) any more than we need something specific against infanticide, uxoricide, genocide or suicide. The general commandment against killing covers all other forms of taking innocent human life. Thus the humanity of the unborn is crucial to the ultimate determination of foeticide. If the unborn child is a human being, then the issue is resolved since a civilised society cannot tolerate the intentional killing of helpless innocent human beings. By shifting to personhood, some argue that the only relevant issue is whether such a child, irrespective of its humanity, is a person and thus has value under the constitution.

What is a 'Person'?
"To get away from the focus on the biological certainty that a foetus is a human life, many have shifted the argument to personhood. Since arguing against humanity is increasingly difficult when it comes to the foetus, they now resort to making a differentiation between person and human being. According to the Hebrew and Christian Scriptures (Old and New Testaments of the Bible), this is purely an arbitrary, artificial distinction".[8]

The word person is not used in the Bible. Latin versions have used the Latin term *persona* to translate Hebrew and Greek words for man, soul, and face. But this is not equivalent as *persona* referred originally to the mask through which an actor spoke his part (*persona*; literally, through-mask). This word changed from being applied merely to the mask to being applied to the actor, then to the character acted to an assumed character, and eventually to anyone having character or status.[9]

Some describe the word person as the individual in functional terms. It describes his expressions and actions, his roles and functions in all these uses. The word person thus came to refer to an individual as he performs in society. "Since this sees the individual in terms of his thinking, feeling, and acting, when any such characteristics are absent, that individual's personhood is questioned".[10]

To make such a distinction, therefore, is artificial and devilish in that it gives an intellectual excuse to set ourselves up as tin gods with the authority and right to get rid of what we deem unworthy, less than useful, less than a fully developed person. "Such technical distinctions open up the Pandora's Box of indiscriminate judgment. Once the unborn is labelled less than a person by such a standard, then the deformed, the disabled, the ill, the elderly have reason to fear for their lives. Life becomes expendable! And this is exactly what has happened and is still happening to our society".[11]

The Bible, as we saw, does not have the equivalent term for person as used in the abortion controversy. Instead the "Bible uses deeper and broader terms such as man and woman, life and soul in referring to individuals made in the image and likeness of God". This false dichotomy between human life and personhood, between sanctity of life and quality of life formed the basis of the *Roe vs Wade* Supreme Court decision.[12] "The perception of personhood became the litmus test in the *Roe vs Wade* Supreme Court decision since they stated that the law did not need to protect those who are not persons in the whole sense. This distinction is the key since in constitutional law, a person is an entity entitled to rights and equal protection under the law".[13]

The Court attempted to redefine man by a quality of life ethic. In so doing she removed that which has always been characteristic of civility: the sanctity of human life. The Court argued that legal personhood and value belong only to those capable of "meaningful life outside the womb."[14] Archibald Cox, former law professor and Watergate prosecutor, justly criticised the Supreme Court following its decision in 1973: "The [Court's] opinion fails even to consider what I would suppose to be the most compelling interest of the state in prohibiting abortion: the interest in maintaining that respect for the paramount sanctity of human life which has always been at the centre of western civilisation."[15]

This utilitarian concept – the quality of life ethic – is very dangerous as it was used by the Nazis as well. Pro-abortion author Beverly Harrison puts it: "The question 'When does human life begin?' Or . . . the more precise moral question 'When shall we predicate full human value to developing foetal life?' has become pivotal to the debate about the morality of abortion for reasons having to do with moral consensus. The moral status of foetal life simply is not the obvious fact that many 'pro-life' proponents contend . . . To conclude that foetal life, admittedly a form of human life, is already full human life does not follow. Because predicating the intrinsic value of human life and opposing killing are the least controversial aspects of the moral debate, the question of the value of foetal life has become the core issue on which everything else appears to hinge."[16] "It is the value of foetal life rather than the intrinsic value of the foetus which has become the core issue of pro-abortion advocates. This has shifted the whole debate".[17]

Thus Harrison ends with the statement: "Reproductive choice for women is requisite to any adequate notion of what constitutes a good society. Transformed social conditions of reproduction are absolutely critical to all women's well-being. No society that coerces women at the level of reproduction may lay claim to moral adequacy."[18] A woman's freedom to kill her unborn baby is a sign of "moral adequacy!"

Criteria for Personhood
"If everything that is genetically *homo sapiens* is not really a person, who or what is? To say that a foetus is living, but not a person is unrealistic since if it is not a person, it must be a plant or an animal or a non-being. If so, what qualifier do we use to determine whether a human being is a person in the full sense of the word? What is the criteria? As can be expected, there are numerous opinions among pro-abortion people as to what these criteria are and how much development is necessary for personhood to be considered as such. What is the *sine qua non*, the essential element, without which there is no legitimate person?"[19] Such criteria usually fall into three groups: the physical, the social and the mental.

The Physical Criteria
"Time is the key element in ascertaining this criterion. Actual personhood – a fully human being – does not come about until a certain stage of physical development is reached. Historically, viability has been the crucial criteria based on the assumption that this is the time that an unborn can survive outside the womb".[20] Since this was the criteria used by the Court in its *Roe vs. Wade* decision, it therefore outlined a three-stage approach: no regulation of abortion needed before the first trimester; some regulation of abortion is allowed after

the first trimester, and more after the second trimester – at which point, the Court said, the foetus is viable and the state's interest in protecting it becomes compelling.

"But there have been babies born prematurely as early as the fourth month of pregnancy who have survived and grown into normal, healthy children. On the other hand, abortions are being performed on perfectly healthy babies much older than that – and they are usually left unattended to suffer and die".[21]

Sandra Day O'Connor, has argued that because of medical advances, the trimester approach is "on a collision course with itself." In the *Roe vs. Wade* decision, it appears that the Court considered the unborn as having only "potential" life until the point of viability: "The difficulty with this analysis is clear: Potential life is no less potential in the first weeks of pregnancy than it is at viability or afterwards . . . The choice of viability as the point at which the state interest in potential life becomes compelling is no less arbitrary than choosing any point before viability or any point afterward. Accordingly, I believe that the States' interest in protecting potential human life exists throughout the pregnancy."[22] She thus questions the choice of viability. Dr. Magda Denes has concluded: "Abortion based on viability is as logical as maintaining that drowning a non-swimmer in a bathtub is permitted because he would have drowned anyway if he would have fallen into the sea."[23]

"Others have argued that personhood begins when all the organs are present in rudimentary form, sometime between the sixth and eighth weeks of development. Some point to the beginning of blood circulation and movement of brain waves (5-6 weeks). Others such as Peter Wenz (author of a recent book, *Abortion Rights as Religious Freedom*, 1992) view personhood at the eighth month because it is at this time that the unborn is most like the newborn. Still others, increasingly the majority of pro-abortion advocates, see full personhood only occurring at birth when the unborn is born, when he takes his first breath. This is why abortions are routinely performed up to the very point of birth".[24]

The health of the person is another physical criterion used. This means 46 chromosomes must be present in each cell and they must develop normally to be acknowledged as fully a person. Ethicist James Gustafson of the University of Chicago puts it: "Respect for life does not necessarily indicate the preservation of human physical life at the cost of unbearable pain to individuals, and even to families around them."[25] Thus, birth defects may very well make it virtually impossible for an organism to live "a meaningful life." In fact, the most outlandish repercussion of such a theory of criteria for personhood is illustrated by none other than Francis Crick, the Nobel Prize winning biologist who discovered DNA. He daringly argues that children need to be at least two days old before we should legally declare them as persons. Only by such time will we be able to determine medically whether they are healthy.[26]

"Eugenics – the belief that true humanity and good health are identical – seems to be the underlying principle at work in such suggestions. This smacks of Aryanism and its Super Race as it expresses a yearning for a perfect world in which only perfect people (usually Anglo-Saxons) who are free from any physical deformities and genetic diseases are allowed to live".[27]

The Social Criteria
"Social criteria are also used in judging personhood. Interaction with other people on a non-biological level is necessary for a human life to be a person. Therefore, capacities such as love, self-consciousness, and the ability to communicate and relate with others are crucial".[28]

"This opens up the way to all kinds of exceptions to personhood. Certainly newborn children as well as severely ill and disabled people cannot relate in a meaningful way".[29] Ashley Montague, a British anthropologist, argues that a baby does not become fully human until he is "moulded by social and cultural influences."[30] This means that college graduates are more human than kindergartners. He sees man's cultural accomplishments as that which sets him apart from the animal world.

A leading geneticist, Joshua Lederberg, believes that an infant's intellectual development is the most important criteria. Thus, the acquisition of language and the ability to participate in "a meaningful, cognitive interaction with his mother and with the rest of society" is what sets him apart from the rest of creation.[31]

"Michael Tooley, a philosopher, argues that personhood is legitimatised only when a human being is consciously aware of his "continuing existence" and is free to "desire its continuance." Therefore, as he puts it, 'a newborn baby does not possess the concept of a continuing self, any more than a newborn kitten possesses such a concept."[32]

Thus, infanticide is morally permissible. Tooley holds that some animals qualify for personhood whereas infants do not. He argues that animals such as cats, dogs, and polar bears may possess properties that endow them with the consciousness of a continuing self and to dispose of them may be equivalent to "murdering innocent persons."[33] Therefore, to kill certain animals is "morally indefensible" while killing infants is morally defensible.

The Mental Criteria
"Of the three criteria of physical, social and mental ability, mental ability is the most popular criteria by which personhood is judged. Scholars commonly hold that it is the intellectual prowess of human beings that make them superior to the rest of the animal kingdom. Therefore, the individual who fails to demonstrate some degree of reason, self-awareness, and volition is not really a person".[34] Rudolp Ehrensing sees the commencement of brain activity to be the first sign of personhood since death is now defined as the cessation of brain activity.[35] Roy Schenk, another scholar, reasons that the foetus becomes an actual person when the cerebral cortex is developed to a level of self-awareness (about the sixth month).[36]

A Combination of Criteria
Probably the most popular view is that personhood is made up of human beings who possess a combination of characteristics. Mary Anne Warren, professor at Sonoma State College in California, gives five criteria:

1. Consciousness – of objects and events external and/or internal to the being, and specifically the capacity to feel pain.

2. Reasoning – the developed capacity to solve new and relatively complex problems.

3. Self-motivation – activity which is relatively independent of either genetic or direct external control.

4. Communication – the capacity to communicate by whatever means, messages of an indefinite number of possible contents, but on indefinitely many possible topics.

5. Self-Concepts and Self-Awareness – the presence of self-concepts and self-awareness either individually or racially, or both.[37]

Warren backpedals as she calls her list "very rough" and admits the difficulty of construing such a list: "there are apt to be a great many problems involved in formulating precise definitions of these criteria."

Then she adds three more qualifications:

1. Not all five criteria are needed. Perhaps one or two alone may be sufficient.

2. We should not insist that any one of these criteria are "necessary" for personhood, although the first three are the most important".[38]

Then she strangely adds the third criteria which contradicts her previous criteria (no.2):

3. Any individual who does not satisfy any of the five criteria is certainly not a person.[39] While admitting the difficulty of "formulating precise definitions of these criteria" she still has the audacity to decide who lives and who dies by her faulty understanding of what it means to be a person.[40]

Arbitrariness marks all such arguments. Is it any wonder that pro-abortionist Garrett Hardin stated: "People who worry about the moral danger of abortion do so because they think of the foetus as a human being and hence equate foeticide with murder? Whether the foetus is or is not a human being is a matter of definition, not fact, and we can define any way we wish."[41] According to Hardin any definition of what a foetus is will do![42]

The pro-abortionist forces say that we all should be properly humble and admit that the matter of when human life begins is a mystery beyond our poor power of comprehension. Still they pontificate that "birth" is the indicator that a foetus is a person?[43]

Milestones in the Development of Personhood

When bio-ethicists struggle to answer the question of what it means to be human, they are not trying to determine what constitutes human life. They attempt to answer the question of personhood, or when a human life attains moral standing. Philosophers and ethicists have proposed a number of thresholds for determining when a human being becomes a person. The different views of personhood can be enumerated as genetic, embryological, neurological, technological and ecological, physiological, post modern and pastoral.

The Genetic View

The genetic view of personhood believes that a human being is always a human person, thus personhood comes at conception.

The Embryological View

The next milestone for moral standing comes 14 days after fertilisation, when the process of gastrulation begins. Bioethicists call the perspective that personhood begins when the process of gastrulation commences the embryological view of personhood. Gastrulation is the process when the three germ layers of the body form (cells differentiate into three categories) and establish the basic body plan. In humans, gastrulation occurs after the embryo implants into the uterine wall of the mother. The mark of this stage is the appearance in the embryo of the primitive streak, a precursor of the spinal column. Before gastrulation, an embryo can split and become identical twins. After gastrulation, an embryo is an ontological individual and can no longer form more than one human being. Regulations in many countries, including Great Britain, treat 14 days after fertilisation as the limit for conducting scientific research on embryos.

Those who reject gastrulation as the important milestone for defining personhood argue that twinning does not alter moral standing: one human life has simply become two human lives. Since at least one human life may begin after fertilisation, fertilisation is the important milestone in determining personhood, not gastrulation.[44]

Soon after gastrulation is complete, specialised cells such as blood cells form and the embryonic heart starts beating around 21 days after fertilisation. So some people feel that the appearance of blood in the embryo marks the attainment of personhood. These people use the teaching in the Bible that "the life of a creature is in the blood" (Leviticus 17:11) to define the point at which research on developing embryos becomes unacceptable.

The Neurological View

Another view on personhood is the neurological view. Doctors define brain death as the loss of the pattern produced by a cerebral electroencephalogram (EEG). Those who hold to this argument reason that if we base life and death on the same standard of measurement, then personhood starts when a foetus acquires a recognisable EEG pattern, which occurs about 24 to 27 weeks after fertilisation.

The argument against this view of personhood, however, is that the lack of brain activity at the end of human life is not the same as the lack of brain activity at the beginning of human life. The brain dead individual has permanently lost the ability to function as a human being, with no hope of reviving brain waves. Although an embryo may not have reached the stage in development at which we can detect brainwaves (which might be possible at later time with more advanced technology), a healthy developing human embryo possesses the inherent capacity to have these brain waves at some point in the future.

The lack of brain waves in a healthy human embryo is only a temporary condition. Most important, the developing embryo is able to integrate his or her basic life functions as an organism, which the brain dead individual can no longer do.[45] We cannot write-off the possibility of developing an EEG which may be able to measure pattern at an earlier stage of development. This will amount to saying that the point at which a foetus becomes a person changes as technology improves.

The Technological and Ecological Views

Scientists base the technological view of personhood on when the developing foetus becomes viable (able to live outside the mother's womb). The most important factor in whether or not a foetus is viable is not neurological development, but maturation of the lungs. Advances in medical science make it possible for a premature baby to breathe after only 25 weeks of gestation, prior to when functioning lungs have fully developed.

People sometimes base laws related to when a person can legally abort a foetus on this view of human personhood. But advances in medical technology have moved the point of foetal viability to earlier points in gestation, thus the point at which a foetus becomes a person changes as technology improves. Real biological limitations on when breathing is possible exist, however, regardless of technological advances. For this reason, we can also call using viability to determine personhood an ecological view of personhood, since personhood rests with the ability of the developing human being to exist apart from biological environment of the mother.

The Physiological View

The physiological view of personhood argues that personhood commences at birth, when the baby has his own functioning circulatory, respiratory, and alimentary system independent of the mother. The traditional Jewish view confers personhood during childbirth, when the head emerges from the birth canal.

The Post-modern View
Another way to view personhood is in relation to the functions of the neo-cortex of the brain: rationality, self-awareness, and relationship with others. Many consider this approach to defining personhood as the post-modern view. This view considers the essential functional capacities that set humans apart from other animals. Yet, humans do not fully develop these capabilities until sometime after birth, during toddler-hood.

When considering the criteria for personhood, we would do well to ponder if we should reduce personhood to a set of capacities or a biological marker. Should moral significance come from who we are or from the functional capabilities we express at a given moment of our existence? From a Biblical viewpoint, does the image of God refer to an intrinsic value that human beings possess or to an extrinsic value measurable by medical science and capable of being lost due to damage of the physical body? Is the natural inherent capacity for self-awareness and a free will sufficient to make us persons, even if disability or disease limits the expression of these functions?

Peter Wenz argues that in the eighth month (or at least in the twentieth week) foetuses qualify for life because they are more functional. He understandably uses different times in determining functionality in his book *Abortion Rights as Religious Freedom* and thus illustrates the impossible effort in determining when a foetus becomes a person if not at conception. Wenz then points out the dilemma of deciding when a foetus becomes a person and concludes that this is a religious question since people logically punch and counterpunch without any agreement. This is unwarranted since the abortion debate is clearly a biological/medical issue as a foetus is a biological creature that has the essential stuff of which human beings are made: DNA. To consign this to religion is a clever way to circumvent the issue at hand and relegate it to the sacred doctrine of privacy which guarantees each mother the decision to determine who lives and who dies.

A Pastoral Perspective: New Human Being at Conception: Not a Matter of Taste/Opinion
Finally, from a pastoral perspective, the use of the concept of personhood to exclude people rather than include people should raise red flags of caution for us. Are we separating human persons from human beings to limit our moral

responsibility as a society? In Luke 10:29, an expert in the Law asked Jesus, "Who is my neighbour?" in an effort to justify himself as having fulfilled his duty to love his neighbour as himself. He was hoping the Lord would provide him with a definition of neighbour that would limit his moral responsibility to his fellowman. Instead, Jesus told the Parable of the Good Samaritan, broadening the moral responsibility required of the expert in the Law. Perhaps, in keeping with the message of this parable, we need to be wary of a too narrow definition in answer to the question, "Who is a person?"

As we said in the beginning, there is no debate as regards to the question, "are the unborn embryos and foetuses human beings?" It is a matter of plain objective science. Our question is, "whether humans be recognised as persons under the law? Yes, because humans are persons. Something is a person if it has a personal nature"[46]. Just as a cat qualifies as a feline simply by being a cat, a foetus qualifies as a person simply by being a human.[47]

So, it is impossible for a foetus to not be a person. The situation we are left with is quite different. There is a huge and singular group of living human beings who have no protection under the law and are being killed *en masse* every day. Is that not astounding?! It is astounding, but not wholly unprecedented.

Norman Geisler logically reasons:
"If we define the humanity of the unborn in terms of its age (so many months in the womb), then why not exclude others from human society, such as the elderly, because of their age?

If humanness is defined in terms of abnormal size, then why not exclude, dwarfs, basketball centres, or the obese from the human community? Each of us began as a tiny one-cell organism.

If humanness is defined in terms of location (life outside the womb), then why can't we discriminate against sections of society by their location (on the wrong side of the tracks)? Geography does not determine humanity; passing through a birth canal does not change one's human status.

If we define humanness in terms of genetic purity (for example, excluding those with Down's syndrome), then other minorities with genetic deformities (like sickle-cell anemia) can be declared non-human.

If humanness is defined in terms of viability, then we must consider severely injured persons, the infirm, and any who can't defend themselves not to be human.

If humanness is defined in terms of consciousness, then drunks, sleepers, drug users, and even some transcendental meditators are non-human.

If humanness is defined in terms of the function of self-consciousness, then any child up to 18 months old is a candidate for infanticide.

If personhood is defined in terms of the ability to think rationally, then we will have excluded all young children, those under great emotional distress, and even some in mystical states of consciousness.

If humanness includes only those who can make moral choices, then young children, the insane, and moral reprobates are not human either.

If we exclude all human beings who are unwanted, then any undesired segment of society, such as AIDS victims, child abusers, or derelicts, can be disposed of as non-human."[48]

It is fallacious to view human beings on the basis of functions. Because to define living beings functionally rather than essentially is to reduce them to the sum total of their parts which brings all human beings to the bar of human evaluation as certain human beings (e.g. adults) stand in judgment of other human beings. In such a case who qualifies to play such a God-like role? The scientific/medical community? The legal community? The governmental/political community? The philosophical community? The theological/religious community? And who determines who qualifies? And who determines who is qualified to determine who is qualified, etc.?

John Jefferson Davis writes: "Man, as *imago Dei*, possessing inalienable dignity and worth, is to be understood not primarily in terms of innate capacities of faculties—whether intellectual, moral, or spiritual—but in terms of his unique relationship to his transcendent Creator and covenant Lord. It is not intrinsic powers of speech, imagination, and rational thought that lend transcendent worth to human nature, but man's unique calling to live in loving fellowship with the triune God for all eternity. Thus there is no place for . . . such criteria as self-awareness, memory, a sense of futurity and time, and a certain minimum IQ,"[49] as Joseph Fletcher has suggested.

To sum up we will say, a new human being has come into being after fertilisation has taken place. It is no longer a matter of taste or opinion...it is plain experimental evidence. Each individual has a very neat beginning, at conception. In spite of all these, some consider accepting personhood from conception may lead to a lot of absurdities.

Absurdities

According to writers like Peter Wenz, accepting personhood from conception can lead to many conceptual conflicts. He calls them absurdities. In his book *Abortion Rights as Religious Freedom,* Wenz argues with the position that a being is a person from the moment it has a human genetic code "entails radical departures from our legal traditions and yield what can only be called absurdities."[50] These absurdities can be logical, practical and legal. Here in this section we shall review the absurdities presented by Peter Wenz in the said book and try to answer them.

The Question of Logic

[50]Glanville Williams argues that the ovum and the sperm were alive in the bodies of the parents before fertilisation took place and "since fertilisation is a process that may take from twenty minutes to over two hours to complete, what we call the "moment of conception" is a myth since it is not a significant point in a person's life."[51] "The argument that life begins with conception is just as un-biological as the old notion that life begins sometime after conception."[52]

"The problem with this argument is that if there is never a point in time when the process is complete, then no one is ever really a person. Yet it seems that pro-abortion advocates view themselves as persons. In fact, they believe they became persons through a process".[53] Therefore, there had to be a point at which time they became a person, or they have always been a person. Or they are not yet persons. Although it is true that growth is a process, a *continuum*, there comes a certain time in the process when what existed formerly, literally ceases to exist and a new conceptus comes into being. This means that there is both a process of fertilisation as well as the point at which that process is completed and a new and unique being begins to exist.[54] To argue that there is no difference between an egg before and after fertilisation flies in the face of scientific inquiry.

Twinning – Individuation is not Indivisibility

To argue against the personhood of the zygote, some take the case of twinning as they ask: Does not twinning show that the human embryo at conception is not an individual human being? The answer to this question depends on one's answer to a related question. Does the lack of the potentiality to give rise to a twin mark the beginning of an individual human life? The answer must be 'no', since any adult human being can in principle be cloned. Cloning is simply an artificial form of twinning which replicates the human genetic code of the donor in order to create a being that is genetically an identical twin. So the individuality of a human being must not arise from the lack of potential to twin.

Twinning does not show that there is no individual human being following conception. Individuation, being an individual, does not require indivisibility.[55] The fact that one being can be divided into two beings does not mean that it was never an individual being. Alfonso Gomez-Lobo provides an example that there is no necessary link between indivisibility and individuality noting that: 'If indivisibility were a necessary condition for individuality, then there would be no material individuals. After all, any material object can be pulled apart or dismantled. No car would be an individual car, but only a collection or package of car parts, likewise no living body would be an individual organism, but only a colony of cells'.[56]

If we cut a flatworm in half and it survives as two flatworms, it does not follow that the flatworm was really two flatworms all along or that the flatworm was never one individual worm. This too shows that the phenomenon of twinning does not undermine the viewing of conception as the beginning of a unique individual human being. That is, individuality does not require indivisibility. It is consistent with the empirical evidence to interpret twinning as form of asexual reproduction in which the original zygote gives rise to another without every falling out of existence.[57] In other words, twinning may be a form of natural cloning or 'budding' in which the original survives giving rise to another human being.

Referring to the possibility of twinning, Peter Wenz asks the following: "First, there is the puzzle about whose human life is deemed to exist from the moment of fertilisation, when a zygote comes into existence with its own human genetic code. The zygote may split within several days to become two (or more) identical zygotes, thus creating monozygotic twins or triplets. Which of these is the 'person' who came into existence at fertilisation? Who are the others? Do they too, have full human rights? If so, does their personhood come into existence not at fertilisation (when there was only one); but at some time (possibly days) later when the zygote splits? How do we know which one became a person at fertilisation and which one(s) attained personhood later? These are all ridiculous questions because they cannot be answered because they cannot be understood. They make no sense within the conceptual scheme available to us. Our normal assumption that full personhood does not begin at fertilisation protects us from such absurdities. Reverse this assumption and we are led to absurd questions. It is a postulate of logic that one should avoid commitments to views that lead to absurdities."[58]

Wenz is correct that his questions are "all ridiculous." Are they ridiculous because "they are based on an illogical presumption? Wenz automatically presumes that only one of these zygotes is a person. Such an assumption leads him to all these other "ridiculous, absurd questions." Wenz correctly points out that it is a postulate of logic that one should avoid commitments to views that lead to absurdities. It was his own assumption, however, that led him to absurd questions. The answer is simple: every one of these zygotes that split creating monozygotic twins or triplets are persons at the point of having their own genotype. How that comes to be is irrelevant. Such knowledge simply is not available to us at this time and has no practical consequences.[59]

Spontaneous Abortion
Abortion may be spontaneous or induced. Spontaneous is called miscarriage. It is usually caused by some abnormality of the developing baby or some other reasons. It usually occurs in the first three months of pregnancy and it seems to be nature's way of preventing abnormal babies from being born. About one pregnancy in seven ends prematurely in this way in a healthy woman. Wenz quotes Joel Feinberg: "Embryologists have estimated that only 58 percent of fertilized ova survive until implantation (seven days after conception) and that the spontaneous abortion rate after that stage is from 10 to 15 percent."[60]

Basing on this fact Wenz argues: "Combined with these facts, the belief that personhood begins at fertilisations yields the conclusion that more than half of all human deaths occur before birth. If these prenatal human lives are to be respected equally with all others, the greatest expenditure of resources in medicine and in medical research should be devoted to saving these lives 'without regard to race, sex, age, health, defect, or condition of dependency.' After all, for every child that suffers from spina bifida, cerebral palsy, or muscular dystrophy, there are thousands who die from a failure to implant on the uterine wall, so medical efforts should be geared primarily to address this problem. If we are successful, we could move from a population where about two percent suffer from relatively minor congenital defects to one where as many as 10 to 20 percent suffer from major defect. When this implication is recognised, how many people really want to attribute personhood from the moment of fertilisation regardless of health or defect."[61]

"The last sentence is telling. The so-called "conceptual" concern is disguised under the thin veil of utilitarian concern. This is due to either ignorance or deception. Since when do we have the right to decide philosophical, moral, and biological (medical) questions based on expediency – ". . . how many people really want to . . ."? What has having resources or the lack of having resources to do with whether a human life with a genetic code is a person or not? What has the percentage of people who suffer from congenital defects have to do with whether that foetus is a human being with rights or not? Absolutely nothing! It is logically absurd to tie either of these issues to the question of personhood".[62]

A being is a person the moment he has a genetic code. To say there is no connection between disregard for the unborn and the born is illogical. "As authority in general came into question *carte blanche*, and precursors of abortion became increasingly evident in the 1960s with the legalisation of abortion-on-demand in 1973, the world has seen the rapid rise of crime".[63] Morality, or more correctly, immorality, is not that easily confined. How we treat some, affects how we treat others. As Mother Teresa said at the National Prayer Breakfast (1994): "If we accept that a mother can kill even her own child, how can we tell other people not to kill each other? . . . Any country that accepts abortion is not teaching its people to love, but to use any violence to get what they want."[64] She concluded with the following words: "Many people are very, very concerned with children in India, with children of Africa, where quite a few die of hunger, and so on. Many people are also concerned about all the violence in this great country of the United States. These concerns are very good. But often these same people are not concerned with the millions who are being killed by the deliberate decision of their own mothers. And this is what is the greater destroyer of peace today – abortion, which brings people to such blindness."[65]

Common Sense and Practices
Peter Wenz then appeals to the absurdities that relate to conflicts with common practice and common sense. The absurdities brought under practical head are: death certificates, population statistics, age adjustments, frozen embryos and in-calculable burdens.

Death Certificates & Funerals

An implication that is at odds with common practice and common sense, according to Wenz, is that we should mourn the death of all these 'people,' and have death certificates and burial requirements (for these little ones). In most cases the only clue that such a death has occurred is a late or particularly heavy menstrual flow.

"A person is a person. All should be treated with respect. Surely none should be flushed down the toilet or thrown into the garbage",[66] says Wenz. Wenz has pointed out the inconsistency of a lot of pro-life people. In some cases, it is physically impossible to do what Wenz suggests (e.g. in case of heavy menstrual flow). However, there is an increase in the practice among pro-lifers of burying foetuses. Wenz is right when he states: "a person is a person. All should be treated with respect." Part of the problem is that when foetuses die they are often in the hands of the medical profession which has not always been sensitive and helpful in showing due respect for that baby that once existed.

Theologian R. C. Sproul acknowledges that one of the problems with our definitions of life and death is seen in the case of stillborn babies. He asks the question, "Are stillborn babies 'dead babies,' or are they 'never-have-been-alive babies?'" Then he points out that "it is commonplace for physicians to speak of stillborn babies as babies who have died."[67] He then shares his experience when his daughter delivered a stillborn baby, an experience of death. "My daughter delivered a stillborn baby. I will relate her experience to show how a nonreligious community dealt with the event. In the ninth month of her pregnancy, my daughter noticed that an entire day had passed with no feeling of foetal movement. She called her doctor, and he examined her immediately. His response was grim. 'I am sorry, but your baby has died,' he told my daughter. The physicians used the language of death to describe the event. The next day my daughter was admitted to the hospital and labour was induced. She endured the labour experience knowing in advance that she would give birth to a stillborn baby. After the baby – a girl – was delivered, the nurses cleansed the body and took photographs. The baby was given a name, and measurements were recorded in the hospital records. The nurses then brought the dead child into my daughter's room – giving her, her husband, my wife, and me the opportunity to hold the baby."

This was not an extraordinary or macabre experience, but the customary practice. "The nurses explained that by giving the parents an opportunity to hold the stillborn baby and to say 'goodbye,' the grief process for the lost child would be less severe. Holding my daughter's stillborn baby was a profound experience for me. Though I had already been convinced that unborn babies are living human persons, any shadow of doubt I might have had was instantly removed. As I held the child, I wondered how it was possible that anyone could think that the baby was not a human being then or two days earlier."[68]

Sproul in his book, *Abortion: A Rational Look at an Emotional Issue*, reasons: "We use the expression: 'If it looks like a duck it walks like a duck, it probably is a duck.'"[69] In case of human foetuses, it is obvious that they look like human persons, they act like human beings, they have the genetics of the human person, and they have sexuality and movement and so they are persons.

Population Statistics
Wenz argues from the vantage point of population also: "Population statistics would have to be revised to reflect the (often brief) existence of these people. According to him, state may gain additional members if it has more pregnant women than do other states. Actuarial tables would have to be revised as well. Since more than half of the human population dies before birth through failure of implantation or spontaneous abortion, a country where the life expectancy is currently thought to be about 70 years would actually be one with a life expectancy under 35."[70]

At this point Wenz sounds like he's being superficial. None of the proposals Wenz is arguing about are necessary. "As a society we already make distinctions between people based on their age. The same would be true in this case. Since these foetuses have not been born yet, they will not be counted as part of the population since they do not take up additional space in society".[71] But such distinctions in no way bring their personhood into question. It is as though he is grasping for straws to try to make the pro-life position as ridiculous as possible.

Age Adjustments
Wenz continues his argument by pointing out that "of course, individuals who survive to childhood would be older than is currently thought, about nine months older in most cases, because we currently date the beginning of life at birth, which is nine months after the person has actually come into existence. Appropriate adjustments would have to be made in the ages at which a person is permitted to drive, vote, drink, and so forth."[72] Wenz doesn't seem to be aware of the fact that this is how much of civilization already counts age.

Counting the age from birth is mostly a Western tradition, whereas much of the Orient and Middle East does what Wenz is suggesting. China is a case in point. Therefore, such a suggestion is hardly new, radical, or absurd.

Chilly People

There is another argument on frozen embryos: "Many thousands of frozen human embryos exist at present. If personhood begins at conception, then these are all chilly people. When decisions are made about their future, they would all need guardians *ad litem* (legal counsel) to protect their rights. If their parents are getting divorced, any dispute over them would be a matter of child custody. If their parents, whether divorcing or not, do not want them to develop further, the court would have to protect their rights by removing them from their parents' custody. As soon as immunosuppressive drugs are available that enable a genetically unrelated woman to carry an embryo to term, these 'children' should be put up for adoption just as other children are."[73]

"It is obvious that Wenz is being cute again as he sarcastically refers to frozen embryos as "chilly" people. His argument on the whole is a dilemma which an immoral society has produced for itself. The pro-lifers do not support this practice of freezing embryos. This is another manifestation of the Brave New World's technology which is creating dilemmas that were never meant to be. The sarcastic answer would be: since you made your bed, you will have to lie in it".[74]

Incalculable Burden

Wenz ends this section on the absurdities that relate to the conflicts with common practice and common sense by pointing out that at times the implications of what he has argued are truly disturbing. "Especially disturbing are the implications concerning the allocation of medical resources. It would be tragic to diminish efforts in areas of postnatal people being subject to lives afflicted with debilitating genetic defects. It is also absurd at a practical level. When health care already consumes a good portion of the gross national product of every country, and millions of (postnatal) people are nevertheless poorly served, it is absurd to add a burden that is incalculable and incomparable".[75] As noted earlier, such concerns have nothing to do with whether a being is a person from the moment it has a human genetic code! "Civility requires that society does its very best in looking out for all its people – whether born or unborn. Money should not be the arbitrator in such instances".[76] Now Wenz appeals to the absurdities that relate to legal questions: abortion and contraception.

Legal Implications

Once we accept personhood from conception we will have to treat abortion and contraception in a quite different way. Wenz moves on to legal questions regarding abortion saying: "by contrast, the legal implications of this view are less absurd than frightening. Abortion would, of course, be illegal. That is the main reason for maintaining, that beings become persons on receipt of a human genetic code. But it is one thing to maintain that abortion is illegal, and quite another to treat it seriously as murder".[77]

Punishment for Murder

"Murder is among the most serious crimes and carries some of the heaviest penalties. Life in prison and even the death penalty is considered to be permissible penalties for murder".[78] If foetuses are considered persons, performing an abortion can be nothing less than premeditated murder, planning an abortion would be conspiracy to commit murder, and having an abortion would be a crime.

"Wherever there is a law that declares people guilty of murder, whenever a crime they commit results in an unlawful death, all women who have abortions would be guilty of murder".[79] Punishing murderers has got two purposes. "One purpose of punishing murderers is to express the community's condemnation of murder. If foetuses are people with equal status, their murder should be condemned as emphatically as anyone else's. Another purpose of punishing murderers is to deter potential murderers, thereby saving the lives of potential victims".[80]

"The only way to give foetuses equal protection of the laws is to punish abortion with the same severity as other murders. Any lesser treatment of abortion would show unwarranted disrespect for foetal people. It would be like punishing those who murder blacks less severely than those who murder whites. This would obviously be immoral". "Thus, if personhood begins at fertilisation, the implication is not that abortion could be treated as murder, but that it would have to be treated as murder."[81]

We agree with the logic of Wenz's argumentation. But we have to disagree with him when he says that such a practice is frightening. Why should not murder be treated as murder and murderers as murderers? What is really frightening is that people get away with murder! And this is happening in epidemic proportions whether in the case of the born or the unborn. Wenz is right when he says that "the only way to give foetuses equal protection of the laws is to punish abortion with the same severity as other murders."[82] Such treatment would bring back justice to the individual and society, and respect and dignity to the unborn.

Some, as Justice Tom C. Clark, may argue that, 'no prosecutor has ever returned a murder indictment charging the taking of the life of a foetus. This would not be the case if the foetus constituted a human life.'[83] The fact that a murder indictment has never been meted out to someone charged with taking the life of a foetus says nothing about the status of that foetus except in the eyes of the beholder. Like many issues in our society, abortion has suffered because of the lack of reflection on the part of the people as they have not really thought through carefully the implications of what it really means to kill a foetus.

Carl Sagan, the creator of the *Cosmos Television* series, asks the typical questions of pro-abortion advocates: "why should legislators have any right at all to tell women what to do with their bodies?"[84] He then adds, "to be deprived of reproductive freedom is demeaning. Women are fed up with being pushed around."[85] Yet Sagan himself understands the critical issue as he is aware of the limits of tolerance: "And yet, by consensus, all of us think it proper that there be prohibitions against, and penalties exacted for, murder. It would be a flimsy defense if the murderer pleads that this is just between him and his victim and none of the government's business. If killing a foetus is truly killing a human being, is it not the duty of the state to prevent it? Indeed, one of the chief functions of government is to protect the weak from the strong."[86]

Moral judgment is not a private affair! If the foetus is a human being, then he is a victim. And if he is a victim – a dead victim – the so-called "pro-choice" philosophy loses all validity.

Contraception
Wenz goes on to the issue of contraceptions: "The implications of treating fertilised eggs as human beings are more ominous where contraception is concerned, because some contraceptives are actually abortifacients (forms of abortion). The IUD (Intra Uterine Device) is the most prominent among these. It prevents fertilised eggs from implanting on the uterine wall, thereby depriving the zygote of the nutrition it requires for further development. The zygote is then expelled in the menstrual flow. If fertilised eggs are human beings, this is murder by starvation and exposure, and would have to be dealt with accordingly if all people are to be given equal protection of the laws.

The woman taking the 'morning after' pill would herself be guilty of murder (if a zygote was actually killed) or reckless endangerment (if there was no fertilised egg). Finding a woman in possession of such a pill would constitute probable cause for an investigation that would have to include collection and inspection of her next menstrual flow to determine whether or not a fertilised egg was present. Surely the difference between murder and reckless endangerment is serious enough to warrant such inspections. The imposition on privacy and the expenditures of police time involved in these inspections are justified by the seriousness of the criminal activity in question. The equal protection of zygotes requires as much.[87]

The pro-life movement has always been against the use of IUDs or the "morning after" pill which clearly are abortifacients. Because society is unable and unwilling to go to every length to investigate the possibility of crimes does not mean that the crimes once found out are not considered crimes and will not be passed over just because they were committed in the past. The same holds for the situation that Wenz has just described.

However some from the pro-abortion camp, especially Peter Wenz is ready to admit that an eighth month foetus is a human person. They do it on the ground that eighth month foetus is similar to the new born and also that their dependence on the mother at that stage is only for a short period. Still they try to make it a religious issue; for by doing so, they can argue that the definition and determination of humanness and personhood all depends upon one's religious viewpoint.

Eight Month Foetuses
Though dependent on mother, Wenz is willing to accord personhood to the eight-month foetus. He considers the dependence on the mother at this stage to be similar to a patient receiving oxygen with the help of a respirator. Besides, he considers the eight month foetus to be similar to a new born baby.

Dependency
"The eighth month foetus, some hold, is literally attached to its mother, from whom it receives oxygen and nutrition, whereas a healthy newborn breaths to extract oxygen from the air. That is, the foetus extracts air indirectly, the newborn receives it directly. The same would be true in terms of its nutrients."[88] That is, the foetus is dependent on its mother. However, this dependence, according to Wenz, is not really very different from the differentiation between how healthy and ill people receive air and nutrition.

Suppose a person is in a hospital and receives oxygen by a respirator and nutrition by intra-venous feeding. Nobody can diminish such a person from the right to life, especially when he is capable immediately of breathing and eating normally.[89] "Therefore the eighth month foetus' dependency which can be ended by his removal from his mother's womb should not deny to such a foetus the same right to life accorded to a newborn."[90]

Notice Wenz's hesitating qualifier: "especially when they are capable *immediately* of breathing and eating normally."[91] "This again shows the quantitative and thus qualitative factor with those who propose death to the unborn (in the case of Wenz, death to the unborn from conception through the seventh month). The implication is obvious: those who quickly get on their own deserve life."[92] What about younger foetuses? Why is the eighth month so significant in terms of personhood?

Hence, Wenz proposes a new criterion: the similarity of foetuses to the newborns. He believes that such a criterion, unlike the criterion of viability, is "immune to technological change, and is morally and legally relevant."[93] Thus "eighth month foetuses normally have the rights of newborns, whereas zygotes and embryos do not."

Similarity with the Newborns

In the *Roe vs Wade* decision foetuses that were viable in that they could "live outside the mother's womb, albeit with artificial aid," were in their general nature considered to be substantially similar to a baby.[94] This shows that the Supreme Court used the argumentation of similarity. Wenz now hypothesises about future technology as he thinks of the possibility of the development of an artificial placenta would enable such zygote to gestate fully outside any human body. Such a technological breakthrough may not be imminent, but may be possible. If such a breakthrough would occur zygotes would be viable, making the viability criterion obsolete. He points to Byron White as being right in rejecting the viability criterion and justified in maintaining that "the possibility of foetal survival is contingent on the state of medical practice and technology, factors that are in essence morally and constitutionally irrelevant."[95] Hence he proposes the criterion for personhood as being "the current nature of the foetus."[96] He argues that such a criterion is as legitimate as "the relevant factor in according many other rights......" He illustrates this by pointing out that five year olds are not given the right to drive a car even though they are potential seventeen-year-olds with adequate driving skills. Their rights are geared to their current state of being. Similarly, the high school biology student does not have the right to practice medicine, even though s/he is potentially a physician. Therefore, "the foetus's right to life is simply geared to its current state",[97] so says Wenz.

Referring to biological complexity Wenz denies personhood to embryos less than eight months old. Wenz points out that zygotes and embryos do not have the organs or the sensitivities of newborns. He points out that except for the genetic code, embryos can be frozen for later implantation, and argues that this shows that they are more like simpler organisms than infants. Wenz continues by arguing from the standpoint of biological complexity: "The current state of being is biologically much more primitive than that of birds and mammals, which lack the right to life in our law, but do have a right to be free of needless cruelty. Unlike birds and mammals, however, embryos cannot feel pain, as they have no central nervous system. As long as an embryo is still an embryo (has not yet developed further), its rights are the same as those of other comparably simple organisms. In short, it has no rights at all because its degree of biological complexity is similar to that of insects to whom we ascribe no rights at all. But whereas an eighth month foetus clearly has all the rights of a newborn (other things being equal), an embryo clearly has none of these rights."[98] Therefore "zygotes and embryos lack the right to life because they are so unlike newborns and other human beings."[99]

Wenz's argument that foetuses less than eight months old are "biologically much more primitive than that of birds and mammals,"[100] is not true unless what is meant is biological independence. "Most animals are biologically more independent than human beings. At birth, or close thereafter, most animals are able to walk, swim, or fly, whereas a newborn infant only lays there crying for attention and food. Yet elephants and giraffes tend to their young for years. They are not independent at birth."[101]

Let me ask: "since when did we ever make such biological independence the criterion of biological complexity? Is it legitimate to argue as Wenz does that a foetus should gain a right to life as its current state of being resembles that of a newborn?"[102] Wenz does not attribute personhood to a foetus until the eighth month. Does this mean that seven or even sixth month foetuses are simple organisms? Hardly. "Basic biology and human anatomy classes make it clear that by four weeks an embryo has a heartbeat and by six weeks it has brain waves. So, hardly a simple organism! Such ignorance about the basics of human development and such simplistic thinking in this regard is astounding, for such an otherwise intelligent person who proposes the right to annihilate any foetus less than eighth month in development."[103]

"Wenz's decision that eight months is the significant time when a foetus becomes a person and should therefore be protected by our laws, is purely arbitrary. Is an eighth month foetus significantly different from a foetus that is seven and a half or seven or six and a half or six months old? Such questions lead to the foolishness and absurdities that Wenz hoped to get away from."[104] Thus, in trying to ward off what he considered the absurdities of the pro-life movement, he ended up with the absurdities of the pro-abortion movement! Zygotes and embryos must have all the rights of infants because the developmental process is a *continuum* in which all cut-off points are arbitrary. Former Surgeon General C. Everett Koop reasons: "The logical approach is to go back to the sperm and the egg. A sperm has 23 chromosomes and though it is alive and can fertilize an egg it can never make another sperm. An egg also has 23 chromosomes and it can never make another egg. So we have eggs that cannot reproduce and we have sperms that cannot reproduce. Once there is the union of sperm and egg, and the 23 chromosomes of each are brought together into one cell that has 46 in one cell with its 46 chromosomes has all of the DNA (deoxyribose-nucleic acid), the whole genetic code that will, if not interrupted, make a human being with the potential for God-consciousness. I do not know anyone among my medical conferees, no matter how pro abortion they might be, who would kill a newborn baby the minute he was born. My question to my pro-abortion friend who will not kill a newborn baby is this: 'Would you kill this infant a minute before he was born, or a minute before that, or a minute before that, or a minute before that?' . . . At what minute can one consider life to be worthless and the next minute consider that same life to be precious?"[105]

At what minute does a foetus become a person? Wenz claims at the eighth month. But at what minute? Or at what hour? Or at what day? Or at what week? Are such questions silly? Not at all since human life is at stake. Where a person arbitrarily draws that line where somehow a nonperson foetus becomes a person determines whether that foetus lives or dies. It should have become obvious by now; arbitrariness is the name of the game of the pro-abortion movement! Here we have seen the futility of trying to assess when a foetus becomes a person. It all depends on whom you ask. Everyone differs? Why? Because this is a contrived dilemma. The only answer that is sensible is that a foetus is a human being (person) from the time of conception.

Foetus versus PVS Patient

Wenz argues that few people are troubled by the fact that patients in a persistent vegetative state are not accorded the right to life that normally accompanies personhood since they are left to starve. He then compares foetuses to such vegetative patients because they are "similarly incapable of the activities that distinguish persons from others."[106] As he points out, "despite their human genetic code, they should be denied the status of personhood and the accompanying right to life."[107]

Blechschmidt, in *New Perspectives on Human Abortion* responds to the above saying that "nothing is proven by the fact that few people are troubled by common medical practices that violate the right to live of permanently vegetative individuals."[108] Wenz acknowledges this objection. So indifference toward the lives of those in a persistent vegetative state should be condemned just as indifference toward foetal life should be condemned. Neither is proof of moral acceptability. Blechschmidt continues saying that "even if indifference were acceptable in the case of persistent vegetative individuals, the same would not follow for the foetus."[109] Why? Unlike the person in a persistent vegetative state whose state is permanent, the foetus' lack of distinctive human activities is only temporary. The foetus only needs time to be allowed to develop and its activities will be distinctively human. This means that a foetus is more like a person who is temporarily unconscious than one who is persistently vegetative. And since "we do not deny personhood and the right to life to the temporarily unconscious, we should not deny personhood and the right to life to the temporarily immature."[110] Wenz acknowledged this objection also.[111]

In Defence of Personhood

An elevated view of human life is a common instinct. Cultural relativism would claim that human societies have no common moral values. This cannot be true for the valuing of life, as a matter of mere prudence.[112] In other words, the statement: "human life has no value" seems incoherent, since it forms a poor basis for the continuation of society.

The Christian affirmation of human personhood goes far beyond this prudential sense, however, to a philosophical and theological honouring of human beings made in the image and likeness of a Creator-God. This has been the traditional anthropology of the Church over the centuries, expounded on by such diverse writers as Augustine of Hippo, Thomas Aquinas, Martin Luther, John Calvin and so on. In the past century, during the rise of the modern bioethics movement (1965- 1980), a number of respected writers such as John T. Noonan, Harold O.J. Brown, and Francis Schaeffer have affirmed this traditional Christian theological position, while adding additional philosophical reasoning to it.

The modern debate over the value of humanity is a relatively new phenomenon. The Enlightenment rationalism of the Eighteenth-Century caused no immediate challenge to the traditional thinking, since it presupposed a lofty view of rational human beings even as it de-emphasised God. Yet the gradual influence of Cartesian scepticism has shaken the foundations for such a value. In our present day, pluralistic and secular views compete with older concepts, and one can no longer claim a unique, protectable, intrinsic human nature as societal given.

Few would disagree that the phrase moral agent should include adult rational human beings. The controversy arises when we try to decide who else to include in the moral community, especially with regard to human beings who cannot act as moral agents, such as the unborn, the mentally challenged, or the persistently unconscious. Furthermore, modern technological advances in genetics, embryology, and human reproduction have called into question traditional understandings, forcing a re-examination of what it means to be human, and what it means to be a person.

Primarily A Scientific Issue
In his book, *Abortion Rights as Religious Freedom* Wenz admitted that the exact time of personhood should be left to the experts. It is explicit from the following: "I cannot say exactly where between twenty and twenty-eight weeks the matter of foetal personhood becomes secular. Those more expert than I must determine when the foetus differs from the newborns. Expert opinions may range from 20-26 weeks. It is important to avoid confusing this issue with one about viability, which turns on the technological ability to foster the development of a foetus outside its mother. Even if such foetuses become viable, then, they are not considered persons on purely secular grounds."[113]

According to Wenz, because of uncertainty, foetuses of 20 weeks and younger cannot be classified as persons on secular grounds: "Secular concepts do not suffice to decide the matter one way or the other. On the epistemological standard, indecisiveness makes a matter religious."[114] He then acknowledges that the objection to abortion is that if we cannot decide on secular grounds how to classify young foetuses, then we must exercise caution. He reasons,

"Feeling of uncertainty about whether abortions early in pregnancy kill a person (the foetus) should lead us to refrain from such abortions, just as uncertainty about whether a movement in the bushes is caused by a person or a deer should lead a hunter to refrain from shooting."[115]

He then dismisses this argument by claiming that "the existence of the danger ... exists only because of uncertainty about the truth of a religious claim. To say that the young foetus may be a person is to say that this religious belief may be true."[116] Wenz, thus, appeals to religious rather than biological ("secular") grounds to circumvent his dilemma. Thus, Wenz hides behind "the religious argument" as he states: "All relevant secular facts of science and common sense can be held in common by people whose attitudes differ and who can justify their different attitudes by appeal to 'facts' of some other kind. One 'sees' the essence of personhood in the fertilised ovum, while the other 'sees' merely the potential for personhood."[117]

"However, scientists, as well as religionists, believe that whether a foetus is a person or not is primarily a scientific (biological) issue. Only secondarily does it become a religious issue as the Bible clearly and overwhelmingly supports the contention that the foetus is a person".[118] The scientific data itself compels us to recognise the foetus as a human being. The problem with Wenz is that he has not given compelling evidence to show that the foetus is not a person. Thus, his argument flies in the face of scientific (biological) evidence.

Challenges by Postmodernism

This discussion is further complicated by postmodernism and religious pluralism. These forces have combined with technological advances to allow a shift from traditional notions of human value and dignity during the past generation. At the beginning of life, we now have abortion on demand, experimentation on human foetuses, the selling of foetal body parts, embryonic stem cell research, and human cloning. At the end of life, we are faced with the devaluation of the elderly and infirm, as well as physician assisted suicide and both voluntary and involuntary euthanasia. In the arena of genetic technology, medicine is moving beyond the traditional focus on healing to an exploration of human enhancement. This may open the door to tinkering with our DNA, the very blueprint that genetically defines us.

Nigel Cameron has divided the contemporary bioethics discourse into three eras or phases. Bioethics 1 focused on "taking" life, with abortion and euthanasia as the main issues. Bioethics 2 deals with "making" life, and responds to the new reproductive technologies, pre-implantation genetic diagnosis, and the possibility of human cloning. Bioethics 3 is the newest arena, mostly yet in the future, and involves "faking" life, the possibility that developments in genetic technology, nanotechnology, and neurotechnology will not only lead to new cures for disease (a very desirable goal), but also to true human enhancement or the redesigning of humanity (much more dubious goals).

A Christian response to these assaults on human dignity has lagged behind technology. Christian voices have done an admirable job in defining the antiabortion debate, but have not responded as forcefully and effectively to the newer challenges. In the emerging areas of Bioethics 2 and 3, Christians must develop more thoughtful strategies to cope with increasingly complex ethical concerns.[119] A Christian defense of life must therefore be nuanced, thoughtful, and led by the Spirit. It must also truly engage postmodern culture. We will describe three possible strategies – the absolutist, the privatisation and the common ground approaches – to respond to the assaults on human personhood, favouring the third as a middle ground between the first two. Then we will discuss the theoretical content that such a strategy may entail, drawing on some insights from natural law.

Strategies for Defending Human Personhood
The modern bioethics era began in the mid-1960s, partly as a religiously grounded response to the debate over abortion. The defence of human life was the province of religious leaders and theologians. The initial foundations were principles of the sanctity of human life, drawn from scriptural and theological sources.[120] The strategy of this period coincided with Cameron's Bioethics 1, and could be dubbed the 'Absolutist Approach'.

The Absolutist Approach
This approach attempted to convince the public of the evils of abortion on the basis of pure truth claims. This approach uses scriptural and logical arguments. A principal champion was Francis Schaeffer. David Hopkins called him "the last of the relevant and the truly great modern theologians."[121] His strong stand made it difficult to accommodate competing views because he considered that the nature of truth itself demands an uncompromising fidelity.

Hence, this view implies that there is only one correct way to think. As columnist Paul Greenberg put it, "Some questions will not be answered until they are answered right."[122] So, the Absolutist Approach cannot always acknowledge the plurality of ideas. But plurality of ideas is characteristic of postmodern society. Some have claimed that Schaeffer has erred in this regard, attempting to use modernist (Enlightenment) methods, creating a rigid, divisive clash of competing absolute truths.[123] The resulting culture wars have reinforced opinions on both sides of the debate. This situation made it more difficult for pro-life and pro-choice forces to consider the strengths and weaknesses of each other's point of view.

This state of affairs has led some to conclude that the Absolutist Approach to defend human personhood has been a failure. One reason, of course, is that it is not universally accepted as right. Summarising the problem Hollinger says: "It is one thing to say that Christianity must have a legitimate voice at the table of public debate . . . but it is quite another to say that Christianity must have the privileged voice."[124] Besides the impact of such arguments in the legal arena, with the broadest possible liberalisation of abortion by the courts was very weak.[125]

A second strategy has therefore developed. It represents a radical rejection of absolute truth, and favours a capitulation to religious plurality. Hollinger named this strategy as, the 'Privatisation Approach'.

The Privatisation Approach
H. Tristram Engelhardt is a proponent of this strategy. In his landmark work *The Foundations of Bioethics*, he pessimistically refers to "the irremedial plurality of postmodernity." Our dialogue with society, on his view, cannot hold any moral content with which some members of society might disagree: Morality according to him is available on two levels: the content-full morality of moral friends, and the procedural morality binding moral strangers. As a consequence, much must be allowed in large-scale secular states that many know to be grievously wrong and morally disordered. This circumstance will disappoint those who hope that the general society would constitute the moral community, which could be guided by the content-full secular bioethics. Their hope is socially ungrounded and, in terms of the possibility of a secular morality, unjustifiable,[126] so says Tristram Engelhardt. A diversity of moral opinions is hard to deny, but Engelhardt uses such diversity as a club to drive any normative theory away from public ethical discourse. His response to pluralism is to impose a radical limitation on secular moral authority, calling this a "content-less" secular bioethics. Those who would hold to even such bioethical basics as beneficence, non-maleficence, autonomy, and justice, Engelhardt dismisses as moral fanatics.[127] This assumes

that the application of common moral norms is somehow odious, that the imposition of beneficence itself (for example) is not beneficent. Implied in all of this is a low view of moral agents, that they cannot be trusted to serve anything but a highly suspect fundamentalist agenda.

However, Dr. Engelhardt, himself has repudiated such an extreme position. His later work, *Foundations of Christian Bioethics*,[128] lays claim to a complete "content-full" bioethics from a Christian perspective. His work is of great benefit among moral friends. But it relegates his voice to just one of many among the plurality of moral strangers.

For some the Absolutist Approach and the Privatisation Approach are equally unsatisfactory extremes: one holds to such a priority to truth that it has no sway over those who do not share its presuppositions; while the other despairs of any commonality, with bioethics not much more than a procedural set of rules for regulating a diversity of opinions. And so the debate has reached an impasse, with armed camps slinging their rhetorical weapons across a philosophical no-man's land from behind the bulwarks of their presuppositions. To enter the no-man's land requires a more optimistic stance, called the 'Common Ground Approach'.

The Common Ground Approach
This approach must acknowledge a diversity of moral viewpoints while holding an epistemic commitment to absolute truth. For this to work we need a shared body of moral knowledge upon which all participants can agree. To Engelhardt's moral friends and moral strangers, a third category seems possible: that of moral acquaintances. These acquaintances must share some common anthropological preconceptions. That will help our discussion of human personhood. This may be possible through the application of natural law. Our moral voice can open up a dialogue that will help us find areas of agreement that allow us to live (for a while) in the no-man's land. As a way of proceeding, we may appeal to a God-given impulse within all men for the rational use of logic, common decency, and civil discourse.

Ordinary People: The Test of Common Ground Approach
The real test of the Common Ground Approach will come from ordinary men and women struggling with real problems. Consider the woman who has had an abortion. Planned Parenthood claims that "emotional responses to legally induced abortion are largely positive."[129] They will either minimise or deny many of the psychological, medical, and emotional costs involved.[130] What

can such a woman do if she experiences grief and guilt? She can deny the symptoms. It will only bury the problem if the guilt is real. Or she can openly acknowledge the guilt, for the woman has gone against the moral law written in her heart. This will be a better approach, I suppose. For it will enable her to grieve and emotionally heal herself if she can face the moral wrong of her actions and seek the forgiveness of God.

Will the Common Ground Approach be able to bring the two sides of the debate closer together? One example comes from the problem of coercive abortions. 30% of women who have abortions have been coerced in some way (by family members or boyfriends). According to some, this can be an area of agreement that provides a way to discuss an otherwise contentious issue: "Pro-lifers will support such a defense of women's rights, and the vast majority of those who describe themselves as pro-choice would also agree that an effort to stop coerced abortions is reasonable and necessary."[131] This approach has a powerful influence on all parties, even among traditional abortion rights advocates. It builds on shared moral values and helps to find common ground in the no-man's land.

Perhaps the best example of the value of natural law in defending the unborn is that of Samuel, a baby boy afflicted with spina bifida, whom we have already referred to. As the surgeon closed the wound after operation, the tiny child reached up and squeezed the doctor's finger. Michael Clancy the photographer was there to capture the moment. The resulting photograph has appeared in newspapers, magazines, and internet sites, and has galvanised the pro-life movement with its emotional depiction of Samuel's personhood.[132]

Samuel, when he was three years old visited Congress with his parents, where Senator Brownback showed him the famous picture and asked him who it was. The child quickly replied: "Baby Samuel." The senator then asked him what had happened at the time the picture was taken. Without hesitation, Samuel said, "They fixed my boo-boo." All this led Pia de Solenni of the Family Research Council to remark: "Perhaps the next time Samuel's visiting in D.C., the Supreme Court justices and many of our congressmen could spend some time with him to better understand the *continuum* of human dignity. After all, if a three-year-old can get it . . ." Is all of this mere emotional hype, or is there a reality here that carries moral authority? The value of life is immediately evident to even the most jaded in our society. Some may argue that Samuel was merely influenced by his parents, but even this little three-year-old knows who he is, and who he was in the womb.

Natural Law and Personhood

Natural law looks at the *telos* (end or purpose) of human beings in an attempt to derive moral guidelines. Aristotle considers the ethical implications of *telos* to be self-evident: "[T]his [*telos*] must be the good and the chief good. Will not the knowledge of it, then, have a great influence on life? Shall we not, like archers who have a mark to aim at, be more likely to hit upon what is right?"[133] An understanding of *telos* implies an order to the universe and also a Creator behind it. Thomas Aquinas argues that the created nature of human beings bestows upon them a special natural habit, which he calls *synderesis*. Like Augustine, he too affirms the presence of certain "rules and seeds of virtue, both true and unchangeable" within human nature. Such rules are acquired through reason.[134]

Natural law, then, is the rational understanding of certain moral truths that are common to all moral agents. It is essentially theistic, for it derives its force from the *telos* built into men by their Creator. God creates all men with the same purpose. So all men can know such shared moral truths. Furthermore, there is nothing relativistic, arbitrary, or subjective about such knowledge. Budziszewski has called it *What We Can't Not Know*, the title of his book on natural law.[135]

According to the natural law theorists Scripture teaches firstly, that certain moral principles are truly known by all men. Though their understanding may be partial, these commonly held truths are clear enough to the unregenerate that they are "without excuse" (Romans 1:20). Secondly, though men may understand moral truth, they may suppress it, as a consequence of the Fall. It is not a problem of knowledge, but of the will. So natural law, though partial and incomplete, may begin a common dialogue, and can help form a common source of moral values.

For illustrating the above, we turn to one of its greatest 20th-century proponents. Clive Staples Lewis, an academic at Magdalen College in Oxford, published a short book entitled *The Abolition of Man*.[136] Its subtitle, *Reflections on Education with Special Reference to the Teaching of English in the Upper Forms of Schools* was obscure. So it has been overlooked or ignored by great many scholars. However, Budziszewski has called *Abolition of Man* "perhaps the greatest work on natural law in the 20th Century."[137]

The premise of this tiny volume is simple: teachers in modern society must not only teach facts but values as well. Lewis is sorry about the attempt to remove the underpinnings of moral values from education. The result is a kind of virtue without value. In other words, it is an attempt to make men moral without any basis. Lewis claims that there is indeed a basis for common morality through a concept of objective value he calls the *Tao* (his synonym for natural law). The *Tao* is not intuition, instinct, or emotion, but something greater. According to Lewis, it is "not one among a series of possible systems of value. It is the sole source of all value judgments. If it is rejected, all value is rejected."[138] Lewis applies this specifically to human personhood. Then he warns that we dare not "step outside the *Tao*." If we do, we will "decide for ourselves what man is to be and make him into that: not on any ground of imagined value, but because we want him to be such."[139] As technology advances, man will be tempted more and more to meddle with his own nature, leading to the final outcome: "Man's final conquest has proved to be the abolition of Man."[140] In arguing for a human nature based on the *Tao*, Lewis envisioned the future in which we now find ourselves. Indeed, technological advances have led some authors to despair of the concept of a unique human nature, even as they admit that we need such a view now more than ever.

One writer in this vein is Francis Fukuyama. He strikes a warning note about the dangers to humanity of recent technological advances.[141] He is a thoroughgoing evolutionist; he is generally optimistic about biotechnology. Yet Fukuyama argues that developments in neuropharmacology and the prolongation of life, coupled with genetic engineering (he prefers this to the more-loaded term eugenics), will present unique challenges to our self understanding. He argues for a strong affirmation of human nature and human dignity, claiming that "denial of the concept of human dignity . . . leads us down a very perilous path."[142]

With naturalistic evolution as his foundation, Fukuyama has a weak warrant for this stand. Excluding religion, on what basis does he make any claim for the dignity of human beings? He does not derive this view; he merely assumes it, or more properly, he says that it is a good idea. William Provine cheerfully admits that if the theory of evolution by random chance is true, then the implications for human society are enormous: there is no God and no foundation for human behaviour, no foundation for law, no unique human nature, and no free will.[143]

Defining human nature via natural law therefore remains a pressing need. According to Mortimer Adler the denial of human nature is one of the great "philosophical mistakes" of our age.[144] This mistake is seen in the ethical debate over human cloning. Leon Kass has written that cloning is "a major violation of our given nature as embodied, gendered and engendering beings."[145] Such an appeal to a given nature is based on a notion of human valuing with great normative power and a long history.

If C.S. Lewis, Francis Fukuyama, Mortimer Adler, Leon Kass and many others are correct, be they theists or agnostics, we desperately need a robust and commonly-held high moral valuing of human beings. Lewis surveys a number of sources to show the moral commonalities across world views.[146] He holds natural law to be self-evident and hence needs no proof. From his survey, we can extract certain commonly held ideas supporting a high view of human life. For example, consider the following extracts: I have not slain men (Ancient Egyptian: *Book of the Dead, Confession of the Righteous Soul*). Do not murder (*Ancient Jewish*: Exodus 20:13). Never do to others what you would not like them to do to you (*Ancient Chinese: Analects of Confucious, xv.23*). Nature urges that a man should wish human society to exist (*Roman: De Officiis* (Cicero), I. iv.). By the fundamental Law of Nature Man [is] to be preserved as much as possible (*Locke: Treatises of Civil Government,* ii. 3). Man is man's delight (*Old Norse: Hávamál* 47). Do to men what you wish men to do to you (*Christian:* Matthew 7:12).[147]

The *Tao* demonstrates that there are universally recognisable truths regarding the value of life, and that these are not restricted to one worldview, philosophy, or religion. The immediate, unstudied recognition of these truths is more than mere custom, for all men agree on them, even if they do not live up to them. Lewis made this clear a few years after writing *Abolition*: "Human beings, all over the earth, have this curious idea that they ought to behave in a certain way, and cannot really get rid of it. [Yet] they do not in fact behave in that way."

We can have an example of this "curious idea" from the abortion debate. A pro-life ethic is often evident despite efforts to suppress it. Consider the statements of two outspoken pro-choice feminists: Naomi Wolf and Gloria Steinem. Naomi Wolf: [What] Americans want and deserve is an abortion-rights movement willing publicly to mourn the evil – necessary evil though it may be – that is abortion. We must have a movement that acts with moral accountability and without euphemism.[148] Gloria Steinem: I do think pro-abortion was the wrong term – since everyone would like to reduce the necessity of abortion. I prefer reproductive freedom – the freedom to have as well as not to have children . . . And in any case, we could work together for contraception and sex education that would diminish the necessity of abortion.[149]

Although Steinem did not herself use the phrase necessary evil, both statements imply that the taking of a human life in the act of abortion is simply wrong. Both writers would justify such an evil as necessary, but an evil nonetheless. Their own writings declare that the taking of a human life (both in the womb and outside the womb) is something to mourn and for which the necessity should diminish.

We have ironic testimonies to the *law written in the heart. The National Review,* gave two letters, written by women about to undergo an abortion. These letters were addressed to the children they were about to abort.[150] The bizarre incongruity of proclaiming love for a baby one is about to destroy, or the need to rationalise such an act to the victim, is an ironic testimony to the law written on the heart.[151] Carol Gilligan, in her survey of pregnant women about to undergo abortion, discovered that many women thought that their actions were morally wrong, even to the point of calling abortion murder. Yet they went through with the procedure because of their economic and social circumstances.[152] These brief examples show that there is a universal sense of the value of life, even in the womb, as a given, even though abortion remains commonplace. One reason, of course, is that other things are going on. As we have seen, Peter Singer the Princeton philosophy professor, teaches that there is no moral distinction between human beings and animals. On Singer's view, it is permissible, even sometimes ethically required, to kill newborn babies less than a month old. Equating moral humanity with mental capacities, he holds that babies have no intrinsic right to life, and that their only value is what is "conferred upon them by their parents."[153] This causes a strong reaction, much more than a mere sentiment. Certainly most people (perhaps excluding philosophers!) find such views offensive and repugnant. This is the power of natural law.

Again to show that the affirmation of life is common to all people, we shall also consider the partial-birth abortion debate. This late-term abortion technique (technically known as intact dilation and extraction) creates such an intense emotional reaction that 30 states in the US, passed laws against it, and the US Congress has twice outlawed the procedure (the current ban was recently upheld by the U.S. Supreme Court).[154] A recent poll showed that 70% of Americans oppose the procedure,[155] which some have called constitutionally sanctioned homicide.[156]

In a local newspaper editorial supporting an Ohio law against partial-birth abortion, Dennis M. Sullivan used a natural law argument: ". . . it is one thing to debate the humanity of a tiny embryo. It is quite another when it comes to a 20-week-old foetus. By then, it surely looks like a baby."[157] Such arguments resonate with a moral nature implanted within each of us. And an appeal to a common view of life does not just apply to certain late-term abortions. Even in the early stages of pregnancy, an ultrasound examination can help a pregnant woman identify with her unborn child as a unique individual. The above discussions have demonstrated a common high view of humanity that is widespread, crosses worldviews, and is difficult to suppress. Further, this is reflected in experience. Geisler and Feinberg have observed that "all persons feel they have intrinsic value and not merely extrinsic value. If so, then one can begin to provide some content from human experience to disclose the meaning of moral law."[158] The image of God in man, though affected by the fall, still not completely obliterated, could provide some basis for moral knowledge.

Natural law can provide a context for a common dialogue for a public ethical discourse. Though there are limitations, natural law should allow moral acquaintances to set some modest goals. Though pro-life and pro-choice forces may never agree on the morality of abortion, a common dialogue may allow both sides to agree that it should be less frequent. However, the search for common moral ground must never be an excuse for moral relativism.[159]

Thus morally, it is essential we presume the humanity of the unborn since any other assumption requires that we define human life in terms that would exclude from the community other "minority" elements in society as well.

The Unborn are Persons
Attempts to distinguish human persons from mere human beings have failed.[160] There is no ethically relevant difference between human beings of various stages of development that renders some human beings non-persons. If the dignity and value of the human person does not begin after birth, or at birth, or sometime during gestation, then human personhood begins at conception.[161] Thus all human beings are also human persons.

Potentialities: Two Kinds
Ethicist Robert Royce points out that there is a confusion of two kinds of potentialities: "the potency to cause something to come into existence is improperly identified with the potency for this new being to become fully

what it is."[162] The sperm and the ovum are not potential life but as Paul Fowler puts it, "potential causes of individual human life.[163] Although they have the potential to cause an individual to come into existence, the zygote has the potential to become what it already in essence is. This means "that there is no such thing as a potentially living organism. Every living thing is actual, with more or less potentiality."[164] Therefore when we are looking at this issue of personhood, we are dealing with an actual person with potential, not a potential person.

Dr. E. Blechschmidt argues for belief in the personhood of young foetuses: "A human being does not become a human being but rather is such from the instant of fertilisation. During the entire ontogenesis, no single break can be demonstrated, either in the sense of a leap from the lifeless to the live, or of a transition from the vegetative to the instinctive or to characteristically human behaviour. It may be considered today a fundamental law of human ontogenesis . . . that only the appearance of the individual being changes in the course of its ontogenesis."[165]

Peter Wenz argues that such a claim is inconclusive. He says that this view is defended by a "fallacious form of reasoning" as it argues that the zygote is a person because the newborn is a person, and the newborn develops from the zygote by a continuous process. This is fallacious "because according to our secular forms of reasoning, continuous processes of change can alter fundamentally what is undergoing change, so that what exists at the end is not the same sort of being as existed at the beginning."[166] Using the analogy of acorn, Wenz argues that, "the possibility of fundamental change cannot be ruled out in the case of the transition from fertilised ovum to new-born child."[167]

"Contrary to what Wenz and others claim, gradual change does not produce a change in essence. In fact, his illustration is a case in point. The acorn that changes (develops or grows) into a tree is not a change in essence. Try to grow anything but an acorn and see if you end up with an oak tree".[168] Blechshmidt similarly argues: "Why does a human ovum always result in a human being, while any other ovum always results in another organism? For instance, no human being originates from a duck's egg. The answer is because in each ovum the essence has already been fixed; only the appearance changes in development. It is characteristic for every ontogenesis that only that develops which is essentially already there."[169]

To argue that "what is present from the beginning in the fertilised ovum's genetic code may be the potentiality for the development of a person, not the essence of personhood"[170] is nonsense. If this were true, then there could be a change in essence, which no one has been able to show. Even if it could be shown to be true in the case of other things, it would not necessarily be true of human beings since they are unique to everything else in creation.

"Joseph Fletcher too, uses the acorn analogy to illustrate his position as it develops through a continuous process into oak trees, and yet we do not conclude that "acorn" and "oak tree" are different words for the same thing".[171] In his words: "An acorn is not an oak tree, even if it has sprouts; and no one in his right mind would equate crushing an acorn with cutting down an oak tree."[172] He also says that to say that the potential is the actual is like saying a promise is its fulfilment or a blueprint is a house. Paul Fowler points out that, "a sapling becoming an oak would be a more accurate analogy than an acorn since a sapling is living and growing like the zygote whereas an acorn is dormant".[173]

The analogy of the blueprint and house is a mechanistic view of life. "The mechanistic viewpoint is seen in that first comes the blueprint, then the foundation, then the walls, the windows and doors, and finally the house. Whereas a blueprint never becomes part of a house, zygotes contain in themselves all that goes into the maturation of a human being".[174] As John Wilke, said, "In truth we did not come from a single cell. Rather, each of us once was a single cell; and all we have done since then has been to grow up."[175]

Similarly, a human being does not develop like a clock which is not fully a clock until, part by part; it is completed and is functioning. In fact, until that point, a clock is worth-less. Thus Fletcher seems to view a human being as though he is not fully human until all the component parts are fully forming and functioning. The problem with this mechanistic view is that a human being is more than the sum total of his parts – organs plus muscles plus bones plus heart plus brain matter, etc.[176]

The 'Already' and the 'Not Yet' Tension
Values lie not in the potential of something but in the actual possession of it. Therefore, there is no reason to demand that someone who will one day be a person must be treated as one now. This is why the pro-abortion movement feels justified in murdering "merely potential human life." Such argumentation is a reminder of the statement, "She is a little bit pregnant." This is an

untenable position. Either a woman is or is not pregnant. The same is true of personhood. Either that foetus is or is not a person.[177]

What exactly is a foetus? John Stott answers this as well as anyone: "The foetus is not a growth in the mother's body (which can be removed as readily as her tonsils or appendix), nor even a potential human being, but a human life who, though not yet mature, has the potentiality to grow into the fullness of the humanity it already possesses."[178] As early as the end of the second century Tertullian expressed the "already" and the "not yet" tension between what a person is and what a person will become: "He also is a man who is about to be one; you have the fruit already in its seed."[179] Lewis Smedes calls this tension "the deep ontological ambiguity – the ambiguity of not being something yet and at the same time having the makings of what it will be."[180] Scottish scientific theologian Thomas Torrance has clarified this tension: "the potentiality concerned is not that of becoming something else but of becoming what it essentially is."[181]

The Bible simply does not allow for a separation between those who are merely biologically alive and those who are fully persons. The womb is holy ground because God is at work bringing a human life into increasing fullness of the humanity he already possesses. And this continues as he is born into this world until the day he dies. Size, age, development has nothing to do with the sacredness of life. A tiny, undeveloped unborn baby is as sacred as any large, older, fully developed person. Dr. Seuss, in his wonderful fable, *Horton Hears a Who*, states the issue clearly: ". . . a person's a person, no matter how small."[182]

Wenz points out that critics of foetal personhood object to the analogy between young foetuses and normal but unconscious, children and adults: "The latter have already engaged in characteristically human activities and are able, typically, to resume such activities at a moment's notice. They are in what Aristotle calls the state of second potentiality. They have already developed and displayed their abilities, but happen not to be displaying them at the moment. They are like car mechanics who are not currently fixing cars. We call on car mechanics in honour of the abilities that they have developed and displayed, ignoring the fact that they are temporarily asleep or on lunch break."[183]

He argues that, in contrast to children and adults, the young foetus has never displayed the abilities distinctive of human beings. According to Wenz, since the young foetus needs to develop further before it can act like a person it should not have the rights associated with the state of being for which they are in a state of first potentiality. This point is illustrated by the medical profession in that those who are not fully trained as doctors may not act as doctors, even those who, because they could acquire such training, are in a state of first potentiality for a medical degree.

This is a ludicrous analogy since the foetal potential for personhood is different from a young person's potential for a medical degree. Firstly, because, one has to do with the issue of life and the other the issue of a career. For one, the young person does not have to become a physician to life. All kinds of career paths are possible. Conversely, the young foetus has no alternative but death to the development of distinctively human traits and activities.

Secondly, becoming a physician has to do with one's own conscious choices of how ability, time and energy are expended whereas the young foetus develops into full personhood automatically. Thus the potentiality is based, not on achievement, but on actuality as it flows naturally from that actuality. Therefore, the potentiality of a foetus is his actuality in that only time (if not interfered with) is required for his manifestation of that actuality.

Wenz then refers to Robert Joyce who argues, "The potential of a human conceptus to think and talk is an actuality." He illustrates this with the statement, "A woman's potential to give birth to a baby is an actuality that a man does not have.[184] Wenz then makes the point that such an illustration shows that potentiality and actuality are not the same thing. Although a woman's uterus is a part of her actuality that underlies her potential for giving birth, a uterus and a birth are different. Similarly, he argues: "The genetic code is an actuality that underlies the young foetus's potential for personhood, but for that very reason it is not the fulfilment of that potentiality. Furthermore, it is logically impossible for the same thing to be at the same time and in the same respect both a potential and actual. So if the young foetus is a potential person, it can't be at the same time and in the same respect an actual person."[185] There is no argument with that point. No one is saying that a young foetus's potential for personhood is the same as his fulfilment of that potentiality. What is argued is that a person's actuality determines how he will develop. For instance, a person with a uterus is defined as being of the female gender. Even if that uterus does not function as it should in giving birth, which is part of its reason for existence; this does not mean that she is not a female. It is not the defect but the actuality – the possession of a uterus – that determines whether that person is a female rather than a male. Similarly, a foetus is not a born baby. But a foetus is an unborn baby because he/she has the essential ingredients (DNA) of becoming a fully developed human being.

We really know that Wenz operates by a functional model and therefore does not agree to such reasoning. He typically refers to "the current ability to engage in distinctively human pursuits."[186] The following 'endowment account of personhood' and the 'constitutive property' argument will be an additional support for our understanding of the personhood of the unborn.

Endowment Account of Personhood

Drawing upon the work of philosopher Robert Spitzer in his book *Healing the Culture* (2000) and John Kavanaugh in *Who Count as Persons?* (2001), we can contrast the endowment account of personhood with the performance account of personhood. The performance account holds that a being is to be accorded respect, if and only if, the being functions in a given way. There are numerous and conflicting accounts of what this function is, but some of the proposed candidates include: self-awareness, rationality, sentience, desirability, ethnicity, economic productivity, gender, nationality, native language, beauty, age, health, religion, race, fertility, birth and national origin.[187]

The endowment account holds that each human being has inherent moral worth simply by virtue of the kind of being it is. By endowment we mean that the being in question has an intrinsic dynamic orientation towards self expressive activity.[188] Beings with endowments that orient them towards moral values, such as rationality, autonomy, and respect, thereby merit inclusion as members of the moral community.

The endowment account applies equally to all human beings who, despite their manifest differences in rational function, for example, remain oriented towards reason and freedom, even when this orientation cannot be expressed because of immaturity, illness, sleep or disability. To be oriented toward reason and freedom is to have one's flourishing and welfare consists in enjoying certain kinds of goods (e.g., friendship, knowing the truth) that can only be achieved through the exercise of reason and freedom.

Endowment of some kind (ability, capacity, disposition) is not just necessary but sufficient for the right to life. Rational endowment is nothing other than the capacity, ability or disposition (though perhaps not realisable) enjoyed only by whole, living beings whose active self – development is aimed towards and whose flourishing consists in freedom and rationality.

Endowment account of personhood need not be taken as some sectarian religious view. Endowment accounts are already implicitly at work in medical arts via the very concept of pathology. Pathology is not simply a lack of something. It is an incapacity, inability, or failure to realise a disposition which, in the relevant circumstances, can and ought to be realized given the endowment of the being in question. Birds that do not speak are not thereby suffering a pathology. A human being of six years old who cannot speak following an accident is suffering a pathology, physical or mental. The practice of medicine, both for humans and non-humans, can and does appeal to endowments, what a being can and should be able to do given the requisite conditions, maturity, and support.

If every human being is recognised as a human person, based simply of personal endowment, then the 'episodic problem', where the personhood of a being comes and goes, is avoided. Valuing personal endowments, avoids the problem of various forms of under-inclusiveness and over-inclusiveness. Once biological humanity is not episodic, so we do not face the problem of one and the same human being getting personhood and then losing it and then regaining it again and so on. Biological humanity is characteristically equally shared by all human beings, so if one's humanity grants personhood, then all human persons are fundamentally equal in a moral sense and should enjoy fundamental equal rights before the law – especially the right to life. Basing the personhood of humans on their shared humanity is not over-inclusive including beings like worms that are obviously not persons, nor under-inclusive, excluding human beings who are in comas, physically or mentally handicapped, sleeping or under anaesthesia. If we understand a person as a member of a kind of being that is rational and free, and since each and every human being is a member of a kind of being (viz. human beings) that is rational and free, then all these problems are avoided. Hence our next step is to show that humans are rational and have membership in a kind.

Humans are Rational
Every single human being is properly described as a rational being; not potentially rational being, but a currently existing actual rational being, though many individual human beings do not function rationally, including the human embryo, the human foetus, the senile, the sleeping, the temporarily

comatose, and the mentally handicapped. Such human beings cannot communicate, and they do not have conscious self-awareness. For clarification, consider human anatomy. A male with testicles or a female with ovaries currently and actually (not later and potentially) possesses genital or reproductive organs. Now not every human being having reproductive organs actually reproduces. Some are too old, others too young. Some are sterile, others never have sexual intercourse. But the reproductive organs of such human beings, as well as the reproductive organs of those who do have, are properly named and described as the reproductive or genital (ordered to generating) organs because these are the kinds of organs that in some circumstances perform the act which uniquely specifies them. The reproductive organs are not merely potentially the reproductive organs, simply because they are not functionally engaged in the act of reproducing. They actually are the reproductive organs. The genital organs remain genital organs even when they are not generating or incapable of generating new life.

In the same way, every single human being is a rational being, even though human beings as individuals do not always function rationally. It is clear that, not all human beings function rationally at any given time, but every human being is a member of a kind of being (human beings) who can, in certain circumstances, perform actions specifically defined as rational. Similarly the genitals of a sterilised adult are still properly called reproductive organs (though they are no longer properly functioning reproductive organs), so too an immature human being is a rational being (thought not yet a properly functioning rational being). The reproductive or genital organs merit a certain kind of respect (e.g., touching someone's hand is appropriate in many situations where touching the same person's genitals would not be) in virtue of the kind of organs they are even if in a given case a person's reproductive or genital organs cannot in fact (yet) generate or reproduce. Like reproductive organs, even when rational animals capable of functioning rationally are not performing their specifying[189] functions are rational.

To say that the human being in utero is not rational being because he or she is not functioning rationally makes as much sense as saying that a human being is not gendered male or female unless in the act of successfully reproducing. Successful reproduction follows from the endowment (from conception) as male or female, and it is from this endowment that the sex organs emerge, secondary sex characteristics develop, and reproductive activity becomes possible. Even if a human being never performs the activity specific to being male or female (reproduction) that human being is still male or female.

Similarly, even if a human being never performs the activity specific to a rational being (reasoning), that human being is still rational.[190]

Membership in a Kind

According to Martha Nussbaum, the species membership gives us a benchmark by which to judge the flourishing of an individual member of a species and so it is morally relevant.[191] For example, for a human being of a certain age to be unable to read indicates a failure of that individual to flourish fully; whereas a squirrel can flourish without the capacity to read. Ethical decisions bear upon promoting or thwarting the flourishing of others. Since there are species-specific kinds of flourishing, the natural kind of the being in question matters ethically.[192] Assigning moral worth to members of species rather than to particular individuals facilitates moral judgement and provides a level standard for equal basic rights.

History can provide strong evidence in favour of an inclusive society in which all human beings are respected as persons having dignity as opposed to an exclusive society. When considered in the light of history it seems apparent that every single time the performance view has been chosen over the endowment view, gross moral mistakes were made. Accordingly, humankind was divided into two classes by some version of the performance evaluation in which one half was permitted to dispose of the other at will – men exploiting women, whites selling blacks, the young dispatching the old, the rich utilising the poor, the healthy overpowering the sickly – and are nearly universally recognised as evil.

In this context, it is good to recall what Adolf Hitler's national socialists called euthanasia, which was a merciless and systematic elimination of people who were labelled by experts *Lebensunwertes Leben* (life not worth being lived) or *Ballastexistenzen* (an existence which is considered a burden to society). A bureaucratic machinery of sifting and judging people was set up, and the hereditary sick, chronic alcoholics, besides schizophrenics, manic-depressives, hardcore criminals, and even homosexuals, who did not seem to be fit to be included in the *Volksgemeinde* were systematically granted mercy-death or *Gnadentod*, mostly by sending them to gas chambers filled with carbon monoxide.[193]

Personhood is tied to moral agency – not that all persons are always acting as moral agents or could at every moment act as moral agents, but that all persons actually have the genetic basis to be moral agents.[194] Liao S Mathew in *The*

Basis of Human Moral Status, suggests that all human beings have rights in virtue of having the genetic basis for moral agency. It (genetic basis for moral agency) is an actual, identifiable, physical attribute of the individual. The genetic basis for moral agency is not a matter of potentiality, but rather of what a being actually possesses.[195] "Since the genetic basis for moral agency is only a sufficient condition for right holding, it avoids the intuitive cost of denying the status of right holding to those non-human animals or other beings who may plausibly qualify as right holders but who may not have the genetic basis for moral agency."[196]

'Constitutive Property' Argument
We can formulate the "constitutive property" argument in the following way: If an individual being has a constitutive property at one point in time, then it has that property at every point in its existence. This is true by definition, since what X has constitutively must always be a characteristic of X, otherwise it is not a constitutive characteristic, but only an accidental one.

We are the same individual living being or organism as the foetus from which we developed. The truth of this premise is a matter of observation and scientific data. You now, you at ten years old, you at ten days following birth, you ten days after conception and you at all stages of your life in between stand in bodily continuity.

Let me bring in Boonin David once again. He notes in his book, *A Defence of Abortion*: "In the top drawer of my desk I keep another picture of (my son) Eli. This picture was taken on September 7, 1993, 24 weeks before he was born. The sonogram image is murky, but it reveals clearly enough a small head tilted back slightly, and an arm raised up and bent, with the hand pointing back towards the face and the thumb extended out toward the mouth. There is no doubt in my mind that this picture too, shows the same little boy at a very early stage in his physical development."[197]

We also have the experience of watching the development of a single human being through various stages after birth and through maturity. If wombs had windows, we would be able to watch this one human being grow throughout various stages of development before birth as well. If a stranger attacks the mother and permanently damages the human foetus within her, then throughout all future phases of life from cradle through kindergarten and from adulthood to grave, this human being will suffer on account of the damage suffered while in utero.

We are human persons constitutively. If one defines a person as an individual substance of rational nature (Boethius) or as a being endowed with freedom even if not exercising it (Kant), then this premise would be true by definition since what is by nature or endowment is constitutively an aspect of the being in question.

If one defines a person as a member of a kind of being that is rational, then it is also the case that you are a person constitutively. A constitutive characteristic is the contrary of all that is conventional, superficial, or learned. But being a member of the species *Homo Sapiens* is just such a characteristic for it is not a matter of convention (like which side of the road to drive on), nor is it a superficial characteristic (like length of hair), nor does it arise from training (we do not learn how to be a member of the species *Homo Sapiens*). Being a member of a kind of being (human) is a characteristic such that to cease being a member of this kind is for you to cease to exist. So, if a person is a member of a kind of being that is rational, and if being a kind of being is a constitutive property, then every person is constitutively a person.

The zygote from which we developed was a human person. If this argument is sound, it would show that every human foetus is also a human person. Thus, as said earlier, the constitutive property argument shows that every human foetus is a person. If an individual human being has a constitutive property at one point in time, then it has that property at every point in its existence. You are a person constitutively, ontologically. Furthermore, you are the same individual living human being as the foetus from which you developed. Thus, it follows that the foetus from which you developed was a person, and since nothing in the argument depends on any of your unique individual characteristics, this holds also for every other human foetus. All human beings, from the zygotic to the geriatric, enjoy the same fundamental rights, including, most fundamentally, the right to life.

However, in an interview published in *Crisis* (January, 1995), a neoconservative journal of lay Catholic opinion, leftist columnist Christopher Hitchens voices his opposition to abortion in spite of his liberal ideology. In fact, he calls for the reversal of *Roe vs. Wade* as he argues that feminists and humanists must not allow their "woman's right to choose" contradict humanism. Hitchens rightly points out that "we don't have bodies," "we are bodies" and then he appeals to the theory of evolution to support his stance as he believes evolution "establishes beyond reasonable doubt that life is a *continuum* that begins at conception because it can't begin anywhere else."[198]

The overwhelming Biblical evidence of the sacredness of the body and the unity of man as soul and body should forever cure anyone of seeing biological life as relevant to a definition of the personhood of man. Once this is clearly seen the idea of development toward personhood becomes nonsensical. The facts of biology themselves determine humanness. A foetus is a human being irrespective of religion! A fact is a fact! If not a Person, What?

Human Persons Begin to Exist at Conception

Do human beings begin to exist at conception? This is not primarily a moral question ("when does personhood begin?") but rather a scientific question ("when do human beings begin to exist?") or "do members of the species *Homo Sapiens* begin to exist at conception?" This is a biological question, and we could quote here, page after page, numerous biologists, scientists and physicians who have provided clear answers to this questions.

In the interest of space, and to avoid repetition,[199] let's consider the following texts only: "The formation, maturation, and meeting of a male and female sex cell are all preliminary to their actual union into a combined cell, or zygote, which definitely marks the beginning of a new individual. This penetration of the ovum by spermatozoon, and the coming together and pooling of their respective nuclei, constitutes the process of fertilisation."[200] Thus, there results zygote. "Zygote. This cell is the beginning of a human being. It results from the fertilisation of an ovum by a sperm. The expression "fertilised ovum" refers to the zygote."[201]

"Embryonic life commences with fertilisation, and hence the beginning of that process may be taken as the point of departure of stage I."[202]

Indeed, summarising hours of testimony, the official U.S. Senate report on Senate Bill 158, the Human Life Bill, stated: "Physicians, biologists, and other scientists agree that conception marks the beginning of the life of a human being – a being that is alive and is a member of the human species. There is overwhelming agreement on this point in countless medical, biological and scientific writings."[203]

Patrick Lee quotes a number of scientists, and then goes on to suggest reasons why it makes sense to hold that fertilisation marks the start of a new human life.[204]

First, to claim that zygote is not the organism as the foetus, new born or child requires positing significant additional changes without need or cause. No outside agency is present changing the newly conceived organism into something else, but rather the human embryo is self developing towards functional rationality. Speaking analogously, the human embryo is therefore not merely a detailed blueprint of the house that will be built but a tiny house that constructs itself larger and more complex through its active self-development towards maturity.[205]

Second, Lee notes a radical discontinuity between sperm and egg, on the one hand, and the human zygote on the other: "The actual coming to be of an organism cannot be a gradual process. As Aristotle noted long ago, there are no degrees of being a substance or a concrete thing: one either is or is not a horse, one either is or is not an amoeba. Even if the changes which lead to the coming to be of a new organism may be gradual, the transition to actually being one must be instantaneous, and therefore involve a discontinuity. Fertilisation is a radical discontinuity in a series of events in which it does not seem possible to place necessary discontinuity anywhere else."[206] The radical discontinuity occurs at the completion of fertilisation because it is then that a being with 46 chromosomes, a being which previously did not exist, first comes into existence and the individual gametes, the sperm having 23 and the ovum having 23, cease to exist.

A human embryo is properly classified as an individual human being rather than a collection of human cells, a member of the kind *Homo Sapiens* rather than simply a 'heap' of cells of human origin.[207] Human person is a self-developing and self-integrated whole whose various parts (skin, eyes, arms, blood) serve the whole. Skin cells are merely parts of a human being without dynamic, intrinsic orientation to develop towards maturity in the human species. The human embryo is a whole, complete organism, a living individual human being whose cells work together in a coordinated effort to self-development towards maturity. If all human beings are persons, then the human embryo is a person. If all human beings are persons and if human beings begin to exist at conception, then persons begin to exist at conception.

Conclusion
The onslaughts of postmodernism and pluralism have caused many ordinary people to doubt their common sense, their shared traditions, and their deep-seated moralities. We made an attempt to peer into the "no-man's land," seeking to find a common basis on which moral acquaintances may build a

view of personhood. Such a Common Ground Approach might help to confer a dignity upon human beings that all parties inwardly know they possess.

We have examined the insights from a number of writers to demonstrate a commonly-held understanding of human value. Yet this moral sense is fragile, and it can be obscured by post modernity and pluralism. It cannot bring about true moral change, for it is only a beginning. It is limited by our own ability to understand the *telos* built into the universe, so it must not be stretched beyond appropriate boundaries.

For defending the personhood of the unborn we began with the endowment account of personhood. It was supported by a 'constitutive property' argument. Defining person as a member of a kind of being that is rational and free, we tried to establish that humans are rational and a member of a species *Homo Sapiens*. This helped us arrive at the conclusion that human beings begin to exist at conception and every zygote is a human person.

In the final analysis, the problem we face is not a lack of knowledge; it is a moral unwillingness to act on it: Most modern ethical thinking goes about matters backwards. It assumes that the problem of human sin is mainly cognitive – that it has to do with the state of our knowledge. In other words, it holds that we don't know what's right and wrong and are trying to find out. But natural law theory assumes that the problem is mainly volitional – that it has to do with the state of our will. It holds that by and large we know what's right and wrong but wish we did not, and that we try to keep ourselves in ignorance so that we can do as we please.[208]

Summary
An elevated view of human life is a common instinct. The Christian affirmation of human personhood goes far beyond the prudential sense, to a philosophical/theological honouring of human being made in the image and likeness of God.

The image of God in man could provide some basis for moral law, with Biblical support. Every individual from fertilisation is known by God. He is under His providential care and is morally accountable. Since human life begins at fertilisation, the full moral worth afforded to every human being is equally afforded from fertilisation onward throughout development. Vague notions of personhood or social utility have no place in decisions regarding the worth, dignity, or rights of any human being. Because, all human beings derive their inherent worth and the right to life from being made in the image of God, standing in relation to God as their personal Creator. Therefore, a human being's value and worth is constant, whether strong or weak, conscious or unconscious, healthy or disabled, socially "useful" or "useless," wanted or unwanted.[209]

The Cartesian scepticism has shaken the foundation for such a value to human life. The present day secular philosophic/ postmodernist views questioned the intrinsic human nature as societal given. Modern advances in genetics, embryology and human reproduction have forced us to re-examine of what it means to be human and person. During the rise of the modern bioethics movement (1965-80) a number of respected writers have affirmed the traditional Christian theological positions, while adding philosophical reasoning to it.

The statement "human life has no value" seems incoherent, since it forms a poor basis for the continuation of society. Again, the denial of the concept of human dignity will lead us down a very perilous path. So we need a strong affirmation of human nature and human dignity. For that we need a robust and a commonly held high moral valuing of human being. We have proposed three strategies to respond to the assaults on human personhood. There is a basis for common morality through a concept of objective value – natural law – the source of all value judgement. If we step outside the objective morality – the source of all value – we will decide for ourselves what 'man' is to be and make him into that which will result in the 'abolition of man'.

All feel that man has intrinsic value. So we can provide some content from our own experience to disclose the meaning of moral law. There are universally recognisable truths regarding the value of life. Human beings have the 'curious idea' that they ought to behave in a certain way; there is a universal sense of the value of life as given. Besides, we have the ironic testimonies to the 'law written in the heart' to attest to the value of life.

We also had recourse to the 'endowment account' and the 'constitutive property' argument. Endowment account holds that each human being has inherent moral worth simply by virtue of the kind of being it is. The human embryo is a whole, complete organism, a living individual human being whose cells work together in a coordinated effort to self-development towards maturity. If all human beings are persons, then human embryo is a person. If all human beings are persons and if human beings begin to exist at conception, then persons begin to exist at conception. The 'constitutive property' argument also will show that every human foetus is a person. If an individual human being has a constitutive property at one point in time, then it has that property at every point in its existence. You are a person constitutively, you are the same individual living human being as the foetus from which you developed. So if foetus from which you developed was a person, and since nothing in the argument depends on any of your unique individual characteristics, this holds also for every other human foetus.

To conclude we quote Dr. Edwin Vieira, (Jr). Taking premises of the proabortionists' argument against the personhood of the unborn, he succeeds in establishing that their assumptions are false. He writes: "The underlying premise in the arguments pro-abortionists give against foetal personhood is that non-persons can change into persons. They are saying that a living being can undergo a radical, essential change in its nature during its lifetime. But there is a logical problem here. If the change was biologically inevitable from conception, given time, then this change is not a change in essential nature. This is because if the being naturally initiates the change, it must be in its nature from the beginning to do so. If it is in its nature to do so, then despite any changes in such characteristics as independence, place of residence, physical development, or demonstration of mental ability, what the being is in later life is what the being is from the beginning of its life. This means that if we are persons with the right to be free from aggression later in life, we are persons even at conception."[210] Eric Versluys also, endorses this view.[211]

Since abortion ends human life, one must ask the question whether abortion is justifiable homicide or murder. Hence a human being's life may not be sacrificed for the economic or political welfare or convenience of other individuals or society. Indeed, society itself is to be judged by its protection of and the solicitude it shows for the weakest of its members and all of us know that the unborn are the weakest one can imagine.

---

1 For this section I am very much indebted to Christina M.H. Powell, Ph.D., author, medical writer, and research scientist trained at Harvard Medical School and Harvard University and also to Dennis M. Sullivan, "Defending Human Personhood: Some Insights from Natural Law," in Christian Scholar's Review, 37:3 (Spring, 2008), pp. 1-17.

2 Leon R. Kass, "Making Babies—The New Biology and the 'Old Morality,'" The Public Interest (Winter, 1972), 53 cited in John Powell, Abortion: The Silent Holocaust, 40.

3 See, John S. Feinberg and Paul D. Feinberg, Ethics for a Brave New World, Wheaton, 1993.

4 R. C. Sproul, Abortion: A Rational Look at an Emotional Issue (Colorado Springs: Nav Press, 1990), p.63.

5 HBVS Person, The Image of God (imago Dei) How We View Ourselves, p.26; seen at www.vitalchristianity.org/docs/Image. This book has helped me a lot in writing this part.

6 HBVS Person, The Image of God (imago Dei) How We View Ourselves, pp26-27; seen at www.vitalchristianity.org/docs/Image

7 HBVS Person, The Image of God (imago Dei) How We View Ourselves, p.27; seen at www.vitalchristianity.org/docs/Image

8 HBVS Person, The Image of God (imago Dei) How We View Ourselves, p.3; seen at www.vitalchristianity.org/docs/Image

9 R. C. Sproul, Abortion: A Rational Look at an Emotional Issue (Colorado Springs: Nav Press, 1990), p.97. See also, HBVS Person, The Image of God (imago Dei) How We View Ourselves, p.3.

10 HBVS Person, The Image of God (imago Dei) How We View Ourselves, p.3; seen at www.vitalchristianity.org/docs/Image

11 HBVS Person, The Image of God (imago Dei) How We View Ourselves, p. seen at www.vitalchristianity.org/docs/Image

12 HBVS Person, The Image of God (imago Dei) How We View Ourselves, p.4; seen at www.vitalchristianity.org/docs/Image

13 HBVS Person, The Image of God (imago Dei) How We View Ourselves, p.4; seen at www.vitalchristianity.org/docs/Image

14 Archibald Cox, The Role of the Supreme Court in American Government (New York: Oxford Press, 1976). For full description and discussion of the Roe vs. Wade, see Death Before Birth by Harold OJ Brown (Thomas Nelson, 1977), pp.73-96.

15 Archibald Cox, The Role of the Supreme Court in American Government (New York: Oxford Press, 1976), p.52.

16 Beverly Harrison, Our Right to Choose (Boston: Beacon, 1983), p.193

17 HBVS Person, The Image of God (imago Dei) How We View Ourselves, p.5; seen at www.vitalchristianity.org/docs/Image

18 Beverly Harrison, Our Right to Choose (Boston: Beacon, 1983), p. 63.

19-21 HBVS Person, The Image of God (imago Dei) How We View Ourselves, p.5; seen at www.vitalchristianity.org/docs/Image

22 See, R. C. Sproul, Abortion: A Rational Look at an Emotional Issue (Colorado Springs: Nav Press, 1990), p.63.

23 See, Vidy Metsker, "Legalized Murder: The Horror of Abortion," Psychology for Living (November, 1984), p.7.

24 HBVS Person, The Image of God (imago Dei) How We View Ourselves, p.6; seen at www.vitalchristianity.org/docs/Image

25 James Gustafson, The Contribution of Theology to Medical Ethics (Milwaukee: Marquette University, 1975), 60 cited in Fowler, Abortion: Toward an Evangelical Consensus (Portland, OR: Multnomah Press, 1987), p.34.

26 Francis Crick, Nature 200 (2 November, 1968), 429,430 cited by Bill Crouse, "Abortion and Human Value," Insight (Dallas: Probe Ministries International, 1979), 2 cited in Fowler, Abortion: Toward an Evangelical Consensus, p.34.

27 HBVS Person, The Image of God (imago Dei) How We View Ourselves, p.7; seen at www.vitalchristianity.org/docs/Image

28 HBVS Person, The Image of God (imago Dei) How We View Ourselves, p.7; seen at www.vitalchristianity.org/docs/Image

29 HBVS Person, The Image of God (imago Dei) How We View Ourselves, p.7; seen at www.vitalchristianity.org/docs/Image

30 Ashley Montague, Sex, Man and Society (New York: G. P. Putnam and Sons, 1967) cited in Fowler, Abortion: A Rational Look at an Emotional Issue, p.35.

31 Joshua Lederberg, "A Geneticist Looks at Contraception and Abortion," Annals of Internal Medicine 67 (September, 1967), 26f. cited in Fowler, Abortion: Toward an Evangelical Consensu, p.35.

32-33 Michael Tooley "Abortion and Infanticide," Philosophy and Public Affairs 2 (Fall, 1972), 63 cited in Fowler, Abortion: Toward an Evangelical Consensus, pp.35, 65.

34 HBVS Person, The Image of God (imago Dei) How We View Ourselves, p.7; seen at www.vitalchristianity.org/docs/Image

35 Rudolph Ehrensing, "When Is It Really Abortion?" The National Catholic Reporter (25 May, 1966), 4 cited in Fowler, Abortion: Toward an Evangelical Consensus, p.36.

36 Roy Schenk, "Let's Think About Abortion," The Catholic World, (April, 1968), 16; cited in Fowler, Abortion: Toward an Evangelical Consensus, p.36.

37 Mary Ann Warren, "On the Moral and Legal Status of Abortion," The Monist (January, 1973), 55f.; cited in Fowler, Abortion: Toward an Evangelical Consensus, p.37.

38 HBVS Person, The Image of God (imago Dei) How We View Ourselves, p.8-9; seen at www.vitalchristianity.org/docs/Image

39 Mary Ann Warren, "On the Moral and Legal Status of Abortion," The Monist (January, 1973), 55f.; cited in Fowler, Abortion: Toward an Evangelical Consensus, p.37.

40 Joseph Fletcher, "Four Indicators of Humanhood—The Enquiry Matures," The Hastings Center Report 4 (December, 1974), pp. 4-7.

42 See, R. C. Sproul, Abortion: A Rational Look at an Emotional Issue (Colorado Springs: Nav Press, 1990), p.67.

HBVS Person, The Image of God (imago Dei) How We View Ourselves, p.9; seen at http://www.vitalchristianity.org/docs/Image

43 I find it curious that in 1973 the Supreme Court (USA) appealed to "humility" as it arrogantly legislated and argued that it could not "resolve the difficult question of when life begins," when, in fact, the Court knew what every high-school biology student knows. So it quickly inserted the adjectives "meaningful" and "useful" and defined viability as the point at which the baby can have "meaningful" and "useful" life. Such pragmatic criteria are very dangerous. After all, who decides what are useful and meaningful?

44 Christina M.H. Powell, at http://www.questionyourdoubts.com

45 See Christina M.H. Powell, Ph.D., at http://www.questionyourdoubts.com

46 Greg Koukl, "Are Humans Persons?" Accessed June 3, 2009; Available from www.str.org/site/News2?page=NewsArticle&id=5117

47 Francis Beckwith, "The Explanatory Power of the Substance View of Persons," Christian Bioethics 10 (2004): pp.33-54.

48 Norman L. Geisler, "The Arguments for Abortion Are Strong If . . ." Moody Monthly (September, 1986), pp.89-90. See also, HBVS Person, The Image of God (imago Dei) How We View Ourselves, p.10; seen at www.vitalchristianity.org/docs/Image

49 John Jefferson Davis in Abortion and the Christian: What Every Believer Should Know [Philadelphia: Presbyterian and Reformed Publishing House, 1984, pp. 36-37.

50 Peter Wenz, Abortion Rights As Religious Freedom (Philadelphia: Temple University Press, 1992), p. 60

51 HBVS Person, The Image of God (imago Dei) How We View Ourselves, p.11; seen at www.vitalchristianity.org/docs/Image

52 Glanville Williams, "The Legalization of Medical Abortion," The Eugenics Review 56 (April 1964), pp. 20-21.

53 HBVS Person, The Image of God (imago Dei) How We View Ourselves, p.11; seen at www.vitalchristianity.org/docs/Image

54 Fowler, Abortion: Toward an Evangelical Issue, p.49.

55 Abortion and Unborn Human Life, Washington, 1996, p.93.

56 Gomez-Lobo, Alfonso, Individuality and Human Beginnings: A Reply to David DeGrazia, The Journal of Law, Medicine and Ethics, 2007, 35 (3), 457-462, p.458

57 Napier Stephen, Twinning, Substance, and Identity through Time: A Reply to McMahan, in National Catholic Bioethics Quarterly, 8(2), 2008, pp.255-264.

58 Peter Wenz, Abortion Rights As Religious Freedom (Philadelphia: Temple University Press, 1992), pp.60-61, 138

59 HBVS Person, The Image of God (imago Dei) How We View Ourselves, p.12; seen at www.vitalchristianity.org/docs/Image

60-61 Peter Wenz, Abortion Rights As Religious Freedom (Philadelphia: Temple University Presss, 1992), p.60.

62-63 HBVS Person, The Image of God (imago Dei) How We View Ourselves, p.13; seen at www.vitalchristianity.org/docs/Image

64 Mother Teresa, Press Conference, Dublin, Ireland, 1982 cited in Smith, When Choice Becomes God, p.225.

65 Mother Teresa, Press Conference, Dublin, Ireland, 1982 cited in Smith, When Choice Becomes God, p.225.

66 Wenz, Abortion Rights As Religious Freedom, p.61.

67 R.C. Sproul, Abortion: A Rational Look at an Emotional Issue, p.61.

68 R.C. Sproul, Abortion: A Rational Look at an Emotional Issue, pp.61-62.

69 R.C. Sproul, Abortion: A Rational Look at an Emotional Issue, p.62.

70 P. Wenz, Abortion Rights As Religious Freedom, pp61-62

71 HBVS Person, The Image of God (imago Dei) How We View Ourselves, p.16; seen at www.vitalchristianity.org/docs/Image

72-73 P. Wenz, Abortion Rights As Religious Freedom, p62.

74 HBVS Person, The Image of God (imago Dei) How We View Ourselves, p.16; seen at www.vitalchristianity.org/docs/Image

75 P. Wenz, Abortion Rights As Religious Freedom, p62.

76-80 HBVS Person, The Image of God (imago Dei) How We View Ourselves, p.17; www.vitalchristianity.org/docs/Image

81-83 P. Wenz, Abortion Rights As Religious Freedom, p63.

84-86 Carl Sagan and Ann Druyan, "Is It Possible To Be Pro-Life and Pro-Choice?" Parade Magazine (April 22, 1989) cited in F. LaGard Smith, When CHOICE Becomes God, p.236.

87 P. Wenz, Abortion Rights As Religious Freedom, p.64.

88 HBVS Person, The Image of God (imago Dei) How We View Ourselves, p23; seen at www.vitalchristianity.org/docs/Image

89 P. Wenz, Abortion Rights As Religious Freedom, p.66.

90 HBVS Person, The Image of God (imago Dei) How We View Ourselves, p.23; seen at www.vitalchristianity.org/docs/Image

91 P. Wenz, Abortion Rights As Religious Freedom, p.66.

92 HBVS Person, The Image of God (imago Dei) How We View Ourselves, p.24; seen at www.vitalchristianity.org/docs/Image

93 P. Wenz, Abortion Rights As Religious Freedom, p.66.

94 P. Wenz, Abortion Rights As Religious Freedom, p.67.

95 Rubenfeld, "Right of Privacy," 790 cited in Wenz, Abortion Rights As Religious Freedom, p.67.

96 P. Wenz, Abortion Rights As Religious Freedom, p.65.

97 HBVS Person, The Image of God (imago Dei) How We View Ourselves, p.21; seen at www.vitalchristianity.org/docs/Image

98 P. Wenz, Abortion Rights As Religious Freedom, pp.66-67.

99-100 P. Wenz, Abortion Rights As Religious Freedom, p.66.

101 HBVS Person, The Image of God (imago Dei) How We View Ourselves, p.24; www.vitalchristianity.org/docs/Image

102 HBVS Person, The Image of God (imago Dei) How We View Ourselves, p.25; at www.vitalchristianity.org/docs/Image

103 HBVS Person, The Image of God (imago Dei) How We View Ourselves, p.24; at www.vitalchristianity.org/docs/Image

104 HBVS Person, The Image of God (imago Dei) How We View Ourselves, p.25; at www.vitalchristianity.org/docs/Image

105 C. Everett Koop, "The Right to Live" Hensley, 49-50.

106-110 Blechschmidt, "New Perspectives on Human Abortion", 12-13 cited in Wenz, Abortion Rights As Religious Freedom, 172

111 P. Wenz, Abortion Rights As Religious Freedom, p.173.

112 See, James Rachels, The Elements of Moral Philosophy, Fourth Ed., Boston, 2003.

113 P. Wenz, Abortion Rights As Religious Freedom, pp.180-181.

114 P. Wenz, Abortion Rights As Religious Freedom, pp.18.

115-117 P. Wenz, Abortion Rights As Religious Freedom, pp.181.

118 HBVS Person, The Image of God (imago Dei) How We View Ourselves, p23; at www.vitalchristianity.org/docs/Image.

119 See, Nigel M Cameron, "Christian Vision for the Biotech Century" in Human Dignity in the Biotech Century, Charles Colson and Nigel M Cameron ed., Downers Grove, 2004.

120 See, Gilbert Meilaender, Bioethics: A Primer for Christians, Grand Rapids, 1996; Wendy Murray Zoba, "Abortion's Untold Story" in Christianity Today, April 27, 1998.

121 See, David Hopkins, "Francis Schaeffer: The Last Great Modern Theologian", in The Words Online, 2007. http//www.the words.com/articles/schaefferdave.htm.

122 Frederica Mathewes-Green, "The Abortion Debate Is Over," in Christianity Today, December 6, 1999.

123 See, Robert C. Greer, Mapping Postmodernism: A Survey of Christian Options, Downers Grove, 2003 and Alister McGrath, "Evangelicals and Post liberals: Pitfalls and Possibilities," Keynote address to Wheaton College, April 21, 1995.

124 Dennis P. Hollinger, Choosing the Good: Christian Ethics in a Complex World, Grand rapids, 2002, p.247.

125 See, Paige Cunningham, "Learning From Our Mistakes," in Human Dignity in the Biotech Century, Charles Colson and Nigel Cameron, ed., Downers Grove, 2004.

126-128 H.Tristam Engelhardt, The Foundations of Bioethics, Second ed., Oxford, 1996, pp.9-10.

129 "The Emotional Effects of Induced Abortion," Planned Parenthood, www.plannedparenthood.org/library/facts/emoteff_010600.html.

130 AUL, "Cutting-Edge Bioethical Issues," Americans United for Life, http://www.unitedforlife.org/hot_topics.htm. Reardon, "The Aftereffects of Abortion."

131 David Reardon, "CoercedAbortions Highlight How Abortion Hurts Women," LifeNews.com, www.lifenews.com/oped14.html

132 "The Hand of Hope," (2006), http://freerepublic.com/focus/f-news/1012548/posts. Pia de_Solenni, "Miracles of Life," National ReviewOnline, www.nationalreview.com/comment/solenni200309301002.asp.

133 Aristotle, Nocomachean Ethics, Book I, The Internet Classics Archive, classics.mit.edu/Aristotle/Nicomachean.1.i.html.

134 Thomas Aquinas, "Summa Theologica," Christian Classics Ethereal Library, www.ccel.org/a/aquinas/summa/FP/FP079.html#FPQ79OUTP1

135 See, J. Budziszewski, What We Can't Not Know , Dallas: Spence Publishing, 2003.

136 See, C. S. Lewis, The Abolition of Man, New York: MacMillen, 1944; reprint, 1974.

137 Budziszewski, What We Can't Not Know, p.13.

138 J. Budziszewski, What We Can't Not Know, p.43.

139 J. Budziszewski, What We Can't Not Know, p.51.

140 J. Budziszewski, What We Can't Not Know, p.64.

141 Francis Fukuyama, Our Posthuman Future: Consequences of the Biotechnology Revolution (New York: Picador), 2002.

142 Francis Fukuyama, Our Posthuman Future: Consequences of the Biotechnology Revolution (NY: Picador, 2002), p.160.

143 William Provine, "Darwinism: Science or Naturalistic Philosophy?," Access ResearchNetwork, www.arn.org/docs/guides/stan_gd1.htm#3a.

144 See, Mortimer J. Adler, Ten Philosophical Mistakes (New York: Touchstone), 1985.

145 Leon Kass, "The Wisdom of Repugnance," in Ethical Issues in Biotechnology, ed. Richard Sherlock and John D. Morrey (Lanham: Rowman and Littlefield), 2002), p.559.

146 See, the appendix to his 'Abolition of Man'.

147 C.S. Lewis, The Abolition of Man, 83-86; C.S. Lewis, Mere Christianity (New York: Harper Collins, 1952), p.8.

148 See, Naomi Wolf, "Our Bodies, Our Souls," The New Republic, October 16, 1995.

149 Gloria Steinem, "Ask Gloria," Feminist.com, http://www.feminist.com/resources/artspeech/interviews/steinem.htm.

150 See, "The Week," National Review, September 1, 2003.

151 Much more could be said on this theme, but the cost of abortion in terms of regret and guilt is well known and documented.

See, R Ashton, "The Psychosocial Outcome of Induced Abortion," British Journal of Obstetrics and Gynaecology 87 (1980); David Reardon, "The After effects of Abortion," Elliot Institute, http://www.afterabortion.org/complic.html.

152 See, Carol Gilligan, In a Different Voice (Cambridge: Harvard University Press), 1982.

153 Peter Singer, "Animal Rights," in Animal Rights and Human Obligations, ed. Tom Regan and Peter Singer (Englewood Cliffs, NJ: Prentice Hall), 1989.

154 Gonzales V. Carhart Et Al, (2007). Following this Court's Stenberg v. Carhart, 530 U. S. 914, decision that Nebraska's "partial birth abortion" statute violated the Federal Constitution, as interpreted in Planned Parenthood of Southeastern Pa. v. Casey, 505 U. S. 833, and Roe v. Wade, 410 U. S. 113, Congress passed the Partial-Birth Abortion Ban Act of 2003 (Act) to proscribe a particular method of ending foetal life in the later stages of pregnancy.

155 See, "Partial Birth Abortion Act Passes House," Minnesota Christian Chronicle, June 11, 2003.

156 See, Michael Uhlmann, "The Supreme Court 2000: A Symposium," First Things, no. 106 (2000).

157 See, Dennis M. Sullivan, "Common Sense Should Rule Debate," The Dayton Daily News 2001.

158 See, Norman L. Geisler and Paul D. Feinberg, Introduction to Philosophy: A Christian Perspective (Grand Rapids: Baker Books), 1980.

159 See, Stephen John Grabill, Rediscovering the Natural Law in Reformed Theological Ethics, Emory University Studies in Law and Religion (Grand Rapids, Mich.: William B. Eerdmans Pub. Co.), 2006

160-161 See, Christopher Kaczor, The Ethics of Abortion: Women's Rights, Human Life, and the Question of justice New York and London, 2010, Chs. 1-4.

162-164 Robert E. Joyce, "When does a Person Begin?" New Perspectives on Human Abortion, edited by T. W. Hilgers, D. J. Horan, and D. Mall (Frederick, MD: Aletheia Books, 1981), 353 cited in Fowler, pp. 51-52.

165 E. Blechschmidt, "Human from the First," in Hilgers, Horan, and Mall, ed., New Perspectives on Human Abortion (Frederick, MD: University Publishers of Amercia, 1981), 12-13 cited in Peter S. Wenz, Abortion Rights As Religious Freedom (Philadelphia: Temple University Press, 1992), p.171.

166 Cited by E. Blechschmidt, "Human from the First," in Hilgers, Horan, and Mall, ed., New Perspectives on Human Abortion (Frederick, MD: University Publishers of Amercia, 1981), pp.12-13 cited in Peter S. Wenz, Abortion Rights As Religious Freedom (Philadelphia: Temple University Press, 1992), p. 171.

167 Cited by E. Blechschmidt, "Human from the First," in Hilgers, Horan, and Mall, ed., New Perspectives on Human Abortion (Frederick, MD: University Publishers of Amercia, 1981), pp. 12-13 cited in Peter S. Wenz, Abortion Rights As Religious Freedom (Philadelphia: Temple University Press, 1992), p. 171

168 HBVS Person, The Image of God (imago Dei) How We View Ourselves, p.29; seen at www.vitalchristianity.org/docs/Image.

169 Blechschmidt, New Perspectives on Human Abortion, pp.12-13 cited in Wenz, Abortion Rights As Religious Freedom, p.171.

170 Blechschmidt, New Perspectives on Human Abortion,12-13 cited in Wenz, Abortion Rights As Religious Freedom, p.172.

171 HBVS Person, The Image of God (imago Dei) How We View Ourselves, p.28; seen at www.vitalchristianity.org/docs/Image.

172 Cited in R.C. Sproul, Abortion: A Rational Look at an Emotional Issue, p. 45.

173 HBVS Person, The Image of God (imago Dei) How We View Ourselves, p.28; seen at www.vitalchristianity.org/docs/Image.

174 HBVS Person, The Image of God (imago Dei) How We View Ourselves, p.28; seen at www.vitalchristianity.org/docs/Image.

175-176 John Willke, National Right to Life News (June 29, 1981), p.5 cited in Fowler, Abortion: A Rational Look at an Emotional Issue, p.51.

177 HBVS Person, The Image of God (imago Dei) How We View Ourselves, p.29; seen at www.vitalchristianity.org/docs/Image.

178 HBVS Person, The Image of God (imago Dei) How We View Ourselves, p.29; seen at www.vitalchristianity.org/docs/Image.

179 Tertullian, Apology, chapter ix cited in Gorman, p.54

180 C. S. Lewis Mere Morality (Grand Rapids: Wm. B. Eerdmans Publishing Co., 1983), p.129

181 Quoted in the Church of Scotland's Board of Social Responsibility, 1985 report to the General Assembly. See also Professor Torrance's booklet Test-Tube Babies(Scottish Academic Press 1984) by Stott, Decisive Issues Facing Christians Today, p.334.

182 Seuss, Horton Hears a Who (New York: Random House, 1954), p.18.

183 Blechschmidt, New Perspectives on Human Abortion,12-13 cited in Wenz, Abortion Rights As Religious Freedom, p.173.

184 Robert Joyce, "When does a Person Begin?" In Hilgers, Perspectives, p.348 cited in Wenz, Abortion Rights As Religious Freedom, p.173.

185 Robert Joyce, "When does a Person Begin?" In Hilgers, Perspectives, p.348 cited in Wenz, Abortion Rights As Religious Freedom, p.174.

186 Robert Joyce, "When does a Person Begin?" In Hilgers, Perspectives, p.348 cited in Wenz, Abortion Rights As Religious Freedom, p.173.

187 Christopher Kaczor, The Ethics of Abortion: Women's Rights, Human Life, and the Question of justice New York and London, 2010, p.93.

188 Clarke W.N (1995) Explorations in Metaphysics, Notre Dame, 1995, p.105.

189 Christopher Kaczor, The Ethics of Abortion: Women's Rights, Human Life, and the Question of Justice New York and London, 2010, p.98.

190 Christopher Kaczor, The Ethics of Abortion: Women's Rights, Human Life, and the Question of Justice New York and London, 2010, p.98.

191 See, Martha Nussbaum, Frontiers of Justice: Disability, Nationality, Species Membership, Cambridge, 2006 and Anderson Elizabeth, Animal Rights and the Value of Nonhuman Life. In Cass R. Sunstein and Martha Nussbaum, (eds.), Animal Rights: Current Debates and New Directions, Oxford, 2004, 277-298, pp281-283.

192 Christopher Kaczor, The Ethics of Abortion: Women's Rights, Human Life, and the Question of Justice New York and London, 2010, p.99.

193 John J. Michalczyk, Medicine Ethics and the Third Reich, Historical and Contemporary Issues, Sheed & Ward, NY, 1994, esp. Pp. 42-49; 64-70.

194-196 Liao S Mathew in The Basis of Human Moral Status , Journal of Moral Philosophy, 7(2) 2010, pp.159-179, p.168.

197 Boonin David, A Defense of Abortion, U.K. 2003, p.xiv.

198 David Neff, "Left Face, About Face," Christianity Today.

199 See, the second part of this book.

200 Arey, Leslie Brainerd, Developmental Anatony, (7th ed.), Philadelphia, 1974, p.55.

201 Moore, Keith L., Before We Are Born, ,Washington DC, 1987, p.9.

202 Larsen, William J., Human Embryology, New York, 1993, p.19.

203 Cited by Alcorn, Randy, Prolife Answers to prochoice Arguments, Portland, 2000, p.55

204 Lee, Patrick, Abortion and Unborn Human Life, Washington DC, 1996, p.71

205 Christopher Kaczor, The Ethics of Abortion: Women's Rights, Human Life, and the Question of justice New York and London, 2010, p.104.

206 Lee, Patrick, Abortion and Unborn Human Life, Washington DC, 1996, p.71

207 Condic, Maureen, Life: defining the beginning by the End. First Things, 2003, (133), 50-54, p.52.

208 See, J. Budziszewski, Written on the Heart: The Case for Natural Law (Downers Grove: InterVarsity Press), 1997.

209 Matt 25:40; James 1:27

210 Edwin Vieira, Jr., "A False Assumption," Libertarians for Life, (1999) at:http://www.l4l.org/

211 Eric Versluys, "South Dakota law is clear," The Rocky Mountain Collegina, 2006-MAR-09, at:http://www.collegian.com/